**225 DELICIOUS RECIPES
GUARANTEED TO WIN RAVE REVIEWS**

CROWD-PLEASING
POTLUCK

FRANCINE HALVORSEN

RODALE

Direct and trade editions are both being published in 2007.

Photographs by Mitch Mandel/Rodale Images
Food Styling by Dan Macey

Book design by Tara Long

Library of Congress Cataloging-in-Publication Data

Halvorsen, Francine.
    Crowd-pleasing potluck : 225 delicious recipes guaranteed to win rave reviews / Francine Halvorsen.
        p.   cm.
    Includes index.
    ISBN-13 978–1–59486–473–5 hardcover
    ISBN-10 1–59486–473–X hardcover
    ISBN-13 978–1–59486–474–2 paperback
    ISBN-10 1–59486–474–8 paperback
    1. Cookery. I. Title.
TX714.H3535 2007
641.5—dc22   2007001038

Distributed to the book trade by Holtzbrinck Publishers

2 4 6 8 10 9 7 5 3 1 hardcover
2 4 6 8 10 9 7 5 3 1 paperback

We inspire and enable people to improve their lives and the world around them
For more of our products visit **rodalestore.com** or call 800-848-4735

For "the kids"—Benjamin, Emilia, Harrison, Isaiah, Jacob, Megan, and Sarah—with love and laughter. You grace any meal with your presence.

ACKNOWLEDGMENTS

With thanks from A to Z to Pamela Adler and Claire Zuckerman for being there, to Jesse Halvorsen; Linda Lee; Lionel Halvorsen; Gail and Barry Cohen; Carol Weaver; Felix Harlan; Susan Lewis; and Elizabeth, Alan, and Song Lee for confirming continuously that food tastes only as good as the people you share it with.

With thanks to the team at Rodale, most especially my editor Karen Bolesta, who has been skillful and good-natured through thick and thin, and Shea Zukowski who shepherded the book from its early stages. Copy editors Rachelle Laliberte and Ellen Bingham kept many a slip from showing and Tara Long and Diane Meckel made order out of chaos, while Lois Hazel kept everything on track. Dan Macey and Melissa Reiss, working with photographer Mitch Mandel, made sure that the food looks good enough to eat. I appreciate all your time, talent, and enthusiasm.

A special word of gratitude to the Thursday Taizé meditation and potluck group at the Cathedral of the Incarnation in Baltimore. Thank you all.

CONTENTS

INTRODUCTION

I ONCE CARRIED A HAM, A TURKEY, and stuffing on a flight from New York to Chicago. My mom was unexpectedly ill and could not travel so we decided to celebrate the holiday at her house. Since I was the one most unflappable about presenting food in a variety of circumstances, I was designated to do the lion's share of cooking and assembling the 'pre-fab' meal. Happily, it turned out to be 'fab.' The secret—dishes that travel well and a very well-insulated thermal bag with lots of cold packs. Though I am sure ham and turkeys are no longer allowable carry-ons, there are almost no limitations to potluck.

THE ART OF POTLUCKING

I never thought that what my friends and family were doing was potluck. We seem much too contemporary and too much into good food, and we have professional and private lives that keep us busy. I was talking to a friend who said she never 'does' potlucks. I asked, well what do you call it when you want to get 10 or 12 people together and you ask me to bring dessert, Liz to please bring the great salad she makes, and Adam to bring some cheese and those spicy olives he mixes. She said "Oh."

At this point I don't think I know anyone who has not been asked to bring something to eat somewhere where other people will share it. That's what potluck is—*a meal at which each guest brings food that is then shared by all.* More and more private and professional events are staged by family and friends with busy lives. These people, who love to cook and give parties but have time to do only one or two dishes really well, will ask others to bring something.

From casual dinners and holidays, to public celebrations and occasions too numerous and varied to list, from studio apartments and commodious houses to conference rooms and gardens, people are sharing the art of potlucking. In cities and in suburbs, everyone is bringing something to the table.

When the burden of an entire meal is lifted, the tasks of shopping, organizing, cooking and serving are simplified and you can focus your attention on a great recipe. Usually a dish can be served "as brought" or needs only to be heated, dressed and plated. Sometimes something you decide to cook may require some assembly and finishing. Tips I've learned from experience and from interviews with chefs and caterers will enable you to prepare and present topnotch dishes that will have people asking for your recipe.

With the recipes and suggestions in *Crowd-Pleasing Potluck* you get the opportunity to show off your specialty and get ideas for new ones. The range of dishes in this book are delicious but none require elaborate last-minute preparations. Planning is as important as your unique seasoning.

Food is both a kindness to others and an instant reward for ourselves. Those "oohs" and "aahs" are very gratifying. Whether you are bringing salad or dessert to a family dinner for eight people or two 12-inch by 20-inch sheet cakes to provide many people with a little something to go with their coffee, it is a nice feeling to shine.

You might think that many people cooking for one occasion would cause inconsistencies, but what I have discovered as I have participated in hundreds of potlucks over the years in this country and others, is that a certain harmonious composition occurs. Everyone enjoys bringing a dish and everyone enjoys eating something made by someone else. Don't underestimate your group. The roasted squash soup with the dollop of curried sour cream and toasted pumpkin seeds will be as much appreciated at your congregation's after-service get together as it was at your book club meeting.

The best meals are composed of established crowd-pleasers and a few new dishes. All the recipes in the main section of the book are for 8 to 12 and almost all of them can be halved or multiplied. Most markets have all the items that you will need; some elements will require special shopping and a few can be made from ingredients found in a convenience store.

That being said, always use the freshest best ingredients that you can get. Omit tomatoes if they feel like wax candles—they will probably taste like wax candles. I once interviewed the executive chef of the Excelsior Hotel on the Via Veneto in Rome and after showing me some remarkably elaborate dishes we went into the cavernous kitchen. Among other questions, I asked him what he did when there were no ripe tomatoes. In less than fifteen minutes a chef made me a tomato sauce from drained, canned peeled tomatoes, pancetta, and broccoli rabe and pasta from a box. The secret ingredient to good cooking is flexibility. Often the simplest dishes seem the most luxurious.

I hope that, as with all really useful guides, this book's attention to detail will free you to be confident and creative as you prepare your dishes. Anyone, from the seasoned pro to the enthusiastic home cook, can follow these recipes. All the practical considerations are covered, but most are common sense, and stress-free.

Give it your best shot. The food made from *Crowd-Pleasing Potluck* will be delicious and much appreciated. Shared occasions are people events first and eating events second, which is why 'the art of potlucking" is always a joy and your contribution always welcome.

Francine Halvorsen

HORS D'OEUVRES AND APPETIZERS

NOT ONLY ARE THE RECIPES IN THIS CHAPTER excellent starters, but these recipes in various combinations—especially when paired with fruit, sweets, and beverages—make more than enough food for many gatherings.

Most of the selections included are very forgiving. The French names give you the right idea—*hors d'oeuvres* means "out of the work"; *amuse-bouche* translates as "to amuse the mouth." Many of these recipes can be made a day or more before they are needed. If you are uncertain about serving supplies at your destination, bring along some small or medium durable paper or plastic plates (most people enjoy grazing with small plates), forks and spreaders, and plenty of napkins. Individually packaged wet towels are not necessary but are very welcome.

If you are hosting an event, ask whoever is bringing starters to come a bit early so people can enjoy them when they arrive.

Seville–Style Olives (opposite)
Spicy Black Olives with Garlic and Herbs (page 4)
Ginger–Roasted Almonds (page 5)
Spicy Pecans (page 6)

SEVILLE-STYLE OLIVES

Try to use Spanish olives for this recipe; they are known for their unique flavor and texture. And if you can find Spanish olive oil as well, it will give an authentic touch. You can use any large green olive and get delicious results.

YIELD | 2 CUPS

1	pound large green Spanish olives	1	tablespoon minced fresh thyme or ½ tablespoon dried
¼	cup extra-virgin olive oil	1	teaspoon crushed red pepper flakes
¼	cup sherry vinegar		
6	anchovy fillets, minced	4	bay leaves
6	cloves garlic, peeled and crushed		

Place the olives in a large bowl and bruise them with the back of a wooden spoon. Add all the other ingredients and stir. Divide the mixture between two 1-pint glass canning jars or any jars with tight-fitting lids. Marinate in the refrigerator for a week. They will keep in the refrigerator for up to 2 weeks.

To serve the dish: These olives are best served at room temperature. Be sure to remove any pieces of bay leaf before serving.

SPICY BLACK OLIVES WITH GARLIC AND HERBS

1	pound black olives	4	sprigs fresh thyme and/or rosemary
3	cloves garlic, minced		Olive oil
2	small jalepeño (or your choice) chili peppers, halved lengthwise and seeded		

In a large bowl, stir together the olives and garlic. Layer them in a 1-quart glass jar with a tight-fitting lid, interspersing the peppers and herbs. Add oil to cover. Secure the lid and refrigerate for up to 2 weeks.

To serve the dish: You can place the olives in a bowl and provide a small spoon so people can help themselves to as many as they want on their plate, or you can arrange the olives on a platter and set out toothpicks. Either way, remember to provide little bowls for the discarded pits and picks.

GINGER-ROASTED ALMONDS

1	pound (4 cups) blanched whole almonds	2	teaspoons ground ginger
½	cup packed brown sugar	2	tablespoons honey
1	teaspoon coarse salt	2	tablespoons safflower oil

Preheat the oven to 350°F.

Toast the nuts on two foil- or parchment-lined baking sheets for 5 minutes. Turn the nuts with a spatula once.

Blend the sugar, salt, ginger, honey, and oil in a small saucepan. Place over low heat and stir until the mixture is just simmering and the sugar is dissolved, 3 to 5 minutes.

Remove the baking sheets from the oven, lower the heat to 325°F, and pour the honey mixture over the warm nuts. Stir and roast for an additional 10 minutes. Turn with a spatula after 2 minutes.

Remove the nuts from the baking sheets and drain on wire cake racks placed over paper towels to catch any dripping.

When the nuts are cool and dry, they can be stored in an airtight container for up to a week.

To serve the dish: Serve the nuts at room temperature.

SPICY PECANS

4	tablespoons butter, melted		A few dashes of hot pepper sauce (optional)
2	tablespoons Worcestershire sauce		
1	teaspoon chili powder	1	pound (4 cups) shelled pecan halves
1	teaspoon salt		
¼	teaspoon cayenne pepper		

Preheat the oven to 300°F.

In a large bowl, mix all the ingredients. Roast on two or three baking sheets until the pecans are aromatic and dark but not burnt, about 20 minutes.

Remove to paper towels to cool. When cooled, the seasoned pecans can be stored in an airtight container for a week.

To serve the dish: Serve at room temperature.

HOMEMADE HUMMUS

Why make your own hummus rather than buy it? Two reasons: freshness of the ingredients and texture. It is the coarseness and blandness of the chickpeas against the tang of lemon and mint that makes this recipe special.

YIELD | 4 CUPS

3	cups cooked or canned chickpeas, rinsed and drained	3	tablespoons minced fresh parsley + sprigs for garnish
1½	cups tahini	2	tablespoons minced fresh mint + sprigs for garnish
⅔	cup extra-virgin olive oil		
½	cup water		Harissa or crushed red pepper flakes for garnish (optional)
	Juice of 2 lemons		
	Salt and pepper to taste		

In a medium bowl, mash the chickpeas with a potato masher or fork and set aside.

In a bowl large enough to hold all the ingredients, blend vigorously with a fork the tahini, oil, water, lemon juice, and salt and black pepper to taste, and stir until creamy. Add the chickpeas and blend, then stir in the minced parsley and mint. If you want to make this a day or two ahead of time, omit the parsley and mint and add them before serving. The hummus can be stored, covered, in the refrigerator for 2 days. Bring to room temperature, place in a serving bowl, and stir in the minced parsley and mint.

To serve the dish: Just before serving, garnish the hummus with the mint and parsley sprigs and, if desired, harissa or red pepper flakes. Serve at room temperature along with warm pita triangles or toasts and/or lettuce leaves to scoop up the dip. The dish can be plated as a salad or served buffet-style with little plates or napkins.

POTLUCK NOTE | *Tahini, a Middle Eastern sesame paste, is widely available. Harissa is a Middle Eastern hot-pepper sauce sold at many specialty stores. If you can't find it, substitute a few pinches of red pepper flakes.*

CHICKEN SATAY SKEWERS

This peanut sauce is popular throughout Indonesia and has been adapted for many dishes.

YIELD | 20 SKEWERS

1½	cups vegetable or chicken stock	⅓	cup chopped fresh cilantro
1½	cups crunchy peanut butter	3	scallions, chopped
2	cloves garlic, minced	2	limes, thinly sliced, for garnish
2	teaspoons chili powder	1	cup unsalted roasted peanuts, chopped, for garnish
½	cup hoisin sauce or light soy sauce		
¼	cup packed brown sugar		
5	skinless, boneless chicken breast halves, cut into 20 strips		

In a medium saucepan over medium heat, combine the stock, peanut butter, garlic, chili powder, hoisin or soy sauce, and sugar. Cook, stirring, until thoroughly blended, 5 to 7 minutes. Stir well and set aside 1½ cups.

Place the remaining sauce in a shallow dish and add the chicken strips. Cover and refrigerate for at least 2 hours or overnight. While the chicken is marinating, soak twenty 10- to 12-inch bamboo skewers in water for 1 hour so they will not burn on the grill.

Add the cilantro and scallions to the reserved 1½ cups satay sauce. *Never cross-contaminate by using marinade that has had contact with raw food as part of any sauce.* Thread 1 chicken strip onto each skewer. If you're not serving right away, wrap the skewered chicken in plastic, cover the sauce, and carry to your destination in a cooler bag.

To broil the satay skewers, wrap any visible wood in aluminum foil and place on a broiling pan 6 inches under the hot oven broiler. Cook, turning once, until the chicken is no longer pink, 8 to 10 minutes. Place on a platter and remove the foil.

To serve the dish: If you have a portable grill such as a George Foreman, bring it with you and grill the skewers for 5 to 7 minutes per side about 20 minutes before serving. On an outdoor grill, cook the skewers over hot coals, turning once, until the chicken is thoroughly cooked, 6 to 8 minutes. Garnish with the lime slices and peanuts, and serve the satay dipping sauce in a bowl alongside.

ROASTED EGGPLANT DIP (BABA GHANOUSH)

Versions of this dish are found throughout the Mediterranean. Don't be too fussy when you make it; bits of charred eggplant skin, pockets of garlic, and bursts of pomegranate seeds only enhance the dip's flavor and texture.

YIELD | 4 CUPS

4	large eggplants
½–¾	cup extra-virgin olive oil + more for preparing vegetables
2	green bell peppers
1	cup tahini
3	cloves garlic

1	teaspoon cumin
1	teaspoon coarse salt
¼	teaspoon black pepper
	seeds of one pomegranate (optional)

Preheat the broiler or the oven to 350°F.

If using the broiler, set the eggplants on foil-lined baking sheets 6 inches under the heat source, turning regularly to char the skin all over, until the eggplants become soft and deflate, about 20 minutes. If using the oven, halve the eggplants lengthwise, rub all over with oil, and place cut side down on foil-lined baking sheets. Bake for 45 minutes. When cool enough to handle, scrape the pulp from the skins into a large bowl. (If some of the charred bits get into the bowl, so much the better.) Discard the skins.

Char the bell peppers in the same manner, baking until the skin is blackened. Remove the peppers from the oven and place them in a paper bag (with the open end twisted shut) for several minutes so the steam can loosen the skins. Remove and discard the skins. Place the bell peppers in the bowl with the eggplant and chop until minced. Stir in the tahini.

Using a garlic press, squeeze the garlic cloves into a small bowl and discard the fibers that do not go through. Mix in ½ cup of the oil, cumin, salt, and black pepper, then stir into the eggplant and peppers. Cover and chill in the refrigerator until ready to serve. This can be refrigerated for 24 hours. If it is thick when you take it out of the refrigerator, add up to ¼ cup of the remaining olive oil.

To serve the dish: This dip is best served at room temperature. If desired, garnish with pomegranate seeds just before serving with Crispy Pita Chips (page 14).

TAPENADE

The quality of your olives is key to the flavor of this rich spread from the Mediterranean.

YIELD | 2 CUPS

1	pound good-quality pitted black olives
1/4	cup salt-cured or in-brine capers, rinsed thoroughly and drained
1	can (2 ounces) flat anchovies, rinsed and drained
1/2	cup extra-virgin olive oil
1/2	teaspoon herbes de Provence
	Juice of 1/2 lemon

Place the olives, capers, and anchovies in a blender and coarsely puree until somewhere between the texture of smooth peanut butter and crunchy. Remove to a bowl with the aid of a rubber spatula. Using a small hand whisk or fork, whisk in the oil, herbes de Provence, and lemon juice. Place the tapenade in a tightly sealed container and refrigerate for up to 1 week.

To serve the dish: Serve at room temperature as a spread for crackers or Crostini (below).

CROSTINI

These thin, crispy little toasts provide the perfect base for a variety of toppings, including Tapenade (above), sliced roasted tomato and basil, blue cheese and honey, or Brie and chutney.

YIELD | APPROXIMATELY 40 CROSTINI

2	baguettes (12–14 ounces each)
1/2	cup olive oil
1/2	teaspoon coarse salt

Preheat the oven to 350°F.

Cut the bread into 1/2-inch-thick slices. Arrange the slices in a single layer on two ungreased baking sheets. Brush with some of the oil and sprinkle with the salt. Bake until the edges are golden brown, about 5 minutes. Brush with the remaining oil and place under the broiler for 1 to 2 minutes, then turn and broil for 1 minute longer.

BAKED BUFFALO CHICKEN WINGS

These wings are not for every event, but if you know your crowd, supply tons of napkins, a place to discard the bones, and have fun!

YIELD | 15 TO 20 SERVINGS

5	pounds (about 30) chicken wings, cut in half at the joint, wing tips removed	8	ounces (1 cup) sour cream
⅓	cup canola oil	16	ounces (about 2 cups) blue cheese, crumbled
1	teaspoon salt + more to taste	2	tablespoons white vinegar
¼	teaspoon cayenne pepper (optional)	¼	teaspoon freshly ground black pepper + more to taste
3–6	tablespoons Tabasco	1–2	large heads celery, strings removed, ribs cut into 3-inch sticks, for serving
1	cup mayonnaise		

Preheat the oven to 425°F.

In a large bowl, combine the wings, oil, the 1 teaspoon salt, cayenne, and 3 to 5 tablespoons of the Tabasco. Arrange the wings in a single layer on two large rimmed baking sheets. Bake until just done, about 35 minutes. Drain on paper towels.

In a medium bowl, combine the mayonnaise, sour cream, blue cheese, vinegar, the ¼ teaspoon black pepper, and up to 1 tablespoon of the remaining Tabasco to taste. Season with salt and black pepper to taste. Cover and refrigerate for up to 24 hours.

To serve the dish: Serve the wings hot and the blue cheese dip at room temperature. If you like, you can make the marinade for the wings a day ahead and refrigerate it. Then you have the choice of making the wings at home and carrying them in a thermal container or preparing them at your destination, along with the celery sticks and blue cheese dip.

POTLUCK NOTE | *Various companies package boneless chicken wings, which make a somewhat less messy version of this dish, but they are not available in every market yet.*

CREAMY BLUE-CHEESE SPREAD

This is not the place to use fancy blue cheeses such as Humboldt Fog or Stilton, which should be served on a cheese platter. Find a reasonably priced blue and you will have a very satisfactory dip.

YIELD | 2½ CUPS

8 ounces (about 1 cup) blue cheese, at room temperature, crumbled	8 ounces (1 cup) plain yogurt Dash of hot sauce (optional)
4 ounces (½ cup) cream cheese, at room temperature	2 cups finely chopped fresh watercress

Place the blue cheese, cream cheese, yogurt, and hot sauce (if desired) in a large bowl and blend with a handheld electric mixer. Stir in the watercress. Cover with plastic wrap and refrigerate for up to 24 hours.

To serve the dish: Serve at room temperature.

CRISPY PITA CHIPS

YIELD | 6 DOZEN TRIANGLES

6 pitas	¼ cup olive oil

Preheat the oven to 360°F.

Cut each pita into six wedges, and separate each wedge into two at the fold.

Place the pita pieces rough side up on baking sheets and brush with the oil. Bake until lightly browned, about 8 minutes. You may want to do them in batches. Remove from the oven and serve, or let the pita chips cool completely and store them in an airtight container for up to 24 hours.

TUSCAN-STYLE WHITE BEAN DIP

YIELD | 4 CUPS

1	head garlic	¼	cup fresh lemon juice
1	tablespoon + ⅓ cup extra-virgin olive oil	1	teaspoon dried rosemary
2	cans (15 ounces each) white cannellini beans, drained and rinsed		Coarse salt and ground white pepper to taste

Preheat the oven to 350°F.

Slice the top from the head of the garlic, exposing the tops of the cloves. Rub the entire head with the 1 tablespoon oil, wrap in aluminum foil, place on a baking sheet, and bake until fork-tender, about 45 minutes. Remove the garlic from the foil, remove the papery skins, slit each clove with a bird's beak or small paring knife, and push the garlic into a small bowl. Mash and set aside.

In a large bowl, mash the beans with a potato masher or the back of a wooden spoon. (You can use a food processor, but do not pulse to a paste, and remove the beans to a bowl before adding the other ingredients.) Add the lemon juice, rosemary, reserved garlic, and the remaining ⅓ cup oil, and season with salt and pepper to taste. Serve immediately or refrigerate, covered, for up to 24 hours.

To serve the dish: Serve this spread at room temperature on Crostini (page 11) or slices of crusty bread.

HOT CRAB DIP

YIELD | 6 CUPS

1	pound backfin crabmeat	1	tablespoon Worcestershire sauce
12	ounces (about 1½ cups) cream cheese, softened	½	cup grated cheddar cheese
8	ounces (1 cup) sour cream	¼	cup dry sherry (optional)
½	cup mayonnaise		Salt and pepper
1	tablespoon Old Bay seasoning		Sweet paprika for garnish

Preheat the oven to 350°F.

In a large bowl, combine all the ingredients, then place in an all-temperature dish that can go from the refrigerator to the oven. Bake until the dish bubbles a bit, about 30 minutes.

Remove from the oven and let stand for at least 20 minutes. Do not serve directly from the oven, as the center will be scalding.

The dip can be made a day in advance, cooled, covered, and refrigerated until ready to use.

To serve the dish: If you've made the dip ahead of time, heat for 15 minutes at 300°F 20 minutes before serving, so it isn't too hot. Serve with spoons so people can place the dip on Crostini (page 11), Toasted Polenta Slices (page 24), or crackers.

POTLUCK NOTE | *Backfin crabmeat is good for this dish because it is a little richer in taste and a little less expensive than lump and much better than canned. It often has some bits of shell that you have to pick out and discard.*

ARTICHOKE-SPINACH DIP

YIELD | 8 CUPS

8	ounces (about 1 cup) cream cheese, at room temperature	2	boxes (10 ounces each) frozen chopped spinach, thawed and drained
3	cloves garlic, minced	2	jars (14 ounces) marinated artichoke hearts, drained and minced
1	cup light mayonnaise		
⅔	cup shredded Parmesan cheese		
⅔	cup shredded Monterey Jack cheese		

Preheat the oven to 325°F.

In a large bowl, using an electric mixer or by hand, blend the cream cheese, garlic, mayonnaise, Parmesan, and Monterey Jack. Fold in the spinach and artichokes.

Place the mixture in an ovenproof serving dish and bake until the edges are bubbling, about 45 minutes.

To serve the dish: This can be served with Crostini (page 11), Toasted Polenta Slices (page 24), or any type of cracker.

Tomato-Peach Salsa (opposite)
Crispy Pita Chips (page 14)

TOMATO-PEACH SALSA

This delicious fruity salsa is perfectly paired with Crispy Pita Chips (page 14).

YIELD | 4 CUPS

4	ripe peaches, chopped, or 8 canned peach halves	1	tablespoon fresh lime juice
8	plum tomatoes, peeled and chopped	1	tablespoon vinegar
1	sweet or red onion, chopped	1	tablespoon grated fresh ginger or 1½ teaspoons ground
1	tablespoon + 1 teaspoon packed brown sugar	2	tablespoons minced fresh cilantro
			Salt

In a large bowl, combine all the ingredients except the salt, cover, and refrigerate for at least 2 hours or up to 24 hours. Taste and season with salt if necessary.

To serve the dish: This is a great accompaniment to Dilled Shrimp (page 21), Chicken Satay Skewers (page 9), or any cheese and cold-cut plates that you may arrange.

DEVILED EGGS

YIELD | 24 DEVILED EGGS

12	hard-cooked eggs, chilled and peeled		Salt and pepper to taste
2	tablespoons mayonnaise	2	tablespoons minced fresh cilantro or flat-leaf parsley, for garnish
1	teaspoon mild curry powder		
2	tablespoons sweet chutney, such as Major Grey's, minced		

Halve each egg lengthwise and remove the yolks to a mixing bowl. Mash the yolks and stir in the mayonnaise, curry, and chutney. Season with salt and pepper to taste.

Gently spoon the egg-yolk mixture back into the egg whites and mound the filling with a butter knife. Place the deviled eggs in an egg holder or platter and cover.

To serve the dish: When you're ready to serve, garnish each egg with a little sprinkle of the cilantro or parsley.

POTLUCK NOTE | *To hard-cook eggs, place them in a pot with water to cover by 2 inches. Do not crowd them. Bring to a boil and cook for 1 minute. Then remove from the heat, cover the pot, and let stand for 12 minutes for one to six eggs, 20 minutes for more. Remove the eggs from the pot with a slotted spoon, place them in a bowl in the sink, and run cold water over them until the shells are cool to the touch. You can refrigerate the eggs in their shells for up to 3 days. To remove the shell, crackle it by tapping the egg gently on the edge of a bowl or cup. Roll the egg between your hands to loosen the shell. If the shell sticks, hold the egg under running water to help ease off the shell smoothly.*

DILLED SHRIMP

YIELD | 12 TO 16 SERVINGS

Shrimp

¼   cup salt + more to taste

½   cup sugar

1   bunch fresh dill or ¼ cup dried

2   pounds medium (30–40 count/ pound) fresh or frozen shrimp

Marinade

½   cup canola oil

¼   cup white wine vinegar

½   cup minced fresh dill or 3 tablespoons dried

Salt and pepper to taste

Sprigs of fresh dill or parsley, for garnish

To make the shrimp: Fill a stockpot with water and add the ¼ cup salt, sugar, and dill. Bring to a boil. Drop the shrimp in and boil rapidly for 4 to 5 minutes. Turn off the heat and leave the shrimp in the pot another 5 minutes.

Drain the shrimp and run under cold water to stop the cooking. Peel and devein the shrimp, then place in a 9-by-13-inch Pyrex baking dish.

To assemble the dish: In a small bowl, combine the oil, vinegar, dill, and salt and pepper to taste, then pour the marinade over the shrimp, stirring until the shrimp are covered. Cover with plastic wrap and refrigerate for 2 to 3 hours or up to 24 hours. If you are transporting the shrimp, carry them in a thermal container with a cold pack.

To serve the dish: Arrange the dill or parsley sprigs on a serving platter. Lift the shrimp from the baking dish with a slotted spoon and load them onto the platter. This simple shrimp dish can be served with a classic cocktail sauce or Tomato-Peach Salsa (page 19).

SMOKED SALMON-POTATO CUPS

YIELD | 40 HORS D'OEUVRES

1–2 pounds fingerling potatoes (about 20), each 1–2 inches in diameter and 3 inches long

1 tablespoon extra-virgin olive oil

Salt

12 ounces smoked salmon, minced

⅓ cup (about 3 ounces) sour cream

3 tablespoons minced chives + more for garnish

1 teaspoon drained small capers + more for garnish

1 teaspoon prepared white horseradish, drained

Preheat the oven to 375°F. Line a large baking sheet with foil.

Parboil the potatoes in boiling water until barely tender, about 5 minutes. Let cool slightly on a plate.

Halve each potato and use a small melon baller to scoop out an indentation, leaving at least a ¼-inch shell. Cut a thin slice from the bottom of each potato cup so it won't wobble. Discard these potato bits or place in a zip-top bag and freeze for use in soup or stock.

In a bowl, toss the potato cups with the oil and season lightly with salt.

Arrange the potato cups scooped side down on the prepared baking sheet and bake in the lower third of the oven until the undersides are golden, about 20 minutes. Let cool slightly.

Meanwhile, in a small bowl, mix the salmon, sour cream, chives, the 1 teaspoon capers, and horseradish. Mound each potato cup with salmon filling.

To serve the dish: Arrange the filled cups on a platter and garnish with chives and capers.

TOASTED POLENTA SLICES

YIELD | 24 SLICES

6	cups water	½	teaspoon salt
2	cups quick-cooking polenta		Coarse salt, for sprinkling
	Olive oil for cooking		

Bring the water to a slow boil over medium-high heat. Pour the polenta and ½ teaspoon salt into the water, lower the heat to medium, and cook, stirring constantly, until the polenta is thick and smooth, 3 to 5 minutes (or cook according to package directions). Remove from the heat.

Spread two sheets of plastic wrap, each about 18 inches long, on two baking sheets and coat lightly with olive oil.

Divide the polenta evenly on the prepared baking sheets. With the aid of the plastic wrap and a spatula, roll the polenta into two logs, each about 2 inches in diameter. Let cool for 1 hour, then refrigerate, tightly wrapped, for up to 2 days.

When ready to bake, preheat the oven to 400°F. Line two baking sheets with foil and coat lightly with olive oil.

Remove the plastic from the logs and cut the polenta into ½-inch slices. Lay the slices on the prepared baking sheets, brush with olive oil, and sprinkle with coarse salt. Bake until the slices are golden and crisp at the edges, about 10 minutes. Turn the slices and bake for another 10 minutes, or until crisp on both sides. If you're not serving them right away, let the polenta slices cool, then layer with waxed paper in a flat carrier.

To serve the dish: Heat the polenta slices on a parchment-lined baking sheet in a 350°F oven for 10 minutes. These are terrific with almost anything, including Creamy Blue-Cheese Spread (page 14), Chicken Satay Skewers (page 9), and Dilled Shrimp (page 21).

SALADS

IN MANY WAYS, this is the easiest and most appreciated course. Large salads with lots of different ingredients are fun to put together, and you don't often get a chance to make them when you're feeding just a few people.

Pretty much all salads are easy to transport. Greens at risk of getting soggy when dressed too early can be carried separately from the dressing and toppings. Salads that benefit from early blending, like slaws and pasta and potato salads, can be made ahead of time, refrigerated, and then carried in an insulated container to your event.

Virtually all the salad dressings included here call for extra-virgin olive oil because it is flavorful, abundant, available at various prices, and quite healthy. That said, there are times when canola or safflower oil can be used if you strongly prefer it or find it convenient. Walnut, almond, avocado, truffle, and other oils can impart a special flavor. These are used so infrequently, though, that it is best to buy them in small amounts and refrigerate them after opening.

Balsamic vinegar seems to have become very popular, but though it is delicious it's not always necessary. Wine vinegars—red, white, and sherry—are good to have on hand, as are apple cider vinegar and plain white vinegar. When mixing salad dressing, it is always better to err on the side of less vinegar or lemon than more. You can always add more bit by bit, but you may need to add a ton of oil and other ingredients to correct an overly acidic dressing. Dip a bit of a leaf in the dressing to test the taste.

It's a good idea to have a few glass jars with tightly fitting screw tops in which to make salad dressing. They're easily transportable, and you just need to shake and pour when ready to serve. Keep in mind that salads are best dressed when they are completely dry.

SALADE NIÇOISE

YIELD | 10 SERVINGS

Vinaigrette

¼	cup white or red wine vinegar	½	teaspoon salt, or to taste
1	tablespoon minced shallots	¼	teaspoon freshly ground black pepper, or to taste
½	teaspoon Dijon mustard		
½	cup extra-virgin olive oil		

Salad

2	pounds fingerling potatoes	1	can (2 ounces) flat anchovies, drained
1	pound haricots verts or tiny green string beans	5	hard-cooked eggs (see page 20), peeled and quartered lengthwise
1	head Boston or Bibb lettuce, rinsed and dried	3	tomatoes, peeled and quartered lengthwise, or 1 pint cherry tomatoes, halved
1	red bell pepper, peeled and julienned (see page 113)	1	cup Niçoise olives
1	yellow bell pepper, peeled and julienned (see page 113)	20	caper berries with stems or 3 tablespoons drained jarred capers
2	cans (6 ounces each) Italian tuna packed in olive oil		

To make the vinaigrette: Whisk all the ingredients in a jar with a screw top. Cover and set aside. Shake before each use.

To make the salad: Place the potatoes in a large saucepan with cold water to cover by 1 inch. Bring to a boil and cook until fork-tender, about 15 minutes. When cool enough to handle, peel and toss with 2 tablespoons of the vinaigrette, then cover and refrigerate until chilled.

Meanwhile, steam the haricots verts, or drop them in boiling water for about 2 minutes; they will be crisp. If using green beans, increase the cooking time by 2 minutes. Drain in a colander and rinse under cold water immediately to stop the cooking.

To serve the dish: Lay out the lettuce leaves on a large platter and carefully arrange the peppers, tuna, anchovies, eggs, tomatoes, olives, and caper berries or capers on top of the lettuce. Drizzle with the vinaigrette and serve.

COBB SALAD

This salad, versions of which are still on menus everywhere, was named for Bob Cobb, the original owner of the derby-shaped Hollywood Brown Derby restaurant, where the salad was first composed in 1926.

Salad

½	head iceberg lettuce (about 4 cups)	2	whole boneless, skinless chicken breasts, boiled and diced
1	small head frisée (curly endive or chicory) (about 2½ cups)	3	hard-cooked eggs, chopped into small pieces
½	head romaine (about 2½ cups)	1	ripe avocado, peeled and diced just before serving
1	bunch watercress, bottom stems removed	¾	cup (6 ounces) crumbled Roquefort or blue cheese
2	tomatoes, peeled and diced	2	tablespoons finely chopped chives
6	strips crisp bacon, crumbled		

Dressing

¼	cup water	½	teaspoon sea salt
¼	cup red wine vinegar	¾	teaspoon Worcestershire sauce
1	teaspoon sugar	1	teaspoon Dijon mustard
1	teaspoon freshly squeezed lemon juice	1	clove garlic (any center green stem removed), finely minced
¾	teaspoon freshly ground black pepper	¾	cup extra-virgin olive oil

To make the salad: Cut all the iceberg lettuce, frisée, and romaine and half of the watercress into fine pieces and arrange in a large salad bowl. Arrange the tomatoes, bacon, chicken, eggs, avocado, and cheese in strips on the greens. Sprinkle the chives over the entire salad and garnish with the remaining watercress.

To make the dressing: In a medium bowl, blend together all the ingredients except the oil. Add the oil and mix well.

To serve the dish: Just before serving, drizzle the salad with the dressing.

GREEK SALAD

YIELD | 10 SERVINGS

Salad

1	large head green-leaf lettuce	1	cucumber
1	large head romaine lettuce	1	cup (8 ounces) crumbled feta cheese
1	green bell pepper		
6	plum tomatoes		

Dressing

3	tablespoons fresh lemon juice		Salt and freshly ground black pepper to taste
¾	cup Greek olive oil		
1	tablespoon minced fresh oregano leaves or ½ teaspoon dried		

Accompaniments

1	cup kalamata or other Greek olives, drained	1	cup pepperoncini, drained

To prepare the vegetables: Wash, spin, and dry the lettuce and tear into bite-size pieces. Cut the bell pepper in half lengthwise, remove the seeds and white ribs, and slice. Cut the tomatoes into six slices lengthwise. Peel the cucumber, cut it in half lengthwise, and remove the seeds with the tip of a teaspoon, then slice. Place all the vegetables in a large salad bowl.

To make the dressing: Whisk the lemon juice, oil, oregano, and salt and black pepper to taste in a screw-top jar. Cover and reserve. Shake before each use.

To serve the dish: Mix the vegetables and cheese, toss with the dressing, and top with the olives and pepperoncini.

FENNEL-ARUGULA-PARMESAN SALAD

There is a debate about using lemon or vinegar with Parmesan cheese. If the cheese is of the finest quality, it is probably better to omit the acid, as the cheese will have some bite to it.

YIELD | 10 SERVINGS

½ cup extra-virgin olive oil

2 tablespoons fresh lemon juice (optional)

½ teaspoon coarse salt

3 fennel bulbs, trimmed top and bottom, halved lengthwise, and very thinly sliced with a mandolin or chef's knife

3 bunches arugula, thick stems discarded

8 ounce wedge or block Parmesan cheese

In a shallow bowl large enough to hold the fennel, whisk together the oil, lemon juice (if using), and salt.

Rinse the fennel slices, dry thoroughly with a cloth towel, and toss in the oil mixture. Rinse, spin, and dry the arugula. With a V-shaped vegetable peeler, shave slices of the cheese onto a clean plate.

To serve the dish: On a large platter or individual plates, arrange a bed of the arugula, then layer on the fennel-and-oil mixture and top with the shaved cheese. Provide a pepper mill so people can help themselves to seasoning. Components can be carried separately and assembled at any destination. Carry the cheese in something that won't bend so that it doesn't crumble too much.

POTLUCK NOTE | *The pieces above the fennel bulb and some of the fronds can be wrapped and frozen for future use in soup or stock.*

COUNTRY SALAD WITH LARDONS

YIELD | 10 SERVINGS

½	pound slab bacon, rind removed	2	heads frisée lettuce
2	tablespoons minced shallots	1	log (8 ounces) room-temperature chèvre, crumbled
⅓	cup balsamic vinegar		
½	cup extra-virgin olive oil	2	cups croutons
	Salt and pepper		

Cut ½-inch cubes from the bacon and brown in a heavy skillet over medium-high heat for 10 minutes. Remove the lardons to paper towels with a slotted spoon.

Pour out the drippings and return ⅓ cup to the skillet. Lower the heat to medium, add the shallots and vinegar, and cook, stirring constantly, about 5 minutes. If you are serving the salad immediately, turn off the heat and stir in the oil. Lightly salt and pepper to taste.

To hold everything for a few hours, reserve the lardons in one container and the shallot-vinegar mixture in another. When ready to serve, heat the mixture in a small saucepan over low heat. When it is warm, stir in the lardons and remove from the heat.

Tear the frisée into bite-size pieces, wash, spin, and dry. If not serving immediately, refrigerate in a cloth salad bag or loosely wrapped in paper towels in a plastic bag.

To serve the dish: Place the lettuce in a large salad bowl, top with the chèvre, add the lardons and dressing, toss the salad, and top with the croutons.

POTLUCK NOTE | *Stale challah or brioche makes very good croutons. Remove the crust and cut the bread into ½-inch cubes. Toast on a baking sheet for 10 minutes in a 375°F oven. Use immediately, or let cool and store in an airtight container for 2 or 3 days.*

SPINACH-STRAWBERRY SALAD
WITH POPPY SEED DRESSING

YIELD | 10 SERVINGS

Dressing

½	cup extra-virgin olive oil		1	tablespoon + 1 teaspoon poppy seeds
¼	cup balsamic vinegar			Salt and pepper
2	tablespoons honey			
2	teaspoons coarse mustard			

Salad

2	pints (4 cups) ripe strawberries		1½	pounds prewashed baby spinach

To make the dressing: In a bowl, whisk together the oil, vinegar, honey, mustard, poppy seeds, and salt and pepper to taste. Transfer to a screw-top jar. Refrigerate for up to 24 hours. Before serving, let the dressing return to room temperature, then shake well.

To make the salad: Rinse the strawberries, remove the hulls, and cut the berries in sixths (or quarters if they aren't very large) from top to bottom. Place in a covered container and refrigerate for up to 24 hours.

To serve the dish: Place the spinach and strawberries in a salad bowl and toss with the dressing.

POTLUCK NOTE | *The best way to rinse all berries without bruising them is to fill a bowl with water, add the berries, and let sit for a few minutes. Gently lift the berries out onto paper towels and discard the gritty water.*

BASIC MIXED SALAD

1	head red-leaf lettuce	½	teaspoon sea salt
1	head green-leaf lettuce		Up to ½ cup extra-virgin olive oil
1	head radicchio	3	tablespoons wine vinegar
1	bunch watercress		Freshly ground pepper
1	red onion, thinly sliced		
1	cucumber, peeled, seeded, quartered lengthwise, and thinly sliced		

Separate the leaves of all the greens, rinse, and dry. If not using right away, store in a cloth bag in the refrigerator.

To serve the dish: When ready to serve, toss the greens, onion, and cucumber in a large salad bowl and sprinkle with the salt. Add the oil and toss to coat thoroughly. Add the vinegar and toss again. Grind a few turns of a pepper mill over the salad and serve immediately.

POTLUCK NOTE | *The proportion of dressing to salad is more or less ¾ cup of dressing to 1 pound of salad. Depending on how many other dishes are being served, this amount of salad will serve 10 and can easily stretch to accommodate a few more.*

MIXED SPRING SALAD

Mixed spring salad—also called mesclun, field greens, or spring mix—consists of an assortment of readily available young salad greens. Commercial mixes, sold year-round, often include young, small forms of arugula, mizuna, tatsoi, frisée, oak leaf, red chard, mustard greens, and radicchio.

YIELD | 10 SERVINGS

10	ounces (8 cups) mixed spring salad	Salt and pepper
½	cup salad dressing (recipes follow)	

Rinse and dry the greens, and keep in a cloth bag in the refrigerator until ready to serve.

To serve the dish: Place the greens in a large salad bowl and toss with ½ cup salad dressing or to taste, and season with salt and pepper.

BASIC VINAIGRETTE

This quick dressing can be made on short notice with "on hand" ingredients. Either balsamic vinegar or fresh lemon juice makes a fine substitute for wine vinegar, and shredded basil, chives, or tarragon are good additions. The recipe can be doubled easily.

YIELD | ¾ CUP

3	tablespoons red wine vinegar	1	teaspoon Dijon mustard
½	cup + 2 tablespoons extra-virgin olive oil	¼	teaspoon salt
½	teaspoon sugar		Freshly ground pepper

Place the vinegar, oil, sugar, mustard, salt, and a few twists of freshly ground pepper in a screw-top jar and shake to blend. There's no need to refrigerate it if it's used within 12 hours.

BLUE CHEESE DRESSING

YIELD | 2½ CUPS

1	cup extra-virgin olive oil
⅓	cup white vinegar
6	ounces (¾ cup) blue cheese, crumbled
4	ounces (½ cup) sour cream or buttermilk
	Salt and pepper

Mix the oil, vinegar, blue cheese, sour cream or buttermilk, and salt and pepper to taste in a refrigerator container. Leave the cheese crumbly or mash it, whichever you prefer. Cover and refrigerate for up to 2 days. Bring to room temperature and mix well before serving. If the mixture has thickened, add a couple of tablespoons olive oil and stir.

OLD-FASHIONED THOUSAND ISLAND DRESSING

YIELD | 2 CUPS

1	cup mayonnaise
¼	cup extra-virgin olive oil
⅓	cup bottled chili sauce
2	teaspoons minced shallots
½	teaspoon sweet paprika
2	tablespoons finely chopped pimiento-stuffed olives
⅛	teaspoon freshly ground pepper

Whisk all the ingredients and refrigerate, covered, for up to 3 days. Stir before serving.

QUICK CROUTONS

YIELD | 5 TO 6 CUPS

8	slices loaf bread	2	teaspoons dried thyme
⅓	cup canola or safflower oil + more if needed		Salt and pepper
1	clove garlic, crushed		

Preheat the oven to 300°F.

Trim the crust from the bread and cut the bread into ½-inch cubes.

Pour the oil to a depth of about ¼ inch in a heavy 10- or 12-inch skillet and heat over medium-high heat. Place the garlic in the skillet, add one layer of bread cubes, and lower the heat. Cook, turning with a spatula, until browned, 2 to 3 minutes. (Don't worry if the cubes are not browned on all sides.) Remove to a paper towel, sprinkle with the thyme, and season with salt and pepper to taste. Repeat until all the bread cubes are browned.

Place on a baking sheet and bake for 10 minutes.

If you're not using the croutons right away, let them cool completely before storing in an airtight container. You can keep these for 2 days, but 1 is better.

RED-SKINNED-POTATO SALAD

YIELD | 12 SERVINGS

Salad

4	pounds red-skinned potatoes, scrubbed	⅓	cup bread-and-butter pickles, chopped
4	hard-cooked eggs, peeled and chopped	2	tablespoons capers, drained and rinsed (optional)
1	medium/large red onion, chopped	⅓	cup minced fresh flat-leaf parsley, for garnish
1	bunch scallions, chopped		
3	ribs celery, strings, leaves and fibers removed, chopped		

Dressing

1	cup mayonnaise	2	tablespoons sugar
¼	cup olive oil		Salt and pepper
2	tablespoons white vinegar		

To make the salad: Place the potatoes in a large pot and cover with cold water. Bring to a boil over high heat, then lower the heat to medium-low and boil until the potatoes are fully cooked but still firm, about 20 minutes. Test the potatoes occasionally with a fork so you can get them out of the water before they are too soft for the salad. Drain and rinse in cold water or an ice bath until cool enough to handle.

Slice the potatoes and place in a large bowl. Gently stir in the eggs, onion, scallions, celery, pickles, and capers.

To make the dressing: In a small bowl, mix the mayonnaise, oil, vinegar, and sugar. Stir well; then, with a rubber spatula, gently stir into the potato mixture. Season with salt and pepper to taste. Cover with a lid or plastic wrap and refrigerate until ready to use, up to 24 hours.

To serve the dish: Top with the parsley and serve chilled.

POTLUCK NOTE | *See page 20 for how to hard-cook eggs.*

COLESLAW WITH RAISINS AND CARAWAY SEEDS

YIELD | 8 CUPS (10 TO 12 SERVINGS)

¾ cup raisins

1 cup orange juice or water

1 head firm, fresh green cabbage

2 medium/large carrots

½ cup finely diced green or red bell pepper

1 teaspoon salt

1 cup mayonnaise

1 teaspoon ground cumin

1 teaspoon caraway seeds

¼ cup cider vinegar

¼ cup olive oil

2 tablespoons sugar

¼ cup water

Soak the raisins in the orange juice or water for at least 1 hour. Drain and discard the liquid.

Remove and discard the outer leaves of the cabbage. Cut the cabbage into quarters and remove the hard core. Shred the cabbage either by hand or on the coarse shredding disk in a food processor. Shred the carrots the same way.

In a large bowl, mix the cabbage, carrots, raisins, and bell pepper. Sprinkle with the salt.

In a medium bowl, mix the remaining ingredients. Pour over the slaw and incorporate thoroughly. Refrigerate, covered, and mix again in 30 minutes. Cover and keep refrigerated until ready to serve, up to 24 hours.

To serve the dish: Place the slaw in a large bowl and serve with a slotted spoon to prevent excess liquid on people's plates.

COLD SESAME NOODLES

These ingredients are usually available in the Asian food section of large supermarkets or Asian speciality stores.

YIELD | 10 SERVINGS

3	tablespoons Chinese sesame paste
2	tablespoons oil from sesame paste
⅓	cup light soy sauce or tamari
¼	cup honey
4	tablespoons sesame oil
1	teaspoon hot chili oil, or to taste
½	cup boiling water
1	pound narrow Asian buckwheat noodles
6	ounces plain or flavored extra-firm tofu, diced
¼	cup light sesame seeds
¼	cup minced fresh cilantro

In a heatproof bowl, mix the sesame paste and its oil with the soy sauce or tamari, honey, sesame oil, and chili oil. Stir in the boiling water and mix until smooth.

Boil the noodles according to the package directions, drain, and place in a large serving bowl. Pour the sesame dressing over all and toss until the noodles are coated. Cover and refrigerate for up to 12 hours.

To serve the dish: When ready to serve, mix in the tofu, sesame seeds, and cilantro. Serve cold but with the chill off.

MEDITERRANEAN PASTA SALAD

YIELD | 10 SERVINGS

Pasta

1	pound farfalle or rigatoni	8	ounces smoked mozzarella cheese, diced
¼	cup olive oil	¼	pound pitted black olives, sliced
	Pinch of salt	1	red onion, diced
12	ounces frozen or drained marinated artichoke hearts	½	cup minced fresh flat-leaf parsley
2	ounces sun-dried tomatoes	1	tablespoon minced fresh basil (optional)
12	ounces (about 1½ cups) ricotta cheese		

Dressing

½	cup + 1 tablespoon extra-virgin olive oil	1	tablespoon sugar
3	tablespoons balsamic vinegar		Salt and pepper

To make the pasta: Cook the pasta in a large pot of boiling water according to the package directions, or until al dente. Drain, run under cold water, and pat dry with paper towels. Place in a bowl large enough to hold all the ingredients and toss with the oil and salt.

In a medium saucepan, bring the artichoke hearts (cut in quarters top to bottom if not already quartered) to a boil, then lower the heat and simmer for 3 minutes. Drain and add to the pasta.

Place the tomatoes in a heatproof bowl and cover with boiling water. Let stand for 5 minutes, then drain. Mince and stir into the pasta, then stir in the ricotta, mozzarella, olives, onion, parsley, and basil, if desired.

To make the dressing: In a small bowl, whisk the oil, vinegar, and sugar. Pour the dressing over the salad and toss, then season with salt and pepper to taste. Cover and chill for 1 to 2 hours and serve cold.

To serve the dish: If you are carrying this to another destination, transport the completed salad, covered, in a thermal container with a cold pack.

COUSCOUS SALAD

YIELD | 6 CUPS

3	cups vegetable or chicken broth	¾	cup shredded fresh mint leaves
1	teaspoon ground cumin	5	scallions, finely chopped
1	teaspoon ground cinnamon	½	cup coarsely chopped pistachios
2	cups instant couscous	½	cup slivered almonds, toasted
1	can (15 ounces) chickpeas, rinsed and drained	1	cup dates, pitted and chopped
½–¾	cup extra-virgin olive oil, as needed		Salt and pepper
	Juice and grated zest of 1 lemon (see page 316)		

In a medium pot, heat the broth with the cumin and cinnamon over medium heat until simmering, about 5 minutes. Stir in the couscous until thoroughly moistened. Remove from the heat and transfer to a bowl large enough to hold all the ingredients.

Toss the couscous with the chickpeas and ½ cup of the oil. Let cool, then add the lemon juice and zest and the mint. Mix in the scallions, pistachios, almonds, and dates. Season with salt and pepper to taste. Add up to ¼ cup additional oil, if needed.

To serve the dish: This dish is best served within 2 hours or so, at room temperature.

MIXED BEAN SALAD

This is a year-round favorite. You can combine any variety of beans and use your own dressing.

YIELD | 10 SERVINGS

Salad

¾   cup cooked orange lentils

1⅓   cups cooked black beans or 1 can (15 ounces), rinsed and drained

1⅓   cups cooked white beans or 1 can (15 ounces), rinsed and drained

1⅓   cups cooked chickpeas or 1 can (15 ounces), rinsed and drained

5   walnut-size red radishes, halved and sliced lengthwise

2   large tomatoes, peeled, seeded, and diced (omit if out of season)

1   red onion, diced

3   large ribs celery, strings removed, diced

2   tablespoons minced fresh basil or up to 1 teaspoon dried

¼   cup minced fresh flat-leaf parsley

Vinaigrette

⅓   cup extra-virgin olive oil

1–2   cloves garlic, minced

2   tablespoons fresh lemon juice

3   tablespoons red wine vinegar

2   teaspoons Dijon mustard

¼   teaspoon crushed red pepper flakes

Sea salt and freshly ground black pepper to taste

To make the salad: In a bowl large enough to hold all the ingredients, mix the lentils, black beans, white beans, and chickpeas. Add the radishes, tomatoes, onion, celery, basil, and parsley and stir to combine.

To make the vinaigrette: In a tightly covered jar, mix the oil, garlic, lemon juice, vinegar, mustard, red pepper flakes, and salt and pepper to taste. Shake well. Pour over the bean mixture and stir to combine. Cover and refrigerate for up to 24 hours.

To serve the dish: This salad is best served at room temperature.

PASTA

PASTA IS THE UNIVERSAL comfort food. It is a blank canvas on which the world's palate is exhibited. Pasta in all its many forms is easy to cook, and most of the sauces included here can be made several days ahead. Many of the composed dishes can be assembled a day before you want to serve them. The dish can be made at home and then transported in an insulated carrier or cooked at your destination. (Pyrex and other companies make insulated meal carriers that have covered, variously sized freezer-to-oven dishes with hot or cold gel packs.) It is generally a good idea to use short pasta such as ziti or rigatoni instead of spaghetti or linguine if food is being served buffet- or family-style, because it retains an al dente quality and is easy to portion out.

Pasta will vary in size according to the manufacturer, so use these measurements as guidelines. When using shaped, small to medium pasta such as bow ties, elbow pasta (macaroni), farfalle, fusilli, penne, rigatoni, rotelle (wagon wheels), shells, and ziti: One-half pound will yield 4 cups of cooked pasta. Long pasta will be about the same: One-half pound of spaghetti, linguine, fettuccine, or similar pastas will also yield 4 cups cooked. For egg noodles, ½ pound will yield about 2½ cups. Depending on how it is served and what accompanies it, ½ pound of pasta will serve four to six people.

Traditionally, 1 pound of pasta is boiled in 4 quarts of water with 1 teaspoon of salt and 1 tablespoon of oil. However, both the salt and the oil can be omitted.

When boiling pasta, taste a bit to make sure that it is al dente, not raw. As a rule, fresh store-bought pasta needs to be in boiling water for 5 minutes; packaged dry pasta, 10; and whole wheat, 12 to 15. For hot dishes, drain but don't rinse the pasta unless otherwise directed, and reserve a cup of the cooking water to use if water is needed in the sauce. For cold dishes, drain, rinse, and toss with a tablespoon or so of good olive oil, then cool.

BOLOGNESE SAUCE

This thick, rich, meaty ragù alla Bolognese derives its name from the Bologna region of Italy, where variations of this sauce are served on pasta or gnocchi.

YIELD | 6 CUPS

¼	cup extra-virgin olive oil	¾	teaspoon salt
1	carrot, finely chopped	½	teaspoon freshly grated or ground nutmeg
2	large ribs celery, diced		
1	medium/large onion, diced	2	tablespoons tomato paste
2	tablespoons unsalted butter	2	cans (28 ounces each) Italian diced tomatoes, 1 drained
1	pound ground beef		Salt and freshly ground pepper
1	pound skirt steak, minced	½	cup heavy cream
1	cup dry Italian white wine		
1	cup whole milk		

Heat the oil in a Dutch oven (which will hold a uniform temperature without scorching) over medium-high heat. Add the carrot, celery, and onion. Reduce the heat to medium and cook, stirring, until the pan becomes dry, about 10 minutes. Stir in the butter. Add the ground beef and steak and cook, stirring occasionally, until the meat browns evenly, about 20 minutes.

Add the wine and cook, stirring, for 5 minutes. Gradually add the milk. Stir in the salt, nutmeg, and tomato paste, then pour in the tomatoes. Stir to scrape the bottom of the Dutch oven. Reduce the heat to medium-low and cook, uncovered, for 30 minutes, stirring occasionally. Reduce the heat to low and simmer, stirring occasionally, for 3 hours. Add salt and pepper to taste. Stir in the cream.

The sauce can be cooled, covered, and refrigerated for up to 3 days. To heat, simmer on low heat for 20 minutes, stirring frequently, before serving.

POTLUCK NOTE | *To grate nutmeg, you can use either a small grater meant for this purpose, or a Microplane. You can also use a nutmeg mill, which looks like an oversize pepper mill. You can find these items at any kitchenware store or online.*

SAUSAGE-AND-PEPPERS PASTA CASSEROLE

YIELD | 10 SERVINGS

5	tablespoons olive oil	1½	cups water
1½	pounds Italian sausage (sweet, hot, or a combination), cut into 1-inch pieces	1	teaspoon dried oregano
		1	teaspoon dried thyme
		1	teaspoon dried rosemary
2	red bell peppers, cored and sliced	½	teaspoon black pepper
2	green bell peppers, cored and sliced	1	pound penne, cooked al dente and drained
2	large onions, sliced	¼	cup shredded Parmesan cheese
1	can (28 ounces) roasted or regular diced tomatoes		
1	can (6 ounces) tomato paste		

Preheat the oven to 350°F.

Heat 3 tablespoons of the oil in a large skillet over medium heat. Cook the sausage until brown, about 10 minutes. Remove the sausage from the skillet and set aside.

Place the red and green bell peppers and onions in the skillet and sauté until the onions are transparent and golden brown, about 10 minutes. Return the reserved sausage to the skillet and add the tomatoes, tomato paste, water, oregano, thyme, rosemary, and black pepper. Mix very well. Cook and stir for 5 minutes over low heat.

In a bowl large enough to hold all the ingredients, stir the penne with the remaining 2 tablespoons olive oil. Stir in the sausage-and-peppers mixture. At this point, the mixture can be covered and refrigerated for up to 24 hours.

To serve the dish: Transfer the mixture to a casserole and bake until piping hot and the sausage is cooked through, about 45 minutes. Remove from the oven and sprinkle with the cheese.

LASAGNA WITH BÉCHAMEL SAUCE

This is another of those amazing Italian classics that seems complicated the first time you prepare it, and yet some version of this dish is the mainstay at a great many potlucks. Make it your own. Use your favorite tomato sauce instead of those suggested here. Try the "no cook" lasagna noodles available at many supermarkets, using 24 sheets from two 8-ounce packages. You might even try spinach lasagna, if your supermarket carries it.

YIELD | 10 SERVINGS

¼	cup extra-virgin olive oil or spray, for coating pan and pasta
2	packages (8 ounces each) lasagna noodles
4	cups Thick Tomato and Meat Sauce (see page 60) or Bolognese Sauce (see page 40)
1	container (15 ounces) ricotta cheese, drained
1½	cups diced mozzarella cheese
4	cups Parmesan Béchamel Sauce (recipe follows)
½	cup grated Parmesan cheese, for topping

Preheat the oven to 375°F. Oil the bottom and sides of a 12-by-16-inch lasagna pan or 3½-inch deep roasting pan and set aside.

Cook and drain the lasagna noodles according to package directions. Brush or spray with olive oil.

Place a thin layer of tomato sauce in the pan and spread with a rubber spatula. Place a single layer of noodles over all, overlapping them slightly. Cover with a layer of tomato sauce, then dot with teaspoons of the ricotta and about one-fourth of the mozzarella. Cover with 1 cup of Béchamel Sauce. Continue layering until all the noodles are used, ending with mozzarella cheese and Béchamel.

Bake until the top is golden brown, about 20 minutes. Let the lasagna rest for 15 minutes before serving.

The dish can be assembled at home and baked at your destination.

To serve the dish: Cut the lasagna into squares in the baking dish and place on a heat-proof mat or trivet. Serve with an angled spatula or two serving spoons. Put the Parmesan in a bowl alongside. Accompany with warm sliced Italian or garlic bread—or both.

POTLUCK NOTE | *Both the tomato and Béchamel sauces are best used warm to assemble the lasagna. If you are not using them immediately, they can be cooled, covered, and refrigerated. (Freeze any extra tomato sauce.) The tomato sauce can be heated over a low flame. The Béchamel scorches easily, so it is best to heat in the top of a double boiler or on a heat tamer—an inexpensive gadget that looks like a hollow disk of light metal with a lot of air holes. It keeps the cooking pot from direct contact with the heat source.*

Parmesan Béchamel Sauce

3½	cups whole or 2% milk	¼	teaspoon salt
6	tablespoons unsalted butter	½	teaspoon nutmeg
4	tablespoons instant flour	¾	cup grated Parmesan cheese

In a saucepan over medium heat, scald the milk (bring it to a very low boil; just small bubbles around the edge) and remove from the heat.

In a heavy-bottomed saucepan large enough to hold all the ingredients, melt the butter and stir in the flour until the mixture is well incorporated, just before the flour starts to color, about 2 minutes. Slowly stir in the hot milk, ½ cup at a time. Add the salt and nutmeg and stir in the cheese.

SHELLS STUFFED WITH BROCCOLI, RICOTTA, PINE NUTS, AND RAISINS

YIELD | 10 SERVINGS

Pasta

20	jumbo pasta shells	2	cups shredded mozzarella cheese + more for garnish
3	tablespoons extra-virgin olive oil	⅓	cup grated Parmigiano-Reggiano cheese
1	cup diced fresh mushrooms	2	large eggs, lightly beaten
3	cups shredded and chopped broccoli, thick woody stems removed	½	teaspoon salt
½	cup minced shallots	¼	teaspoon pepper
2	tablespoons pine nuts	¼	cup chopped fresh basil or 1 teaspoon dried
3	tablespoons raisins		
1	container (15 ounces) ricotta cheese, drained		

Sauce

1	can (28 ounces) crushed tomatoes	½	teaspoon garlic powder
2	tablespoons extra-virgin olive oil		Salt and pepper
1	teaspoon sea salt	⅓	cup fine, unseasoned dry bread crumbs
1	teaspoon sugar		

Preheat the oven to 350°F.

To make the pasta: In a large pot of boiling water, cook the shells, 10 at a time if necessary, for 8 minutes, or according to package directions. Gently transfer with a slotted spoon to a bowl of cold water until you've made the filling.

In a sauté pan, heat the oil over medium heat. Add the mushrooms, broccoli, and shallots and sauté until the broccoli is crisp-tender, about 10 minutes. Stir in the pine nuts and raisins and cook for 2 minutes longer. Remove from the heat.

(continued)

In a large bowl, combine the ricotta, mozzarella, Parmigiano-Reggiano, eggs, salt, pepper, and basil, then stir in the sautéed vegetables.

Remove the cooked shells from the water with a large slotted spoon and drain. Set them on a waxed paper–lined baking sheet. Gently spoon the vegetable-cheese mixture into the shells and reserve.

To make the sauce: In a saucepan large enough to hold all the sauce ingredients, bring the tomatoes, oil, sea salt, sugar, and garlic powder to a simmer over medium heat, and cook for 15 minutes, stirring occasionally. Season with salt and pepper to taste. Stir in the bread crumbs and remove from the heat.

At this point, both the reserved stuffed shells and the sauce can be cooled, covered, and refrigerated for up to 24 hours.

To assemble the dish: Spread a thin coating of the sauce on the bottom of a 15-by-11-inch baking dish. Set the stuffed shells in the dish open side up and top with the remaining sauce. Bake for 45 minutes. You can bake the dish at home and carry it in a thermal container, or bake it at your destination.

To serve the dish: Serve right from the baking dish. Garnish with mozzarella cheese.

FRESH FETTUCCINE WITH CRIMINI MUSHROOMS

YIELD | 10 SERVINGS

2	cups boiling water	½	cup pine nuts	
3	ounces dried porcini mushrooms, washed		Salt and black pepper	
4	tablespoons extra-virgin olive oil	1½	pounds fresh fettuccine	
3	tablespoons chopped shallots	½	pint (1 cup) heavy cream	
6	cloves garlic, minced	¼	cup shredded fresh basil	
½	teaspoon crushed red pepper flakes	½	cup coarsely grated Parmigiano-Reggiano cheese	
1	pound cremini mushrooms, sliced			

In a heatproof bowl, pour the boiling water over the porcini mushrooms and let soak for 30 minutes. Meanwhile, bring a large pot of water to a boil for the fettuccine.

In a large sauté pan, heat the oil over medium heat and add the shallots, garlic, and red pepper flakes. Sauté until the shallots and garlic are golden brown, about 3 minutes. Add the porcini and crimini mushrooms and sauté for 5 minutes, then stir in the pine nuts and cook until lightly browned, about 3 minutes. Season with salt and black pepper to taste, stir, and reduce the heat to low.

Cook the fettuccine for 6 minutes, or according to package directions. Drain but do not rinse.

Slowly stir the cream into the mushroom mixture and cook until heated through, 3 to 5 minutes.

To serve the dish: Stir the cooked pasta into the sauce and immediately pour into a warmed serving dish. Top with the basil and cheese.

POTLUCK NOTE | *If you like, you can serve this dish as a casserole. Place the finished product in a large bake-and-serve dish, cover with plastic wrap, and refrigerate for up to 24 hours. At your destination, heat covered with foil in a 325°F oven for 20 minutes. Remove the foil for the last 5 minutes.*

GREEN PASTA WITH POTATOES AND PESTO

This dish is best served when you are hosting or when you can make everything but the Pesto (which can be made ahead of time) at your destination.

YIELD | 10 SERVINGS

1	teaspoon sea salt	1½	cups Pesto (recipe follows)
4	medium/large red potatoes, peeled and diced	1	cup freshly grated Parmigiano-Reggiano cheese, for serving
1½	pounds fresh or dried spinach fusilli or other short pasta		Freshly ground pepper, for serving
3	tablespoons olive oil		

Bring a large pot of water to a boil with the sea salt. Add the potatoes and cook for 5 minutes, then add the pasta and continue cooking for 5 minutes for fresh pasta, 10 minutes for dried.

Drain the potatoes and pasta, reserving ½ cup of the cooking water. Place the potatoes and pasta in a large bowl and stir with the oil and reserved cooking water. Stir in the Pesto and toss lightly.

If you prepare this dish at home, carry it in a thermal container to your destination.

To serve the dish: Serve with the cheese and freshly ground pepper.

Pesto

This recipe is best made with a mortar and pestle, but it's fine to use a blender. Just be sure to grate the cheese separately and stir it into the basil mixture by hand when it has been removed from the blender. Feel free to vary the recipe to suit your own tastes. Not to worry: Everyone in Genoa has his or her own version.

YIELD | 3 CUPS

5	cloves garlic, halved, center green cores removed	1	cup extra-virgin olive oil, preferably Italian
½	teaspoon sea salt, or to taste	½	cup finely grated pecorino cheese
3	cups shredded fresh basil leaves, center stems removed	½	cup finely grated Parmigiano-Reggiano cheese
¾	cup pine nuts		

If you are using a blender, pulse all the ingredients together except the cheeses. With a rubber spatula, remove the mixture from the blender and place in a bowl. Thoroughly mix in the cheeses.

If you are using a mortar and pestle, crush the garlic and salt until a paste forms. Gradually add the basil and keep grinding until all the basil is incorporated. Add the pine nuts and continue grinding. When a coarse paste forms, add the cheeses and gently incorporate. Add the oil and quickly blend all together with a wooden spoon.

Divide the Pesto into two 1½-cup portions. Use one portion for the Green Pasta with Potatoes, and reserve the rest for another use.

Use immediately or refrigerate, covered, for 3 days.

POTLUCK NOTE | *Pesto can be made without the cheese when basil is in season and frozen in airtight plastic containers until needed. The cheese will keep in the refrigerator for several weeks if well-wrapped. Thaw the pesto and stir in the cheese as needed.*

THE BEST SPAGHETTI AND MEATBALLS

Spaghetti is the traditional pasta for this dish, but there are many delicious alternatives if you think it will be a little hard to handle for your event. Two good pasta options for this dish are bucatini, long tubes of pasta that can be broken into 3- or 4-inch pieces, and rigatoni.

YIELD | 24 SMALL MEATBALLS

2	pounds ground beef	2	tablespoons minced fresh flat-leaf parsley
2	large eggs		Salt and freshly ground pepper
1	tablespoon olive oil + more for cooking meatballs	1½–2	pounds spaghetti
2	cloves garlic, crushed		Thick Tomato and Meat Sauce (see page 60), for serving
⅓	cup fine dry bread crumbs		
2	tablespoons grated Parmesan cheese	1½	cups freshly grated Parmigiano-Reggiano cheese, for serving

To make the meatballs: In a large bowl, with a light touch, mix the beef, eggs, the 1 tablespoon oil, garlic, bread crumbs, Parmesan, and parsley and season with salt and pepper to taste. Do not overmix, or the meatballs will be tough. Form into twenty-four 1- to 1½-inch meatballs.

In a large heavy skillet, with up to ¼ inch of oil over medium-high heat, add the meatballs in a single layer and sauté, turning carefully so that they keep their shape and are evenly cooked, for 15 minutes, or until cooked through. If you do not have a large skillet, cook the meatballs in batches. Remove from the skillet with a slotted spoon and drain on paper towels.

If you are not using the meatballs immediately, let cool, then refrigerate in a covered container for up to 3 days. They can also be frozen for up to 1 month. Thaw in the refrigerator before using.

To make the pasta: Bring a large pot of water to a boil and cook the pasta according to package directions. This is not a dish that requires the pasta to be al dente. However, it is best if cooked just before serving.

To serve the dish: Drain the pasta and place in a warm, deep platter; toss with Thick Tomato and Meat Sauce; and top with the meatballs. Serve with a generous bowl of Parmigiano-Reggiano. Warm Italian bread makes a good accompaniment.

POTLUCK NOTE | *Dried pasta can be boiled until al dente, drained, and tossed with a light coating of extra-virgin olive oil. Let cool and refrigerate for up to 2 days. Before serving, place in a large pot of boiling water, stir, bring the water back to a boil, remove after 1 minute, drain, and proceed with the recipe directions.*

THICK TOMATO AND MEAT SAUCE

This versatile sauce can be used for any recipe calling for a rich tomato sauce, not just spaghetti and meatballs.

YIELD | 2 QUARTS (8 ONE-CUP OR 16 HALF-CUP SERVINGS)

½	cup olive oil	5	tablespoons tomato paste
4	pork chops	1	head garlic, peeled and crushed
1	large onion, diced	2	tablespoons chopped fresh oregano or 2 teaspoons dried
3	large ribs celery, diced		
2	carrots, shredded	½	cup chopped fresh flat-leaf parsley
1	pound fresh mushrooms, sliced	1	cup dry red wine
4	pounds tomatoes, peeled, seeded and crushed, or 2 cans (28 ounces each) Italian crushed tomatoes	½	lemon, quartered and seeded
		2	tablespoons sugar

Heat ¼ cup of the oil in a large heavy saucepan over medium-high heat. Cook the pork chops until browned on both sides, about 2 minutes per side. Add the onion, celery, and carrots and cook until slightly browned, about 2 minutes. Stir in the mushrooms and add more of the remaining oil as needed. Add the remaining ingredients and simmer for 3 hours, stirring frequently. (If using canned tomatoes, drain 1 can and use the liquid from the other.)

After 2½ hours, remove the pork chops. Remove the pork from the bones, shred it, and return the meat to the sauce. Remove the lemon pieces and discard. If the sauce is too thick, add some wine or some water splashed with balsamic vinegar.

The sauce can be cooled and refrigerated for 3 days if you are not using it immediately. To freeze it, ladle the cooled sauce into two tightly sealed 1-quart containers and label them with the contents and the date. The sauce can be kept frozen for 1 month.

If you make this sauce ahead of time and refrigerate it, simmer it on low heat for 15 minutes, stirring frequently, before serving.

MINESTRONE WITH PESTO

There are many versions of this delicious soup. If you don't have cannellini beans, substitute any white bean or even red ones. No turnip? Use carrots and zucchini. To make this meatless, omit the bacon and use 4 tablespoons of extra-virgin olive oil. You will soon make this recipe your own. With bread and a salad, dinner is ready.

YIELD | 4 QUARTS (16 ONE-CUP SERVINGS)

¼	pound bacon, diced
1	large onion, chopped
3	leeks, white and light green parts only, well rinsed and chopped
1	turnip, peeled and chopped
3	cups shredded cabbage
2	teaspoons coarse salt
½	teaspoon freshly ground pepper
8	cups water
3	large tomatoes, diced
2	cloves garlic, minced
6	basil leaves

1	cup fresh peas (frozen may be substituted)
1	cup cut string beans, (1-inch pieces)
1½	cups cooked, rinsed, and drained canned cannellini beans
1	large red potato, peeled and diced
¼	pound tubetti pasta or small macaroni
	Pesto (see page 57), for topping
1	cup freshly grated or store-bought Parmesan cheese, for topping

In a heavy-bottomed soup pot large enough to hold all the ingredients, over medium heat, sauté the bacon, onion, leeks, turnip, and cabbage. Stir continuously until the onion is golden brown, about 7 minutes.

Stir in the salt, pepper, water, tomatoes, garlic, and basil and increase the heat to medium-high. Stir in the peas, string beans, cannellini beans, and potato. Bring to a slow boil, lower the heat, and simmer uncovered for 30 minutes. At this point the soup can be cooled, covered, and refrigerated for up to 2 days.

Before serving, bring to a low boil, add the pasta, and cook until the pasta is cooked through, about 12 minutes. As an alternative, the pasta can be cooked separately and added to the simmering soup 10 minutes before serving.

To serve the dish: Serve hot, with the Pesto and the cheese in serving bowls alongside.

PASTA SQUARES WITH ROASTED VEGETABLES

YIELD | 10 SERVINGS

½	cup extra-virgin olive oil, in various uses	2	cloves garlic, minced
2	zucchini, scraped and sliced	⅓	cup best-quality balsamic vinegar, preferably aged
1	eggplant, quartered lengthwise and sliced	1	pound lasagna noodles, broken into 4-inch pieces
1	large red onion, halved and sliced	½	cup chopped fresh flat-leaf parsley, thick stems removed
3	Belgian endives, halved lengthwise, each half cut into 3 long sections		Salt and freshly ground black pepper
1	head radicchio, halved lengthwise, each half cut into 3 long sections	⅔	cup freshly grated pecorino or Parmigiano-Reggiano cheese

Preheat the oven to 400°F. Brush two baking sheets with some of the oil.

Arrange the zucchini, eggplant, onion, endives, and radicchio on the prepared baking sheets and brush with more of the oil. Roast until lightly browned at the edges, 30 to 40 minutes. Check the vegetables from time to time and turn two or three times during cooking. As they are cooked, transfer to a large bowl.

Heat 2 tablespoons of the oil in a small saucepan over medium heat and sauté the garlic until lightly browned, about 3 minutes. Add the vinegar and continue to cook, stirring occasionally, until slightly reduced, about 10 minutes. Pour over the vegetables and stir.

In a large pot of boiling water, cook the pasta until al dente, about 10 minutes. Drain but do not rinse. Mix the pasta with the vegetables in their vinegar sauce, add the remaining olive oil and the parsley, and season with salt and pepper to taste.

You can serve the dish from the bowl or as a casserole: Place the finished dish in a 9-by-13-inch deep-sided bake-and-serve dish, cool, cover with plastic wrap, and refrigerate for up to 24 hours. Bring to room temperature, remove the plastic, and cover with foil. Heat at home in a 325°F oven for 45 minutes and transport in an insulated carrier, or heat at your destination.

To serve the dish: Serve hot, with the cheese at the table.

PASTITSIO: GREEK MACARONI AND CHEESE

At first glance, this dish may seem a little complicated—it isn't. There are three easy steps: 1. Cook the macaroni. 2. Make a meat sauce and a white sauce. 3. Layer them in a baking pan. It is a real crowd-pleaser, in part because it isn't something made every day. Use Greek ingredients if they are available because the aromas and textures of each country bring something unique. Most supermarkets have international sections, and there are a growing number of specialty food stores.

YIELD | 12 SERVINGS

Pasta

1½	pounds macaroni, such as ditali or small ziti
¼	cup + 2 tablespoons Greek (or other) extra-virgin olive oil
3	cups any combination Greek mizithra or kefalotyri cheese (Italian hard ricotta or Romano may be substituted)

2	large eggs, lightly beaten
1	cup fine bread crumbs
	Freshly ground nutmeg to taste or ½ teaspoon ground

Meat Sauce

3	tablespoons extra-virgin olive oil
1	onion, diced
1	pound lean ground lamb or beef
1	clove garlic, minced
½	cup dry red wine
1	can (16 ounces) diced tomatoes, drained

2	tablespoons tomato paste
1	teaspoon dried basil
1	teaspoon ground cinnamon
1	teaspoon salt + more to taste
¼	cup chopped fresh flat-leaf parsley

White Sauce

¼	cup instant flour
4	tablespoons (¼ cup) unsalted butter
2	cups milk

½	teaspoon ground nutmeg
	Salt and ground pepper
2	extra-large eggs, lightly beaten

Preheat the oven to 350°F.

To cook the pasta: In a large pot of boiling salted water, cook the macaroni until almost tender, 12 to 14 minutes. Drain thoroughly but do not rinse.

In a large bowl, combine the macaroni, the ¼ cup oil, 1 cup of the cheese, and eggs. Set aside.

To make the meat sauce: Heat 1 tablespoon oil in a large heavy saucepan with a lid over medium heat. Stir in the onion and cook until translucent, about 4 minutes. Stir in the ground lamb or beef and cook, breaking up the meat and stirring until lightly browned, about 5 minutes. Add the garlic and wine, then cover and simmer for 5 minutes. Stir in the tomatoes, tomato paste, basil, cinnamon, and 1 teaspoon salt, cover, and simmer for 20 minutes. Add the parsley and cook uncovered for another 20 minutes. Stir frequently to allow excess liquid to evaporate; the sauce should be thick.

To make the white sauce: In a small saucepan over medium-low heat, stir the flour and butter together, then slowly stir in the milk. Stir constantly until thick, about 5 minutes. Stir in the nutmeg and season with salt and pepper to taste. Remove from the heat and let cool, stirring occasionally. Stir in the eggs.

To assemble the dish: With the remaining 2 tablespoons oil, grease a 15-by-11-inch baking pan. Spread half of the macaroni mixture on the bottom of the pan, then sprinkle with ½ cup of the remaining cheese. Add all the meat sauce in a layer, then top with the rest of the macaroni. Sprinkle with another 1 cup of the cheese. Top with all the white sauce and spread it gently into the corners. Sprinkle the remaining 1 cup of the cheese and top with the bread crumbs, then grind nutmeg over all. Bake for 45 minutes.

This dish can be carried in a thermal container to your destination—it doesn't have to be piping hot. As an alternative, you can cook it completely, cool, cover, and refrigerate for up to 24 hours. Before serving, heat in a 325°F oven for 20 minutes.

To serve the dish: Let rest 15 minutes before serving directly from the baking pan.

CINCINNATI CHILI

Cincinnati Chili is the creation of chef Tom Kiradjieff, who opened the Empress, a Greek restaurant in Cincinnati, in 1922. His ever-popular dish can still be ordered one of several ways: two-way, which is chili over spaghetti; three-way, which adds shredded cheddar cheese; four-way, which brings chopped onions; and five-way, with heated kidney beans on top, not mixed in.

YIELD | 10 SERVINGS

2	tablespoons olive oil		2	ounces unsweetened or dark chocolate
¼	pound bacon, diced		¾	teaspoon salt + more to taste
1	large onion, diced		4	cups tomato sauce
2	cloves garlic, smashed		¼	cup cider vinegar
2	pounds ground beef			Pepper
1	tablespoon chili powder		1½	pounds spaghetti
2	teaspoons ground cumin			Shredded sharp cheddar cheese, chopped onion, hot kidney beans, and oyster crackers, for serving
2	teaspoons paprika			
1	teaspoon ground allspice			
1	tablespoon ground cinnamon			

In a large heavy-bottomed skillet or an uncovered Dutch oven, heat the oil and bacon over medium heat until the bacon begins to crisp, about 5 minutes. Add the onion and garlic and cook until the onion is golden brown, about 5 minutes. Spread the beef in the pan and cook until it begins to brown, about 5 minutes.

Stir in the chili powder, cumin, paprika, allspice, cinnamon, chocolate, and the ¾ teaspoon salt. Blend well. Add the tomato sauce, reduce the heat, and simmer for 45 minutes, stirring occasionally. When all the liquid has been absorbed by the beef, stir in the vinegar and season to taste with salt and pepper. At this point the chili can be cooled, covered, and refrigerated for 24 hours.

In a large pot of boiling water, cook the spaghetti for 10 minutes, or according to package directions. Drain but do not rinse.

To serve the dish: Transfer the hot spaghetti to a large, deep platter and pour the chili over it, but do not mix. Accompany with bowls of cheese, onion, beans, and oyster crackers.

CHINESE DAN DAN NOODLES
(OLD-FASHIONED STREET SELLER'S NOODLES)

We know that pasta existed in Italy before Marco Polo made his famous journey to China, and there is now archaeological evidence that noodles existed in China as far back as 4,000 years ago. The excavated noodle was made of millet, not wheat, as is common in China today.

YIELD | 10 SERVINGS

Noodles

1½	pounds fresh or dried medium-width Chinese noodles or standard packaged egg noodles		1	tablespoon white Chinese vinegar
2	cups cold water		1	teaspoon ground Sichuan peppercorns (fagara) or ½ teaspoon ground black pepper
2	tablespoons sesame oil		1	cup unsalted homemade or canned chicken stock
3	tablespoons light soy sauce			

Sauce

3	tablespoons peanut or other cooking oil		½	cup unsalted peanuts, coarsely chopped
1	pound ground pork		¼	cup light soy sauce
1	tablespoon minced fresh ginger		1	tablespoon sugar
3	cloves garlic, minced		¼	cup Shaoxing wine or dry sherry
2	tablespoons sesame seeds			

Accompaniments

5	scallions, thinly sliced		½	cup chopped peanuts (any kind)
⅓	cup chopped fresh cilantro			

To make the noodles: If using fresh noodles, bring a large pot of water to a boil, add the noodles, stir, and bring to a boil again. Boil for 3 minutes, then add the cold water to stop the boiling. Bring to a boil again and boil until the noodles are tender, about 3 minutes. Drain but do not rinse. If using dried noodles, follow package directions.

In a large bowl, mix the noodles with the oil, soy sauce, vinegar, ground peppercorns or black pepper, and stock. Set aside.

To make the sauce: Heat the oil in a wok or large sauté pan over medium-high heat. When the oil is hot, crumble in the ground pork so it is separated and grainy, then stir in the ginger and garlic. Lower the heat to medium and cook, stirring from time to time, until none of the pork shows pink, about 12 minutes. Add the sesame seeds and peanuts and cook for another 3 minutes, stirring. Stir in the soy sauce, sugar, and wine. Keep warm until ready to serve, or chill, cover, and refrigerate until needed, for up to 24 hours.

To serve the dish: If you've made the sauce ahead, heat it for 10 minutes over medium heat. Serve hot over warm or hot noodles, accompanied by bowls of the scallions, cilantro, and peanuts.

POTLUCK NOTE | *Fresh Chinese noodles are available in the refrigerated section of Chinese specialty stores. They will keep in the freezer for 1 month.*

STIR-FRIED RICE-STICK NOODLES

Pad Thai is often called the signature dish of Thai cuisine, and every cook has his or her own version. It is very forgiving. For instance, cubed cooked chicken can be substituted for the shrimp; cashews, for the peanuts. The rice noodles can even be replaced by 1½ pounds of cooked linguine.

YIELD | 10 SERVINGS

2	8-ounce packages dried flat rice-stick noodles (¼ inch wide)	2	tablespoons soy sauce
5	tablespoons safflower or canola oil	3	teaspoons fresh lime juice
		2	teaspoons sugar
3	eggs, lightly beaten	1–2	small chili peppers (preferably Thai), stemmed, seeded, and minced, for garnish (optional)
4	cloves garlic, minced		
1	pound small shrimp, peeled and deveined	¾	cup chopped roasted unsalted peanuts, for garnish
1	bunch scallions, sliced	¼	cup chopped fresh cilantro, for garnish
3	cups bean sprouts, rinsed and trimmed		
3	tablespoons nam pla (Thai fish sauce)	1	lime, cut into thin wedges, for serving
1	tablespoon tamarind paste (optional)		

Put the noodles in a heatproof bowl and pour boiling water over them to cover. Allow to soak until softened, for at least 15 minutes, or until ready to use, then drain. Don't soak them longer than ½ hour, or they may start to fall apart.

Heat 2 tablespoons of the oil in a wok or large skillet, preferably nonstick, over medium heat. Add the eggs and scramble quickly for the first minute or so with a fork, then let sit until a flat omelet forms. Cook just until set, remove to a plate, cut into ¼-inch-wide strips, and set aside.

Increase the heat to medium high and add the remaining 3 tablespoons oil. When the oil is hot, add the garlic and shrimp and cook, stirring occasionally, until the shrimp are cooked through, about 3 minutes. Remove the shrimp from the wok with a slotted spoon and set aside. Lower the heat to meduim. Add the scallions and 2½ cups of the bean sprouts to the wok and cook, stirring occasionally, for 3 minutes. Remove and add to the shrimp.

In the wok, combine the drained noodles, nam pla, tamarind paste (if using), soy sauce, lime juice, sugar, and the reserved eggs and cook, stirring occasionally, until the noodles are heated through, about 10 minutes. Add the shrimp mixture and stir to combine.

To serve the dish: Transfer the stir-fry to a large platter and top with the chilies (if using), peanuts, cilantro, and remaining ½ cup bean sprouts. Serve with the lime wedges on the side.

GRAINS AND BEANS

GRAINS AND LEGUMES, the oldest of foods, have sustained entire civilizations, particularly when combined with the spices and herbs of the region in which they were and continue to be cultivated. It is said that Esau relinquished his birthright for lentil porridge, and when the Dead Sea scrolls were discovered at the ancient settlement at Qumran, lentils were found among shards of pottery bowls. Today, as we have become aware that the carbohydrates we eat should be as wholesome as possible, people are turning to this food group for tasty, healthful dishes for elemental feasts.

Grains are edible seeds from plants in the grass family—among them, wheat, corn, barley, rice, millet, and wild rice (which is not actually rice). Grains, especially whole grains, are excellent sources of carbohydrates (energy), dietary fiber, essential fatty acids, and other important nutrients. Legumes, plants that have pods with tidy rows of seeds inside, are their protein-filled counterparts. They include beans, peas, lentils, and peanuts. In the midst of our nation's plenty, we are privileged to have in our markets grains and legumes in the most convenient forms—in hundreds of strains, shapes, and colors. But it is when grains and legumes are eaten together in certain combinations that they form a complete protein and pack their most powerful nutritional punch.

Grains and legumes are universally eaten whole, crushed, or ground; raw, roasted, or boiled; alone or with whatever is available. These very versatile staples can form the main course of a meal or add texture, color, and flavor to other courses. They are delicious at any temperature and adaptable to many methods of cooking and styles of serving.

Conveniently, most cooked grains can be cooled, covered, and refrigerated for a few days. Many beans can be found not only dried but also canned and partially prepared. Feel free to substitute one form for another, but look carefully at the can and be sure to get those without additives.

POLENTA–FOUR CHEESE CASSEROLE

YIELD | 10 SERVINGS

8	cups water	2	cups (8 ounces) Gorgonzola cheese, crumbled
2	teaspoons salt	¾	cup grated Parmigiano-Reggiano cheese
1	pound coarsely ground cornmeal		
2	cups shredded mozzarella cheese		
1	cup shredded fontina cheese		

Preheat the oven to 400°F. Butter a 16-by-12-inch baking dish. If you are making this in two stages, be sure to use a baking dish that can go from refrigerator to oven.

Bring the water to a boil in a wide, heavy-bottomed pot and add the salt. (At the same time, set a kettle or pot of water to boil in case you need a little extra boiling water toward the end of cooking the cornmeal.) When it is at a steady gentle boil, add the cornmeal in a very slow stream. You don't want the water to stop boiling. Stir the cornmeal constantly with a wooden spoon to keep lumps from forming. Continue stirring constantly, about 30 minutes. The longer you stir, the better the polenta will be.

The finished polenta should have the consistency of firm mashed potatoes. If it seems too thick, add a little more boiling water, being careful never to add more than about ¼ cup water at a time. The polenta is done when it peels easily off the sides of the pot. (At this point you have a delicious side dish. Add some butter and grated Parmigiano-Reggiano, and you can serve it as it comes out of the pot!)

Pour the polenta into the prepared baking dish and smooth the top with a moistened spatula. Let cool until firm. The polenta can be covered and refrigerated for up to 2 days.

To serve the dish: Before serving, mix the four cheeses together in a large bowl and spread over the polenta in the baking dish. Bake until the cheese is melted and bubbles slightly, about 10 minutes. Serve hot.

POSOLE AND CHICKEN CASSEROLE

This Mexican dish is traditionally made with boneless pork cubes, which may be substituted for the chicken thighs. Posole is a specific kind of dried corn; if you can't find it, don't substitute canned hominy for this dish.

YIELD | 10 TO 12 SERVINGS

2	cups blue or yellow dried posole, picked over
1	tablespoon coarse salt + more to taste
½	cup extra-virgin olive oil
2	medium/large red onions, diced
1	head garlic, minced
3½	pounds boneless chicken thighs, cubed
4	ancho chilies, stemmed and seeded
2	teaspoons dried Mexican or any oregano
1	teaspoon ground cumin
1	teaspoon ground cinnamon
½	can (8 ounces) crushed tomatoes
1	can (7 ounces) diced green chilies, drained
2	cups beer
	Freshly ground pepper
½	cup minced fresh cilantro, for serving
2	firm ripe avocados, diced, for serving
16	ounces (2 cups) sour cream, for serving
2	limes, cut in wedges, for serving

Put the posole in a large container and add cold water to cover by 3 inches. Let soak for 8 hours or overnight.

Drain the posole, transfer it to a pot, and add fresh water to cover by 4 or 5 inches and the 1 tablespoon coarse salt. Cover the pot and bring to a boil, then reduce the heat and simmer, covered, for 2 hours. Check every 30 minutes, adding water if needed, until the kernels have softened and begin to burst. Drain the posole and rinse well.

Heat the oil in a heavy 6-quart pot over medium heat. Add the onions and sauté until golden, 3 to 4 minutes. Add the garlic, chicken, ancho chilies, oregano, cumin, and cinnamon. Stir in the tomatoes, green chilies, and beer. Bring to a boil, stir in the cooked posole, then reduce the heat and simmer for 1 hour. Season with salt and pepper to taste.

To serve the dish: Serve from the pot or a warm platter and accompany with small bowls of the cilantro, avocado, sour cream, and lime wedges.

WILD RICE CASSEROLE

Wild rice—which is not rice at all but a cereal grass—is native to North America and grows largely in the Great Lakes region. People have been eating it since prehistoric times; in the north-central plains, the Ojibwa, Menominee, and Cree tribes introduced European fur traders to the grain. It became known as wild rice.

YIELD | 10 SIDE-DISH SERVINGS

3	tablespoons unsalted butter, sliced	6	cups cooked wild rice
3	tablespoons olive oil	1½	cups chopped pecans
3	onions, diced		Salt and pepper
10	ounces white mushrooms, sliced	½	cup minced flat-leaf parsley, for garnish

Preheat the oven to 350°F.

In a heavy skillet over medium heat, combine the butter, oil, onions, and mushrooms. Sauté until the onions are golden brown, 4 to 5 minutes.

Transfer the onion and mushroom mixture to a casserole dish with a cover and stir in the rice and pecans. Season with salt and pepper to taste. At this point, the casserole can be cooled, covered, and refrigerated for up to 24 hours. Bring to room temperature before baking. Bake, covered, in a 350°F oven for 20 to 30 minutes.

To serve the dish: Top with the parsley and serve right from the casserole.

POTLUCK NOTE | *Wild rice is easy to make as a casserole component or as a side dish on its own. Rinse the rice in a colander under running water and drain. Add 1½ cups of wild rice to 6 cups of gently boiling salted water. Return the water to a boil, stir, reduce the heat, cover, and simmer for 30 to 40 minutes, or until the rice fluffs up. This will yield about 6 cups of cooked rice.*

ROASTED BARLEY CASSEROLE

About one-third of all barley grown goes into the making of beer. Funny, this dish doesn't taste like beer.

YIELD | 10 SERVINGS

8	tablespoons (½ cup) unsalted butter	8	cups chicken or vegetable stock
2	large sweet onions, halved and sliced	1	pound white mushrooms, sliced
			Salt and pepper
1	teaspoon sugar	¼	cup minced flat-leaf parsley, for garnish
2½	cups pearl barley		

Heat 5 tablespoons of the butter in a 3- or 4-quart Dutch oven or stovetop casserole over medium-low heat. Add the onions, stir in the sugar, and cook, stirring occasionally, until the onions begin to caramelize, about 10 minutes.

In a sauté pan, heat the remaining 3 tablespoons butter over medium heat and stir in the barley. Continue to cook and stir until the barley is roasted and has turned a pale brown, 3 to 4 minutes.

Add the barley to the onions and gradually stir in the stock, then the mushrooms. Bring to a low boil, cover, lower the heat, and cook, stirring occasionally, until the stock is absorbed and the barley is tender, about 45 minutes. Season with salt and pepper to taste.

To serve the dish: Place in a serving bowl and toss like a salad to distribute the ingredients. Garnish with parsley.

RICE AND BEANS WITH FRIED PLANTAINS (MADUROS)

¼	cup Spanish (or other) extra-virgin olive oil	1	teaspoon dried thyme
1	large Spanish onion, diced	1	teaspoon crushed red-pepper flakes
3	cups cooked or canned black beans, rinsed and drained		Salt and black pepper
4	cups cooked rice		Fried Plantains (Maduros) (recipe follows), for serving
2	pounds tomatoes, chopped		

Heat the oil in a large heavy-bottomed saucepan over medium heat. Add the onion and cook until golden brown, about 4 minutes. Mix in the beans, rice, tomatoes, thyme, and red-pepper flakes and season with salt and black pepper to taste. Cook over medium-low heat, stirring occasionally until heated through, about 15 minutes.

To serve the dish: Transfer to a large serving dish and serve with Fried Plantains alongside.

Fried Plantains (Maduros)

Though they resemble bananas, plantains are regarded as a vegetable, not a fruit. They are a staple in many hot climates and are always eaten cooked, either fried, boiled, or roasted.

3	large, firm plantains	3	cups canola or safflower oil

Peel the plantains and slice them on a diagonal, ½ to ¾ inch thick. If they seem very tough, roll a rolling pin over each slice before cooking.

Heat the oil in a heavy saucepan or cast-iron skillet over medium heat until a drop of water sizzles. Add the plantain slices and cook in batches, so that the pan is not too crowded, until golden brown on both sides and fork-tender, about 2 minutes per side. Drain on paper towels and serve.

If you are not serving them immediately, they can be drained and patted free of oil on both sides, cooled, covered, and stored at room temperature for up to 24 hours.

To serve the dish: Heat the plantains on a foil-lined baking sheet (or two) in a 450°F oven for 10 minutes before serving.

Soaking and Cooking Beans

Same-day bean soaking: Before cooking, soak dried, packaged beans to help soften and return moisture to them as well as reduce cooking time. Some people are reluctant to serve beans to a crowd because of their gas-producing potential. Hot soaking helps break down some of the complex sugars that can cause flatulence and makes the beans easier to digest. Add 10 cups of hot water to each pound of beans and heat to boiling. Boil for 5 minutes, remove from the heat, cover, and let stand for 3 or 4 hours. Rinse, drain, and then rinse thoroughly several more times.

Overnight soak: For each pound (2 cups) of dried beans, add 10 cups of cold water and let soak overnight, or at least 8 hours. It is best not to add salt or baking soda, as this will negatively affect taste and texture. Most beans will rehydrate to triple their dried size, so be sure to start with a large enough pot. One way to see if the beans have soaked long enough is to test one by cutting it in half to see if the inside is translucent.

Bean cooking: Drain and rinse beans and cook in fresh water. In general, cook beans in a ratio of 3 or 4 cups of water for every cup of beans. Beans take 30 minutes to 2 hours to cook, depending on variety. Rinse, drain, and rinse cooked beans before adding to another dish. Check bean packaging for specific cooking times and instructions. Always drain and rinse canned beans.

MEDITERRANEAN STUFFED PEPPERS

YIELD | 10 SERVINGS

Peppers

10	red and/or yellow bell peppers, 3–4 inches high	¾	cup chopped pistachios
⅓	cup extra-virgin olive oil	½	cup raisins
2	sweet onions, diced	⅔	cup chopped green olives
5	cups cooked brown rice	6	plum tomatoes, chopped
1	teaspoon grated nutmeg	¼	cup fresh mint leaves, chopped
1	teaspoon ground cinnamon	¼	cup parsley, chopped
			Salt and black pepper

Sauce

2	cups tomato puree		Dash of cinnamon
	Juice of 1 lemon		Dash of nutmeg
2	tablespoons sugar		Salt and black pepper to taste

Preheat the oven to 350°F.

To make the peppers: Cut "lids" from the peppers and carefully remove the seeds and ribs. Blanch the peppers in boiling water for 3 minutes, remove with a slotted spoon, and drain upside down.

Heat the oil in sauté pan and sauté the onions until they are transparent.

In a large bowl, mix the rice with the onions. Stir in the nutmeg, cinnamon, pistachios, raisins, olives, tomatoes, mint, parsley, and salt and black pepper to taste.

To make the sauce: Mix all the ingredients in a separate bowl.

To assemble the dish: Spread a light layer of the sauce in a baking dish large enough (12 by 16 inches should do it) to hold all the peppers upright. Gently stuff the peppers with the rice mixture and place in the dish. Top each with a pepper lid. At this point, the dish and the sauce in the bowl may be covered and refrigerated for up to 24 hours.

To serve the dish: Pour the remaining sauce over the stuffed peppers and bake until the tops are lightly browned, about 45 minutes. Serve hot or at room temperature.

WHITE BEANS WITH GREMOLATA

YIELD | 10 SIDE-DISH SERVINGS

1 cup minced fresh flat-leaf parsley

4 cloves garlic, finely minced

3–4 tablespoons extra-virgin olive oil

Juice of 1 lemon

Zest of 1 lemon (see page 316)

¼ teaspoon freshly ground black pepper

5 cups cooked or canned white beans (rinsed and drained)

To make the gremolata: In a small bowl, mix the parsley, garlic, oil, lemon juice, lemon zest, and pepper. Set the gremolata aside.

To make the beans: Heat the beans in the top of a double boiler over simmering water until hot, about 15 minutes.

To serve the dish: Transfer the beans to a warm bowl and top with the reserved gremolata.

MUSHROOM AND ASPARAGUS RISOTTO

This risotto is a little more forgiving than the classic one cooked entirely on top of the stove. Because it can be removed from the oven and finished on a flame tamer, it doesn't need constant attention. It is made with Italian arborio or carnaroli rice, which will cook up with a creamy texture.

YIELD | 10 SERVINGS

10	cups chicken or vegetable stock	20	asparagus spears, the top 4 inches cut on an angle into ½-inch slices and blanched for 2 minutes, the rest reserved for another use
3	tablespoons unsalted butter		
3	tablespoons extra-virgin olive oil		
5	small shallots, minced	2	tablespoons chopped fresh flat-leaf parsley
3	cups arborio or carnaroli rice		
¾	cup dry white wine	½	cup grated Parmigiano-Reggiano cheese
	Salt and pepper		
1	pound assorted wild mushrooms, trimmed, cubed, and sautéed		

Preheat the oven to 450°F.

Heat the stock in a 3-quart stockpot over medium heat until it simmers. Keep it simmering as you make the risotto.

In a large, ovenproof, heavy-bottomed casserole with a lid, heat the butter and oil over medium heat. Stir in the shallots and cook until wilted. Lower the heat, add the rice, and stir for 1 to 2 minutes. Add the wine and cook, stirring, until it is absorbed, about 5 minutes.

Stir in the simmering stock in 1-cup increments, season with salt and pepper to taste, and mix in the mushrooms and asparagus. Remove from the heat. Cover and bake for 15 minutes.

Remove from the oven and mix in the parsley and cheese.

To serve the dish: Keep warm on the stove top over very low heat on a heat or flame tamer and serve as soon as possible. You can carry this dish in the casserole in a thermal container with a heat pack.

Aromatic Lentil Soup (opposite)
Cheddar Cheese Bis̲c̲u̲i̲t̲s̲ (̲p̲a̲g̲e̲ 2̲6̲)̲

AROMATIC LENTIL SOUP

YIELD | 3 QUARTS (10 ONE-CUP SERVINGS)

¼	cup olive oil		3	cloves garlic, minced
1	teaspoon ground ginger		2	cups brown lentils, rinsed and picked over
2	teaspoons ground cumin			
¼	teaspoon ground cloves		10	cups water
1	teaspoon ground cinnamon		1	pound plum tomatoes, peeled and diced
	Grated zest of 1 lemon (see page 316)			Salt and pepper to taste
2	onions, finely chopped		½	cup chopped fresh cilantro or flat-leaf parsley, for garnish
2	carrots, finely diced			
2	ribs celery, finely diced			

Heat the oil in a soup pot over medium heat. Stir in the ginger, cumin, cloves, cinnamon, and lemon zest and cook until aromatic, about 3 minutes. Stir in the onions, carrots, celery, and garlic and cook, stirring frequently, until the onions start to brown, about 5 minutes. Add the lentils, water, tomatoes, and salt and pepper to taste. Cook over medium heat, stirring occasionally, until the vegetables are tender, about 45 minutes. The soup is best served immediately but can be cooled, covered, and refrigerated for up to 2 days.

To serve the dish: Serve the soup hot, garnished with the cilantro. A nice accompaniment would be Cheddar Cheese Biscuits (page 261).

POTLUCK NOTE | *To peel a tomato, bring a saucepan of water to a boil. Make a small X on the end of the tomato opposite the stem. Pierce the stem end with a fork, and hold the tomato in the boiling water for 5 to 20 seconds. Peel the skin back and discard. If you need to peel a lot of tomatoes, make an X in each, remove the stem circle, and drop the tomatoes in the boiling water. Remove them with a slotted spoon after 20 seconds. Peel with a very sharply pointed paring knife.*

TABBOULEH

Bulgur is wheat that has been cracked, steamed, and dried. All it needs is boiling water to bring it to a coarse cereal consistency in a very short time. The ratio of water to bulgur is usually 3 to 1. If after about half an hour there is still water visible, simply strain the grain to remove the excess liquid.

YIELD | 10 SERVINGS

1½	cups medium or fine bulgur	3	tomatoes, finely chopped
4½	cups boiling water	1½	cups minced fresh mint leaves
1	teaspoon sea salt + more to taste	1	cup minced fresh flat-leaf parsley
½	teaspoon freshly ground pepper + more to taste	½	cup fresh lemon juice
6	scallions, finely chopped	¾	cup olive oil

Place the bulgur in a large heatproof bowl and cover with the boiling water. Let sit for 15 minutes, stirring lightly with a fork every few minutes. If you see any water, let sit for another 15 minutes, then drain any excess.

In a serving bowl, stir the bulgur with the 1 teaspoon salt, the ½ teaspoon pepper, scallions, tomatoes, mint, and parsley. Toss with ¼ cup of the lemon juice and the oil. Season with more of the remaining lemon juice and salt and pepper to taste.

Refrigerate, covered, for up to 24 hours.

To serve the dish: Serve cold or at room temperature with fresh pita bread or Crispy Pita Chips (page 20).

POULTRY

FROM HENRY IV OF FRANCE, who famously said he wanted no one in the country so poor as not to have a chicken in the pot every Sunday, to Herbert Hoover's campaign pledge of "a chicken in every pot and a car in every garage," hollow promises have ruled the political roost. What is interesting is that in the vast world of cuisine, it is chicken that has been the icon of the good life.

Long a luxury, chicken has become an international staple. Simply roasted with rosemary and garlic or deliciously layered in a Moroccan *bestilla*, poultry is one of the easiest foods to cook. Americans have enjoyed turkey at holidays and feasts for generations, and now it is abundant enough to be eaten at any meal.

ARROZ CON POLLO
(LATIN-STYLE CHICKEN AND RICE)

Growing up in New York provided an opportunity to eat around the world without leaving town. When I attended Columbia University, there was an increasing number of home-style Puerto Rican and Latino restaurants. Each made this dish differently. Sometimes it was accompanied with tostones, which are the same as the Fried Plantains (Maduros) on page 78.

YIELD | 10 SERVINGS

3	tablespoons extra-virgin olive oil	½	teaspoon saffron or 1 teaspoon powdered turmeric
3	pounds boneless chicken breasts and thighs, cubed	3½	cups chicken stock
	Salt and pepper	2	cups corn kernels, fresh or frozen
1	onion, diced	1½	cups mild or medium salsa
4	cloves garlic, minced	½	cup minced cilantro, for garnish
2	teaspoons dried oregano	1	cup sliced pimiento-stuffed olives, for garnish
2	cups long-grain rice		

Preheat the oven to 350°F.

Heat the oil in a Dutch oven or large flame- and ovenproof covered casserole over medium-high heat. Add the chicken and sauté until browned, about 5 minutes. Season with salt and pepper to taste. Transfer to a platter.

Add the onion, garlic, and oregano to the casserole and sauté until the onion has softened, about 3 minutes. Add the rice and cook, stirring, until opaque, about 2 minutes.

Add the saffron or tumeric, stock, corn, and salsa. Bring to a boil and add the chicken, but do not stir. Cover the casserole and transfer to the oven.

Bake until the rice is tender and the chicken is cooked through, about 20 minutes.

To serve the dish: Serve Arroz con Pollo from the casserole or in a large deep platter garnished with the cilantro and olives.

CHICKEN CACCIATORE WITH SAUSAGE AND MEATBALLS

Anyone who often cooks for a lot of people over a long period of time discovers that sometimes he or she just isn't in the mood. That's the best time to make Chicken Cacciatore. You can prepare it a day ahead or at the last minute, but the real reason to make it is that once you start cooking, you are drawn into the delicious aromas and restored to the pleasures of cooking. And as a reward, everyone seems to find this dish the epitome of comfort food. It is also a good choice when you are not sure how many people will be eating because sides of spaghetti, rice, or polenta can stretch it out.

YIELD | 10 TO 20 SERVINGS

1	chicken (3½ pounds), cut into 10 pieces	2	cans (28 ounces each) peeled Italian tomatoes
1	cup fine, dry, seasoned bread crumbs	1	can (6 ounces) tomato paste
¼	cup olive oil	1½	cups dry red wine
1½	pounds Italian-style, pale green, long frying peppers (Cubanelle or standard bell peppers may be substituted), seeded and cut into strips	1	tablespoon dried oregano
		1	teaspoon dried thyme
		½	cup minced fresh flat-leaf parsley
			Salt and freshly ground black pepper
2	onions, diced	20	Meatballs (recipe follows)
6	cloves garlic, minced	2	cups shredded Parmigiano-Reggiano cheese, for serving
1	pound sweet Italian sausage, cut into 1-inch pieces		
1	pound hot Italian sausage, cut into 1-inch pieces		

Dredge the chicken in the bread crumbs and set aside.

Heat the oil over medium heat in a Dutch oven or other heavy pan large enough to hold all the ingredients. Sauté the peppers, onions, and garlic for 5 minutes, or until soft. Add the sweet and hot sausages and cook until brown, about 10 minutes. Add the reserved chicken and cook, stirring, until golden brown, another 10 minutes. Stir in the tomatoes, tomato paste, wine, oregano, thyme, and parsley, and season with salt and black pepper to taste.

Bring to a low boil and gently stir in the Meatballs. Lower the heat and simmer for 1½ hours, stirring occasionally. Serve immediately or cool, cover, and refrigerate for up to 2 days.

To serve the dish: Serve hot with a bowl of the cheese alongside. If you've made the dish ahead, heat over low heat, stirring occasionally, until it starts to bubble, about 20 minutes.

Meatballs

YIELD | 20 MEATBALLS

1	pound ground beef	¼	teaspoon salt
⅓	cup fine, dry, seasoned bread crumbs		Freshly ground pepper
1	large egg, lightly beaten	¼	cup olive oil
¼	teaspoon garlic powder		

In a medium bowl, mix the beef, bread crumbs, egg, garlic powder, salt, and pepper to taste. Form into twenty 1-inch meatballs.

Heat the oil in a large sauté pan over medium heat. Add the meatballs and cook, turning, until evenly browned, 5 to 7 minutes. They do not need to cook through because they will cook in the tomato sauce. Drain on paper towels and reserve until ready to add to the cacciatore.

COQ AU VIN (CHICKEN IN WINE)

When I suggest this dish, I think of Paul Bocuse, one of my favorite French chefs, because he is a confidence builder. He knows that home cooks can prepare delicious meals if they relax a bit. His thinking would be that if the chicken and wine are of good quality and the dish is salted and peppered well, then the brandy can be omitted, and shallots or small leeks can be substituted for the boiling onions, and white mushrooms for the cremini.

YIELD | 10 SERVINGS

20	white boiling onions, peeled	½	cup brandy (optional)
2	chickens (4 pounds each), each cut into 8 to 10 pieces (or 6 pounds chicken sections, no wings)	2	tablespoons unsalted butter
		2	tablespoons olive oil
		2	pounds small cremini mushrooms
4	tablespoons instant flour	6	cups dry red wine
½	teaspoon salt		Bouquet garni (1 minced leek, 6 sprigs fresh thyme, 4 sprigs fresh parsley, and 2 bay leaves)
½	teaspoon freshly ground pepper		
4	slices bacon, cut into 1-inch pieces	2	cloves garlic, minced

Bring a pot of water to a boil and blanch the onions for 2 minutes. Drain and set aside.

Dust the chicken with the flour, salt, and pepper. It is not important for the chicken pieces to be completely coated.

In a Dutch oven or stove-top casserole, cook the bacon over medium heat until done but not crisp, about 5 minutes. Remove with a slotted spoon and set aside.

Place the chicken in the Dutch oven and cook, stirring, until slightly browned, about 5 minutes. Turn off the heat and pour the brandy, if using, over all. Using a long fireplace match, ignite the brandy and step back. The flame will go out in less than 2 minutes.

Return the heat to medium and add the butter and olive oil. Stir in the mushrooms and the reserved onions and cook for 10 minutes, stirring once or twice. Stir in the wine, bouquet garni, and garlic and bring to a low boil, stirring constantly. Add the reserved bacon, cover, lower the heat to medium-low, and simmer for 45 minutes. At this point the dish can be cooled, covered, and refrigerated for 24 hours.

To serve the dish: Remove the sprigs and the bay leaves. Slowly bring the Coq au Vin back to the boiling point on the stovetop and serve hot, perhaps with Garlic Roasted Mashed Potatoes (page 167).

CHICKEN POTPIE WITH BISCUIT TOPPING

YIELD | 12 SERVINGS

1½	pounds skinless, boneless chicken breasts and thighs, cut into bite-size chunks	4	carrots, scraped and cut into ½-inch slices
2	cups chicken stock	3	tablespoons unsalted butter
1	cup heavy cream	3	tablespoons instant or all-purpose flour
2	leeks (white and light green parts), rinsed well and cut into ½-inch slices	¼	teaspoon ground nutmeg
4	cloves garlic, minced	¼	cup chopped fresh flat-leaf parsley
1	pound new potatoes, cleaned and cut into bite-size chunks		Salt and freshly ground pepper
1	pound small white or cremini mushrooms, cleaned and halved		Biscuit Topping (recipe follows)

Put the chicken, stock, cream, leeks, garlic, potatoes, mushrooms, and carrots in a Dutch oven or heavy-bottomed saucepan or casserole. Bring to a low boil over medium heat, stir, reduce the heat to medium-low, cover, and simmer until the chicken is tender and cooked through, 25 to 30 minutes. Pour the pan contents into a colander set over a large heatproof bowl. Reserve the liquid.

Clean and dry the pan, add the butter, and melt gently over medium heat. Stir in the flour until bubbling, but do not let the mixture brown. Add the hot poaching liquid about a third at a time, heating and stirring well between additions, until the mixture is thick and smooth, about 5 minutes. Stir in the nutmeg and parsley, then season with salt and pepper to taste. Add the chicken and vegetables and toss gently in the sauce until well coated. Cook over low heat for 10 minutes, then remove from the heat.

If you are not taking this dish anywhere right away, let the chicken-and-vegetable filling cool, transfer to a covered container, and refrigerate until needed, up to 48 hours. If you are transporting it right away, place it in a thermal container with a hot pack.

To serve the dish: At your home or theirs, preheat the oven to 375°F. Place the chicken-and-vegetable mixture in a 13-by-9-inch baking pan (or two smaller ones) and cover with the cut biscuits. Bake for 30 to 40 minutes, or until the biscuit tops are golden brown. Remove from the oven and serve warm.

Biscuit Topping

YIELD | 16 SMALL BISCUITS

2	cups self-rising flour	¾	cup milk or buttermilk
1	tablespoon sugar		
6	tablespoons cold unsalted butter, sliced		

Measure the flour and sugar into a medium bowl. With two table knives or a pastry blender, cut in the butter until the mixture resembles course oatmeal. Add ¾ cup of the milk or buttermilk and stir until the liquid is absorbed. The dough will be moist.

Place the dough on a floured work surface. Fold it over three or four times and pat it into a ½-inch-thick square or rectangle. (At this point, the dough can be refrigerated for 24 hours. Shape and bake just before serving.) Cut the dough into twelve 2-inch round or square biscuits but do not bake. Assemble and bake the potpie.

CHICKEN CURRY WITH PEACH CHUTNEY

YIELD | 12 TO 15 SERVINGS

¼	cup olive or canola oil		3	tablespoons curry powder
1	pound small (1½- to 2-inch) potatoes		2	cups plain yogurt
1	pound small (1½- to 2-inch) turnips		1	tablespoon ground cumin
			1	tablespoon ground coriander
1	pound small (1½- to 2-inch) onions, peeled		1	tablespoon ground cardamom
5	large carrots		1	tablespoon ground ginger
	Salt and pepper		2	cans (28 ounces each) peeled tomatoes, 1 can strained and liquid discarded
4	pounds skinless, boneless chicken breasts (4–5 whole breasts)		1½	cups shredded coconut, for garnish
8	tablespoons (½ cup) unsalted butter, softened		1	cup minced fresh cilantro, for garnish
1	piece (2 inches) ginger, peeled and sliced			Peach Chutney (recipe follows), for serving
1	clove garlic, peeled			

Preheat the oven to 375°F. Spread the oil on a large baking sheet.

Cut the potatoes, turnips, and onions into six wedges each. Cut the carrots into 2-inch pieces, then halve each piece diagonally.

Place the vegetables on the prepared baking sheet, sprinkle lightly with salt and pepper to taste, and roast for 45 minutes. (You can roast the vegetables a day ahead and refrigerate them. You can also add the vegetables to the dish without roasting them first. Omit the oil, salt, and pepper.)

Meanwhile, halve the chicken breasts and trim. Cut each half into three strips lengthwise, then each strip into 1½-inch pieces. Place in a Dutch oven.

In a small blender, combine the butter, ginger, garlic, and curry powder and pulse until a loose paste. In a bowl, combine the yogurt, cumin, coriander, cardamom, and ground ginger. Stir the butter mixture into the yogurt mixture, then use your hands

(continued)

or a spatula to thoroughly coat the chicken in the pan with it. Add the roasted vegetables and stir thoroughly. Mix in the tomatoes and the liquid from one of the cans.

Bring the curry to a low boil over medium heat, then lower the heat, stir, cover, and simmer for 3 hours, stirring occasionally.

To serve the dish: Transfer the curry to a serving platter and garnish with the coconut and cilantro. Serve with 4 to 6 cups of Peach Chutney. (You can keep a pint in the refrigerator for 3 weeks and use it as you like, or give it as gift.) Other good accompaniments are hot white or brown rice and/or assorted Indian breads.

Peach Chutney

YIELD | 6 CUPS

2	pounds peaches, halved and pitted, or 2 cans (29-ounces) sliced peaches, drained	1–2	teaspoons crushed red pepper flakes, or to taste
1½	cups dried apricots	2	teaspoons mustard powder
1	cup raisins	1	cup granulated sugar
2	onions, diced	2	cups packed brown sugar
1	piece (2 inches) ginger, peeled and minced	4–6	cinnamon sticks (about 3 inches each)
2	lemons, seeded and diced (including peels)		Cider vinegar to cover

Cut each peach half into about eight pieces. (If using canned slices, cut each into three pieces.) Place in a large stockpot and stir in the apricots and raisins. Add the remaining ingredients and cook, stirring, over medium heat, until the mixture starts to boil. Lower the heat and simmer, stirring frequently, for 2 hours if using fresh peaches, 1½ hours if using canned.

Bring the chutney to room temperature, remove the cinnamon sticks, stir, and transfer to three 2-cup containers. If you will be using the chutney over the course of a few weeks, transfer to hinged or standard preserving jars that have been cleaned with their rubber gaskets in hot soapy water and rinsed thoroughly. Refrigerate for up to 3 weeks.

CHICKEN SALAD WITH GRAPES AND WALNUTS

This year-round favorite is simple to make and serve. It can be dressed up with garnishes such as crumbled bacon, olives, and/or croutons. You can also replace the tarragon with a tablespoon of mild curry and accompany it with Peach Chutney.

YIELD | 10 SERVINGS

6	cups diced cooked white and dark chicken	½	cup chopped walnuts
1	red onion, finely diced	¾	cup mayonnaise
1	red bell pepper, trimmed and finely diced	1	tablespoon minced fresh tarragon leaves or 1½ teaspoons dried
3	ribs celery (strings removed), finely diced	2	tablespoons extra-virgin olive oil
2	cups halved seedless grapes	1	tablespoon white wine vinegar
			Salt and black pepper

In a large bowl, combine the chicken, onion, pepper, celery, grapes, and walnuts. Stir in the mayonnaise, tarragon, oil, and vinegar, then season with salt and black pepper to taste. Cover and chill until ready to serve.

To serve the dish: Serve chilled, perhaps with a sliced tomato salad and a simple potato salad.

POTLUCK NOTE | *Buy the best chicken you can afford because the taste and texture of your dishes depend on it. There are now specific rules and regulations establishing standards for organic, free-range, and kosher chickens. These are the chickens that usually win taste tests and are worth looking for.*

BESTILLA (MOROCCAN CHICKEN PIE IN FILLO)

This pie is very popular throughout Morocco and the Middle East. Each component—the chicken, eggs, and almonds—can be made a day before you need the pie. Alternatively, the pie can be made, cooled, covered with plastic wrap, and frozen for a month or so. Then just bring it to room temperature, heat it, and top it with confectioners' sugar and cinnamon.

YIELD | 10 SERVINGS

Chicken

4	tablespoons (¼ cup) unsalted butter	½	teaspoon turmeric
1	chicken (3–4 pounds), cut up	2	cinnamon sticks
2	onions, grated	1	teaspoon black pepper
½	cup chopped fresh flat-leaf parsley	2	teaspoons salt
1	teaspoon ground ginger	2	cups water
		2	tablespoons sugar

Almonds

⅓	cup canola oil	⅓	cup sugar
1⅓	cups blanched whole almonds	1	tablespoon cinnamon

Eggs

⅔	cup reserved chicken-cooking liquid		Juice of ½ lemon
		4	large eggs, lightly beaten

Pie

1	package (1 pound) frozen fillo dough, thawed according to package directions	Up to	1 cup (½ pound) unsalted butter, melted + more for greasing
		1	egg yolk, beaten

Topping

½	cup confectioners' sugar	1	tablespoon cinnamon

Preheat the oven to 425°F.

To make the chicken: In a large sauté pan, heat the butter over medium heat, add the chicken and cook for 10 minutes, turning once or twice. Add the onions, parsley, ginger, turmeric, cinnamon sticks, pepper, and salt. Mix well and sauté for another 10 minutes, stirring frequently. Add the water, bring to a boil, lower the heat to low, and simmer until the chicken is cooked through, about 30 minutes.

Remove the chicken from the pot. Pull off and discard any skin and bones and shred the chicken with your hands into 1- to 2-inch pieces. In a bowl, toss the chicken with the sugar and set aside. Strain the cooking liquid from the pot and set aside ⅔ cup. Discard the rest.

To make the almonds: In a sauté pan, heat the oil over low heat and cook the almonds, stirring constantly, until lightly browned, about 3 minutes. Remove and drain on paper towels. Put the almonds, sugar, and cinnamon in a food processor and pulse to the consistency of coarse meal.

To make the eggs: Warm the reserved cooking liquid in a sauté pan over medium-low heat and add the lemon juice. Bring to a slow boil and slowly add the eggs, stirring constantly. Cook until they are the consistency of scrambled eggs. Drain any extra liquid and let cool.

To assemble the pie: Brush a 12-inch round cake pan or a 13-by-9-inch baking pan with melted butter. Have on hand a clean, damp dish towel. Open the package of fillo and lay it on a counter.

Remove 4 or 5 fillo sheets and lay them, overlapping, in the pan, brushing each sheet with some of the melted butter. (Cover unused fillo with the damp dish towel.) Some of the fillo will drape over the edges of the pan.

Spread half the chicken in a layer on the fillo, making sure it goes to the edges all around, and cover with 2 or 3 fillo sheets, each brushed with butter. Spread half of the almonds edge to edge, cover with another couple of sheets of fillo, each brushed with butter, and top with a layer of the eggs. Place the remaining chicken over the eggs. Top with 2 sheets of brushed fillo, add the remaining almonds, cover with several sheets of buttered fillo, and tuck them into the bottom of the pie, encasing the whole thing. Brush with the beaten egg yolk.

Bake the pie in the middle of the oven until golden, about 15 minutes.

To serve the dish: Remove the pie from the oven and let cool in the pan for 10 minutes. Lift it out carefully, with the aid of an oversize spatula, onto a serving plate. Let rest for 15 minutes, sprinkle with the sugar and cinnamon, and serve.

OVEN-COOKED JERK CHICKEN BREASTS

YIELD | 10 TO 12 SERVINGS

1	tablespoon ground allspice	2	tablespoons minced fresh ginger
1	teaspoon ground nutmeg	4	cloves garlic, finely minced
1	teaspoon dried thyme	1 or 2	chipotle chili peppers*, soaked for 2 hours and finely minced
½	teaspoon salt	⅓	cup fresh lime juice
¾	teaspoon black pepper	⅓	cup rum
10–12	chicken breast halves, skin pierced	⅓	cup turbinado or packed brown sugar
3	tablespoons olive oil		Banana or plantain slices for garnish (optional)
2	onions, diced		

In a small bowl, mix the allspice, nutmeg, thyme, salt, and pepper. Rub on the chicken.

Place the oil, onions, ginger, garlic, and chili peppers in a small blender and pulse until the mixture resembles a thick paste with small bits in it. In a medium bowl, mix the lime juice, rum, and turbinado or brown sugar until the sugar dissolves. Stir in the oil mixture.

Place the chicken skin side up in a large baking dish and pour the oil-and-lime mixture over it. Cover and marinate in the refrigerator overnight or all day, turning once or twice.

Preheat the oven to 400°F. Remove the chicken from the marinade and roast on a broiling pan, basting with the marinade several times, until cooked through, 30 to 35 minutes. A meat thermometer inserted in one of the breasts should read 175°F. Serve immediately.

To serve the dish: You can carry the marinated chicken in a thermal container with a cold pack and cook at your destination. Garnish with banana or plantain slices, if desired, and accompany with white rice mixed with cubed oven-roasted yams.

---

* Slightly hot on the Scoville Scale (page 317). The chipotle is much hotter than the jalapeño—a definite bite but not burning for most palates.

ROASTED ROSEMARY-GARLIC CHICKEN

YIELD | 10 SERVINGS

2	roasting chickens (5 pounds each)	2	lemons, cut in eighths, seeds removed
16	cloves garlic, peeled and sliced lengthwise		Freshly ground pepper
2	teaspoons coarse salt + more to taste	2	cups dry white wine
3	tablespoons unsalted butter	1	cup water
1	bunch fresh rosemary, a few sprigs reserved for garnish		

Preheat the oven to 400°F. Remove the giblets, neck, and visible fat from the chickens and freeze for future use or discard. Rinse the chickens under cold water and pat dry with paper towels. Starting at the neck cavity of each, loosen the skin from the breast. Using the tip of a paring knife, make small slits in skin that you can't get to with your fingers, such as the drumsticks. Slip the garlic beneath the skin of the breast and drumsticks of each bird.

Lift the wing tips of each chicken up and over the back, then tuck them under. Rub the chicken cavities with the 2 teaspoons salt and place 1 tablespoon of the butter, 2 sprigs of the rosemary, and half of the lemon in each. Rub the remaining 1 tablespoon butter over the chickens and sprinkle with some rosemary leaves. Season with a bit of salt and pepper. Pour the wine and water in the bottom of a roasting pan with a rack large enough to hold both chickens. Set the chickens on the rack and roast for 30 minutes.

Reduce the oven temperature to 350°F and roast for 1 to 1½ hours, or until a meat thermometer registers 180°F. (Insert the thermometer into the meaty part of a thigh, making sure not to touch bone.) Lift the rack from the roasting pan and remove the lemon and rosemary. Let the chickens sit for 15 minutes before carving and serving.

Meanwhile, pour the wine mixture from the bottom of the pan into a small saucepan, including any bits that have stuck to the bottom. Simmer over low heat for 15 minutes, taste for seasoning, and strain into a warm gravy boat or pitcher.

To serve the dish: Serve the chickens on a large platter and the sauce in a warm gravy pitcher. Accompany with crisp Pan-Roasted Potatoes (page 140).

MAPLE-BOURBON ROASTED CHICKEN
WITH APPLE AND SWEET POTATO WEDGES

YIELD | 10 SERVINGS

4	whole boneless, skinless chicken breasts, split	4	large Golden Delicious or Granny Smith apples
4	cloves garlic, minced	3	large sweet potatoes
2	tablespoons unsalted butter, melted	¼	cup minced shallots
1	tablespoon Dijon or any mustard	¼	cup bourbon
¾	cup pure maple syrup		A few dashes of hot pepper sauce to taste
	Salt and black pepper	¾	cup heavy cream

Preheat the oven to 400°F.

Dry the chicken and trim the fat. Cut each half into three lengthwise slices and place in a shallow platter. In a small bowl, mix the garlic, butter, mustard, ¼ cup of the maple syrup, and salt and black pepper to taste and rub over the chicken. Cover the chicken and let marinate in the refrigerator while you prepare the apples and sweet potatoes. Wash and core the apples, then cut into eight wedges. Wash the sweet potatoes and cut them into pieces about the same size as the apple wedges.

In a large bowl, mix together the shallots, bourbon, hot pepper sauce, and the remaining ½ cup maple syrup. Stir in the apples and sweet potatoes. Mix well and place in a roasting pan. Roast for 35 minutes.

Remove the apples and sweet potatoes from the oven and set the marinated chicken on top. Return the pan to the oven and roast until the chicken is cooked through, another 20 minutes.

To serve the dish: If you are serving immediately, stir in the cream. Set out on a large serving platter. This dish can also be covered and placed in an insulated carrier. If you make it a day ahead, don't add the cream then. Cool the chicken, apples, and sweet potatoes in the roasting pan, cover with plastic wrap, and refrigerate for up to 24 hours. Pour the cream over all after you have heated the dish in a 350°F oven for 30 minutes or until hot.

TURKEY CHILI MOLE

YIELD | 10 SERVINGS

¼	cup canola oil		1	tablespoon ground cinnamon
3	onions, diced		1	teaspoon ground cloves
1	large head garlic, cloves peeled and sliced		1	tablespoon ground cumin
2	dried chili peppers such as Anaheim or ancho, stemmed and minced, seeds reserved for accompaniment		1	teaspoon black pepper
			6	ounces bittersweet chocolate, broken up
				Up to 3 cups water or stock, if necessary
3	tablespoons chili powder		6–8	cups cooked rice, for serving
4	pounds ground turkey			Sliced pimiento-stuffed olives, pine nuts, raisins, chilies, and minced fresh cilantro, for serving
1	can (28 ounces) crushed tomatoes			
1	can (6 ounces) tomato paste			

In a Dutch oven or other heavy pot large enough to hold all ingredients, heat the oil over medium heat. Add the onions and garlic, and cook until soft but not brown, about 5 minutes. Stir in the chilies and chili powder, then gradually add the turkey and tomatoes. Stir in the tomato paste, cinnamon, cloves, cumin, and black pepper.

Cook, stirring frequently, until the chili starts to simmer, about 20 minutes. Add the chocolate, stir, lower the heat, and cook, stirring frequently, until the chili is dark and thick, 2 to 3 hours. Add water or stock only if the chili starts sticking to the pot.

To serve the dish: Serve immediately or cool, cover, and refrigerate for up to 2 days. Heat uncovered over medium-low heat for 15 to 20 minutes, stirring frequently. Serve from the pot or a large serving bowl with a big bowl of the hot rice. Accompany with individual bowls of olives, pine nuts, raisins, chilies, and cilantro.

POTLUCK NOTE | *Though it is not entirely necessary to wear gloves when handling chilies, be certain not to touch your face or any sensitive area until you thoroughly wash your hands.*

ROASTED TURKEY BREAST WITH ORANGE-CRANBERRY STUFFING

Often 4-pound turkey breasts are found frozen and on sale. They are very practical and will serve a crowd with this or your favorite stuffing.

YIELD | 10 SERVINGS

4	cups dried corn bread cubes*			Salt and pepper
½	cup minced celery		2	whole boneless turkey breasts (4 pounds each)
½	cup thinly sliced scallions			
1	cup chicken stock		2	teaspoons coarse salt
2	large eggs, lightly beaten		3	tablespoons extra-virgin olive oil
2	cans (11 ounces each) mandarin oranges, drained and coarsely chopped (liquid reserved)		½	cup orange marmalade
			2	tablespoons Dijon mustard
			2	tablespoons unsalted butter
1½	cups dried cranberries, soaked in mandarin orange liquid for 15 minutes and drained well			

Heat ¾–1-inch cubes of corn bread in a 200°F oven for 1 hour.

Preheat the oven to 350°F.

In a large bowl, mix the bread cubes, celery, and scallions with the stock and eggs. Stir in the oranges and cranberries. Season with salt and pepper to taste.

Place the turkey breasts skin side down on a cutting board. Slightly flatten with your hands, and rub each with ½ teaspoon of the coarse salt and 1 tablespoon of the oil. Spread half of the stuffing on top of each and bring the sides of the turkey around it. Wrap and tie tightly with kitchen twine. Transfer to a roasting pan, skin side up, and rub them with the remaining 1 teaspoon coarse salt and 2 tablespoons oil.

In a small saucepan over low heat, melt the marmalade, mustard, and butter and set aside.

Roast the turkey breasts, brushing with the glaze several times, until the internal temperature of a turkey breast is 170°F and the juices run clear when the meat is pierced with a fork, about 2 hours.

To serve the dish: Let the stuffed turkey breasts rest for 15 minutes, then remove the twine. Slice and serve on a warm, deep platter.

MEAT

THERE IS NOTHING random about the following selection of dishes, which have been favorites of friends and family for years. Almost all of them can be made in your kitchen and finished there or before serving at a potluck. I know many vegetarians, and most of them understand that there may be meat served at an event. They are usually the ones who bring a fabulous meatless favorite and have a wonderful time. There are some vegetarians, however, who are offended by the sight of meat on their table. In a crowd, there is not much to be done about this. If you know beforehand that the diners are primarily vegetarians—skip to another chapter.

That said, buy the best-quality meat you can; you don't want food that has been treated with hormones and other chemicals, so your preference might be organic and grain fed. One pound of boneless meat will serve three to four, as opposed to the old guideline of two servings. This isn't a diet book by any means, but it's good to remember that the most delicious pleasure of any dish is in the first five or six bites, so approach the buffet table with a light hand.

FIVE-FLAVOR BEEF

YIELD | 10 SERVINGS

4	tablespoons peanut or canola oil	3	tablespoons hoisin sauce
3	pounds boneless beef, cut for stir-fry	½	cup light soy sauce
1	package (12 ounces) firm tofu, drained and cubed	½	cup Shaoxing wine or dry sherry
		1	cup beef stock or water
2	tablespoons Chinese five-spice powder	1	tablespoon packed brown sugar
		1	tablespoon sesame oil
½	teaspoon black peppercorns, freshly ground	1	cup unsalted peanuts
		6	scallions, sliced
1	teaspoon minced fresh ginger	6–8	cups hot rice, for serving
2	star anise pods		

Heat the peanut or canola oil in a wok or large sauté pan over medium-high heat. Add the beef in batches and cook until browned, about 7 minutes. If the pan gets too crowded, remove the beef as it cooks and return to the pan for the final 10 minutes. Stir in the tofu and sprinkle with the five-spice powder, pepper, and ginger. Add the star anise and stir.

In a small bowl, mix the hoisin and soy sauces, wine or sherry, stock or water, sugar, and sesame oil. Stir and pour over the meat mixture. Cook for 3 minutes and stir in the peanuts and scallions. Cook and stir for about 10 minutes more, until well mixed. Remove the star anise pods.

To serve the dish: Transfer to a warm platter and serve with 6 to 8 cups of hot rice.

CHILI MOLE

This is a North American version of a dish from Puebla, Mexico, where mole poblano has been made for centuries, using shredded turkey as a base. The hundreds of varieties that have developed in the United States are often called chili Americano. Among the differences is that instead of using whole dried chili peppers and shredded poultry, we shortcut with ground chili powders and ground meat or poultry.

YIELD | 12-PLUS SERVINGS

2	tablespoons canola oil	1	teaspoon ground cinnamon
2	medium/large onions	½	cup grated dark chocolate
6	cloves garlic	¾	cup slivered almonds
1	teaspoon coriander seeds	¾	cup raisins
1	teaspoon anise seed	2–3	cups tomato juice or water, if necessary
4	pounds ground beef, or 2 pounds beef and 2 pounds pork	6	cups hot cooked rice, for serving
1	teaspoon sea salt	2½	cups hot cooked pinto beans, for serving
2	tablespoons ancho chili powder	⅓	cup chopped fresh cilantro, for garnish
3	tablespoons blended chili powder, such as New Mexico blend		Chopped olives, sour cream, and crumbled queso fresco or shredded Jack cheese, for serving (optional)
1	can (28 ounces) crushed tomatoes		
1	pound tomatillos, husked and rinsed, or diced green tomatoes		
¼	teaspoon ground cloves		

Heat the oil in a flameproof casserole or large heavy-bottomed saucepan over medium-high heat. Sauté the onions and garlic until golden brown, about 5 minutes. Stir in the coriander and anise seeds, ground meat, and salt. Blend in the chili powders, then add the tomatoes and tomatillos. Stir and bring to the boiling point. Lower the heat and add the cloves, cinnamon, chocolate, almonds, and raisins. Stir thoroughly and simmer, uncovered, for 2 hours, stirring from time to time. Add up to 3 cups liquid if the chili seems dry.

To serve the dish: If you've made the dish ahead of time, heat the chili over medium-low heat for 20 minutes, stirring frequently. Serve piping hot, accompanied by large bowls of the rice and beans and a bowl of the cilantro. Set out bowls of olives, sour cream, and cheese, if you like.

ROPAS VIEJAS (AROMATIC SHREDDED BEEF STEW)

When I lived in Santa Eulalia on Ibiza, off the coast of Spain, there were hundreds of recipes for this dish, which refers not only to the shredded meat or "old clothes" but also to the casual way in which the dish is served.

YIELD | 10 SERVINGS

1	flank steak (3 pounds), trimmed of excess fat	½	teaspoon crushed red pepper flakes, or to taste
1	large onion, coarsely chopped	1	teaspoon ground cinnamon
1	large carrot, coarsely chopped	½	teaspoon ground cloves
2	bay leaves	1	can (28 ounces) diced tomatoes, drained
½	teaspoon salt + more to taste		
¼	teaspoon freshly ground black pepper + more to taste	1	green bell pepper, skinned and julienned
3	tablespoons extra-virgin olive oil	1	yellow bell pepper, skinned and julienned
2	onions, chopped	1	red bell pepper, skinned and julienned
1	head garlic, cloves peeled and crushed	2	tablespoons capers, rinsed and drained
½	teaspoon finely chopped fresh hot chili pepper, or to taste	½	cup chopped fresh cilantro

Preheat the oven to 350°F.

Place the steak, onion, carrot, bay leaves, the ½ teaspoon salt, and the ¼ teaspoon black pepper in a 6-quart roasting pan with a cover. (Alternatively, use a baking dish covered with heavy aluminum foil.) Add just enough water to cover the steak by ½ inch.

Cover the pan and roast for 1½ hours. Remove the steak from the pan and set aside 2 cups of the strained liquid. Using two forks or your fingers, shred the beef into "rags."

Heat the oil in a large flameproof casserole over medium-high heat. Add the onions and garlic and cook until browned, about 5 minutes. Add the shredded beef and stir in the chopped chili pepper, red pepper flakes, cinnamon, and cloves. Slowly add the tomatoes and reserved roasting liquid. Lower the heat and stir in the bell peppers, capers, and cilantro. Season with salt and pepper to taste.

If not serving right away, let cool, cover, and refrigerate for up to 24 hours.

To serve the dish: If you've made the dish ahead, heat in a 300°F oven or on top of the stove, stirring frequently, until heated through, about 20 minutes. In this country, Ropas Viejas is often served with yellow rice and tortillas.

POTLUCK NOTE | *To remove the skin from a pepper, halve it lengthwise and remove the seeds. Place skin side up on a foil-lined broiler pan and broil 4 inches from the heat source for about 5 minutes, until the skin starts to blister and char. With tongs or a fork, transfer the pepper halves to a paper bag and fold the top over securely. The peppers will steam in the bag. Remove the pepper halves one by one and pull off the fine skin with a paring knife. Don't worry if some of the skin adheres, as long as most of it is removed. Use immediately or refrigerate in a closed container, covered with olive oil, for several days.*

STEAK FAJITAS WITH TOMATO LIME SALSA

⅓	cup olive oil	2	wooden skewers, soaked in water for 30 minutes
¼	cup red wine vinegar		
1	teaspoon salt + more to taste	18	flour tortillas
⅓	cup fresh lime juice		Tomato Lime Salsa (recipe follows), for serving
2½	pounds flank steak		
2	large onions, cut into wedges	2	cups sour cream, for serving
½	teaspoon coarsely ground black pepper	18	lime wedges, for serving

In a shallow dish, stir together the oil, vinegar, the 1 teaspoon salt, and lime juice. Add the steak and onions. Cover with another plate or plastic wrap and refrigerate for 1 hour, turning once.

Coat a grill rack with cooking spray. Preheat the grill.

Remove the steak from the marinade and pat dry. Rub with the pepper and sprinkle with salt to taste.

Grill the onions on a medium-hot grill, turning occasionally, until tender, 16 to 20 minutes. Meanwhile, thread the steak onto the soaked skewers and place on the grill after the onions have cooked for about 10 minutes. Cook the steak for 6 to 10 minutes total for medium-rare. Remove the onions from the grill and set aside. Transfer the meat to a cutting board. Let stand for 5 minutes before thinly slicing across the grain.

While the steak is resting, place the tortillas directly on the grill, turning once, until puffed slightly and browned in spots, about 1 minute.

To serve the dish: Divide the steak and onions among the tortillas, then top with about 2 tablespoons each of Tomato Lime Salsa (use a slotted spoon to avoid excess liquid) and sour cream. Wrap the tortilla around the filling, and garnish with a lime wedge.

(continued)

Tomato Lime Salsa

YIELD | 2 CUPS

1½ cups seeded and finely chopped tomatoes, (about 3 medium)

1 large ripe avocado, peeled, pitted, and chopped

1 tablespoon seeded and chopped jalapeño chili pepper

Zest of 1 fresh lime (see page 316)

Juice of 1 fresh lime

3 tablespoons chopped fresh cilantro

½ teaspoon coarse salt + more if needed

Few turns of a pepper mill

Place all the ingredients in a glass bowl and mix well. Let stand for 30 minutes. Taste and adjust salt and black pepper. Refrigerate until needed. The salsa can be made ahead, covered, and refrigerated for up to 1 day.

BARBECUED BRISKET

YIELD | 10 TO 12 SERVINGS

2	cups ketchup	½	teaspoon sea salt
½	cup packed brown sugar	½	teaspoon freshly ground black pepper
3	tablespoons soy sauce	3½–4	pounds beef brisket (not corned beef)
1	tablespoon honey		
4	cloves garlic, minced	⅓	cup extra-virgin olive oil
1	teaspoon crushed red pepper flakes, or to taste	2	large onions, sliced
	Dash of liquid smoke (optional)	2	cups dry red wine or stock

Preheat the oven to 450°F.

In a bowl, mix the ketchup, sugar, soy sauce, honey, garlic, red pepper flakes, liquid smoke (if using), salt, and black pepper.

Place the brisket in a roasting pan with a cover and top with the sauce. Roast uncovered for 20 minutes.

Meanwhile, heat the oil in a skillet over medium-high heat and sauté the onions until golden brown, about 5 minutes.

Add the onions and wine to the brisket and cover. Reduce the heat to 350°F and roast until tender, about 2 hours.

If you like, you can cool, cover, and refrigerate this dish overnight. When ready to go, remove any visible fat from the dish and discard. Slice the brisket. Place a layer of sauce in an oven-to-table baking dish. Place overlapping slices of brisket over the sauce and top with the remaining sauce. Cover with foil and heat in a 350°F oven until hot, 15 to 20 minutes.

To serve the dish: Slice the brisket (if it isn't already sliced), and serve on a platter with sauce from the roasting pan over all. You might accompany the meat with a big basket of warm rolls cut in half so that guests can make their own sandwiches. Serve with sides of potato salad and pickles.

OVEN-BROILED BLUE CHEESE BURGERS

YIELD | 10 BURGERS

3	pounds lean ground round or sirloin	10	hamburger or kaiser rolls
1	teaspoon sea salt	10	strips bacon, well cooked and crumbled
2	teaspoons Worcestershire sauce	10	slices tomato
¾	pound (about 2½ cups) blue cheese, crumbled	10	slices onion, raw or fried
2	tablespoons unsalted butter, at room temperature	10	leaves Boston lettuce
2	tablespoons extra-virgin olive oil		Ketchup, mayonnaise, mustard, and sliced pickled jalapeño chili peppers, for serving
	Freshly ground black pepper		

Preheat the broiler for 10 minutes.

In a large bowl, mix the ground beef with the salt and Worcestershire sauce and shape into 20 four-inch-diameter patties. Place 10 of the patties on a baking sheet lined with waxed paper.

In a small bowl, mix the blue cheese and butter, and divide the mixture among the 10 patties (about ¼ cup per patty). Smooth to within ¼ inch of the edge. Cover with the remaining 10 patties and pinch the edges closed. Cover with plastic wrap until ready to cook, up to 24 hours.

Brush a perforated broiler pan with the oil, arrange the burgers in a single layer, and season with black pepper to taste. Broil 5 inches from the heat source for 5 minutes, turn with a metal spatula, and broil for another 4 minutes. Remove from the broiler and turn the heat off.

While the burgers are cooking, place the rolls on a baking sheet. As soon as the burgers are out of the broiler, put the rolls in the oven (with the heat off) to warm. Remove them after 5 minutes.

To serve the dish: Set the burgers on the rolls on a large platter. Arrange the bacon, tomato, onion, and lettuce on another platter, and set out the ketchup, mayonnaise, mustard, and chili peppers in bowls. Let people choose their own toppings and dressings.

TENDERLOIN ROAST WITH ROSEMARY-CHOCOLATE-WINE SAUCE

It may seem unusual to use chocolate in this sauce, but it lends a nice rich flavor. People won't guess what the special ingredient is.

YIELD | 10 SERVINGS

1	cup minced shallots	½	teaspoon sea salt
½	cup minced celery, strings removed	½	teaspoon freshly ground pepper
½	cup minced carrots	4	teaspoons fresh thyme leaves + a few sprigs for garnish
6	cloves garlic, minced	4	teaspoons fresh rosemary leaves + a few sprigs for garnish
2	cups dry red wine		
1	cup water	4	ounces bittersweet or dark chocolate, grated
3	tablespoons extra-virgin olive oil		Salt and pepper
1	beef tenderloin (4–4½ pounds)	¼	cup chopped fresh flat-leaf parsley, for garnish
2	tablespoons unsweetened cocoa powder		

Preheat the oven to 425°F.

Place the shallots, celery, carrots, and garlic in a heavy roasting pan with a cover and stir in the wine and water.

Heat the oil in a heavy skillet over medium heat. Add the beef and brown it on all sides, about 10 minutes total. Transfer to the roasting pan. Sprinkle and rub with the cocoa, sea salt, freshly ground pepper, the 4 teaspoons thyme leaves, and the 4 teaspoons rosemary leaves and cover the pan.

Roast for 1½ hours. Remove the meat to a cutting board and let stand a few minutes.

Strain the sauce from the roasting pan into a saucepan over medium-low heat. Add the grated chocolate and stir until blended. Taste and adjust for salt and pepper.

To transport this dish, roast the tenderloin, let it cool, then cover and refrigerate. Cool, cover, and refrigerate the sauce separately.

To serve the dish: Slice the roast onto a warm platter and top with the warm sauce. Garnish with the thyme and rosemary sprigs and chopped parsley, and serve immediately. If you've made the dish ahead of time, slice the beef in a bake-and-serve dish, top with the sauce, cover loosely with foil, and heat in a 425°F oven for 10 minutes. Remove the foil and heat for another 5 minutes. Serve hot.

POTLUCK NOTE | *In place of the 4 teaspoons each of fresh thyme and rosemary, you can use 1 teaspoon each of dried herbs.*

MOUSSAKA

This classic layered Greek entrée is a little bit of a fuss but one of the best potluck dishes to add to your list of dependable favorites. Rich and custardy, it is a nice change from lasagna and eggplant parmigiana, though it combines some of the qualities of each.

YIELD | 10 SERVINGS

Eggplant

2	large eggplants (about 3 pounds total)	½	cup fine, dry, unseasoned bread crumbs
	Coarse salt	¼	cup extra-virgin olive oil

Meat

3	tablespoons extra-virgin olive oil	½	teaspoon ground cinnamon
1½	onions, diced	8	plum tomatoes, chopped, or 1 can (15 ounces) diced tomatoes, drained
4	cloves garlic, minced		
2	pounds ground lamb or beef		
1	teaspoon dried oregano	1	can (28 ounces) diced tomatoes, drained
⅛	teaspoon ground allspice		
¼	teaspoon ground cloves	2	tablespoons tomato paste

Topping

4	cups yogurt	6	egg yolks
¼	teaspoon sea salt	3	tablespoons instant flour
	Pinch of ground nutmeg		

Preheat the oven to 360°F.

To make the eggplant: Cut the eggplants lengthwise into ¼-inch-thick slices and sprinkle with coarse salt. Arrange layers of eggplant in one large colander or two regular ones and cover with a heavy plate or pan. Let drain in the sink for 2 hours. This step will ensure that the eggplant has a good texture.

To make the meat: While the eggplant is draining, prepare the meat layer. Heat the oil in a heavy skillet over medium heat. Add the onions, garlic, and meat and sauté until the meat is no longer pink, about 10 minutes. Stir in the oregano, allspice, cloves, and cinnamon and cook until the meat is slightly browned, about 5 minutes. Stir in the tomatoes and tomato paste and simmer for 10 minutes more.

When the eggplant has drained, rinse it thoroughly and press down on it to remove excess water. Lay it out on paper towels to remove all moisture, and dust with the bread crumbs. Heat the oil in large clean skillet over medium-high heat and lightly sauté the eggplant in a single layer until golden brown, about 3 minutes per side. Remove to paper towels as slices cook, adding more oil and eggplant until done.

To make the topping: In a medium bowl, mix together the yogurt, salt, and nutmeg and whisk the egg yolks in, one at a time. Gradually incorporate the flour.

To assemble the dish: Brush a 10-by-13-by-3-inch baking dish with oil. Lay half of the eggplant slices in the pan, overlapping them. Cover with half of the meat sauce and smooth with a spatula. Repeat with the remaining eggplant and meat sauce. At this point, you can cover it tightly with foil and refrigerate for up to 24 hours. Refrigerate the topping separately.

Bring to room temperature and pour the custard topping over the layered mixture. Smooth with a spatula.

Bake until the top is lightly browned and the custard is set, about 1 hour. Remove the Moussaka from the oven and let rest for 10 minutes before cutting.

To serve the dish: Cut the Moussaka in squares like lasagna and serve right from the baking dish.

SOUTHERN HAM CASSEROLE
WITH STEWED PEACHES

YIELD | 10 SERVINGS

Roux

4	tablespoons unsalted butter	½	teaspoon garlic powder
4	tablespoons instant flour	½	teaspoon ground paprika
3	tablespoons minced onion	2	cups milk
	Pinch of cayenne pepper		

Casserole

4	cups diced cooked ham	½	cup shredded cheddar cheese
2	cups kernels, fresh or frozen corn	3	tablespoons parsley
2	cups cooked or canned lima beans, drained		Salt and white pepper
1	teaspoon Worcestershire sauce		

Topping

3	cups water		Stewed Peaches (recipe follows), for serving
1	cup medium cornmeal		
1	cup grated cheddar cheese		

Preheat the oven to 350°F. Butter a 13-by-9-inch baking dish.

To make the roux: Melt the butter in a small saucepan over medium-low heat, then stir in the flour until golden brown, about 4 minutes. Add the onion, cayenne, garlic powder, cinnamon, and paprika and stir until blended. Slowly stir in the stock or water and cook, stirring, until thickened to the consistency of heavy cream, about 3 to 5 minutes. Set aside.

To make the casserole: In a large bowl, mix the ham, corn, beans, Worcestershire sauce, cheese, and parsley. Season with salt and pepper to taste. Add the reserved roux and stir well.

(continued)

To make the topping: Heat the water in a medium saucepan over medium-high heat until boiling. Pour in the cornmeal in a thin stream and simmer over medium-low heat until thickened, about 15 to 20 minutes (or follow package directions). Stir in ½ cup of the cheese.

To assemble the dish: Pour the ham-and-roux mixture into the prepared baking dish and level with a rubber spatula. Ladle the topping over all, spreading from end to end with the spatula. Top with the remaining ½ cup cheese. At this point, the dish can be covered and taken to your destination. Bake, uncovered, until lightly browned, 15 to 20 minutes.

To serve the dish: Serve hot or at room temperature directly from the baking dish with Stewed Peaches alongside. If you're not going far, you can bake it and take it.

Stewed Peaches

YIELD | 10 SERVINGS

6	cups sliced fresh or frozen and thawed peaches (not canned)	4	thin slices of lemon, with peel, halved
1	cup packed brown or white sugar	½	teaspoon ground cinnamon
½	cup water	¼	cup bourbon (optional)

Place all of the ingredients in a saucepan. Bring to the boiling point over medium heat, stirring constantly. Reduce the heat and simmer for 15 minutes. Peaches may be cooled, covered, and refrigerated for 24 hours and heated at your destination, or served at room temperature.

PORK WITH PRUNES AND APPLES

YIELD | 10 SERVINGS

1	rolled boneless pork loin (5 pounds)	15	pitted prunes, halved, any pit parts removed
	Salt and pepper	¾	cup apple jelly
2	cups dry white wine	1	teaspoon dried thyme
3	Golden Delicious apples, sliced into 1-inch wedges	1	bunch watercress sprigs, rinsed and drained, for garnish

Preheat the oven to 350°F.

Rub the pork loin with salt and pepper and place it in a baking dish with a cover. Add the wine and surround the meat with the apples and prunes.

Cover and roast, stirring the fruit once or twice, until a meat thermometer reads 170°F, about 1½ hours. Do not turn off the oven. Uncover the baking dish and leave the pork in the hot oven.

In a small saucepan, heat the apple jelly with the thyme over low heat until melted, about 3 minutes. Pour over the pork and fruit and roast, uncovered, for another 15 minutes. Let stand for 10 minutes before slicing.

If you are transporting this dish, carry the unsliced roast and fruit in a covered thermal container with a hot pack. At your destination, heat the apple jelly and thyme and slice the pork.

To serve the dish: Arrange the pork slices and fruit on a warm platter and pour the pan juices over all. Drizzle the apple jelly–thyme glaze over all. Garnish with the watercress and serve.

PORK CROWN ROAST WITH APPLE STUFFING AND MUSTARD SAUCE

A pork crown roast is made from a 10- to 12-rib bone-in pork loin that has been tied in a circle, ribs up, to hold the stuffing. You can substitute your favorite stuffing for the one presented here.

YIELD | 10 SERVINGS

5	teaspoons herbes de Provence	1	loin crown roast (about 6 pounds)
1	tablespoon extra-virgin olive oil		Apple Stuffing (recipe follows)
1	teaspoon sea salt		Mustard Sauce (recipe follows), for serving
1	teaspoon freshly ground pepper		

Preheat the oven to 450°F.

In a small bowl, combine the herbes de Provence, oil, salt, and pepper. Rub the mixture evenly over the roast, wrap the exposed rib bones individually with small pieces of foil, and set the roast upright in a baking pan.

Fill the crown of the roast with the Apple Stuffing, mounding it in the center. Do not pack too tightly; any left over can be baked for 30 minutes in ramekins. Cover the stuffing with a piece of foil to prevent it from drying out.

Roast for 30 minutes, reduce the heat to 325°F, and roast until the meat registers 170°F on a meat thermometer, about 2 hours. About 30 to 45 minutes before the end of the roasting time, uncover the stuffing so that it can brown and crisp.

Gently remove the roast to a serving platter and let rest for 10 minutes before serving. Strain the drippings and reserve ½ to ¾ cup for the Mustard Sauce.

To serve the dish: Remove the foil from the rib bones. If you want to be festive, cover the rib tips with paper frills. Carve the roast, using the ribs as a guide, and serve with spoonfuls of Apple Stuffing and Mustard Sauce.

(continued)

Apple Stuffing

3	tablespoons unsalted butter	4	teaspoons sugar
2	tablespoons extra-virgin olive oil	1	teaspoon grated lemon zest (see page 316)
1	onion, diced		
2	ribs celery, finely diced	1	cup apple cider or juice + ½ cup more, if necessary
¾	cup chopped pecans		
2	slightly tart apples, such as Granny Smith, cored and diced	2	tablespoons minced fresh flat-leaf parsley
4	cups stale bread cubes	1	teaspoon crumbled dried sage
1	cup cranberries		Salt and pepper

In a sauté pan, heat the butter and oil over medium heat. Add the onion and celery and sauté until golden brown, about 3 minutes. Add the pecans and roast slightly for 3 minutes. Stir in the apples and cook until golden, about 12 minutes.

Place the bread cubes in a large bowl and mix with the apple-and-onion mixture, stirring thoroughly. In a small bowl, toss the cranberries with the sugar and lemon zest and mix into the bread cubes. Add the 1 cup cider or juice, parsley, sage, and salt and pepper to taste. The stuffing should be moist but not wet. If it's too dry, add up to ½ cup cider.

Mustard Sauce

½–¾	cup strained drippings from the pork roast or beef stock	⅔	cup Dijon mustard
¾	cup red wine	1¼	cups heavy cream
3	shallots, minced		Sea salt and freshly ground white pepper

Pour the drippings or stock into a small saucepan and add the wine and shallots. Bring to the boiling point over medium heat and simmer over medium-low heat for 20 minutes, stirring occasionally, to reduce the liquid. Add the mustard and cream, return to the boiling point, and immediately reduce the heat and cook, whisking frequently, until the sauce is somewhat thickened, about 10 minutes. Season with salt and pepper to taste. Serve in a sauceboat or pitcher.

OLD-FASHIONED YANKEE POT ROAST

This simple dish requires a tasty cut of meat—there are no embellishments, so each bite stands out. Searing or braising the meat enriches the flavor and takes very little time.

YIELD | 10 SERVINGS

2	tablespoons unsalted butter	1	pound carrots (about 10), trimmed into 2-inch lengths
2	tablespoons canola or safflower oil	½	pound baby bella or shiitake mushrooms, cut in half
1	bottom round roast (about 5-pounds)	1	tablespoon potato starch
2	cups water	½	cup dry red wine
1½	teaspoons salt + more to taste		Freshly ground pepper
1	pound boiling onions, peeled and blanched	¼	cup minced fresh flat-leaf parsley, for garnish
20	red potatoes (about 2 inches in diameter), a strip peeled like a belt around the middle		

In a Dutch oven, heat the butter and oil over medium-high heat and sear the meat on all sides, about 2 minutes per side. Add the water and the 1½ teaspoons salt and bring to the boiling point. Add the onions, potatoes, carrots, and mushrooms, then cover, lower the heat, and simmer until the meat is tender, 2 to 2½ hours. Remove the roast to a cutting board and cover it loosely with foil so it doesn't lose too much heat.

In a small bowl, mix the potato starch with the wine until dissolved. Pour into the Dutch oven and cook over low heat, stirring gently, until it thickens a bit, about 10 minutes. Season with salt and pepper to taste.

To serve the dish: Slice the meat and transfer it to a warm platter. Using a slotted spoon, mound the vegetables on the roast, then ladle the gravy over all. Garnish with the parsley and serve.

POTLUCK NOTE | *To transport this dish, cool the roast when it is cooked. Cover. To serve, slice the beef on a baking dish that you can serve from. Top with the vegetables and sauce and heat in a 350°F oven for 20 minutes.*

FISH AND SHELLFISH

THE EARLIEST DOCUMENTED fish recipe, written in China, dates from 1500 BCE. Around the Mediterranean Sea, the Etruscans had a sophisticated aquacultural system, and Scandinavia claims to have records of cooked fish that go back 4,000 years. All over the world in all societies, fish has been caught, sometimes farmed, dried, smoked, salted, frozen—and always eaten. So jump right in and give it a try. This is your chance, because when you are potlucking, you have only one dish to focus on.

You will be rewarded because fish dishes are always well received. Both delicious and healthy, the recipes in this chapter will deliver dishes that are sure to make your reputation as a fabulous "potlucker."

Fish should never, ever smell fishy—it should never look iridescent or feel slimy. It is best not to buy fish more than a day before you are going to cook it. The best way to buy fish is from a market that has someone to talk to so that if you're uncertain what to buy, you can ask for help. Fish vendors are usually well informed.

Very little special equipment is needed. You don't need a lot of serving dishes—just one or two 13-by-9-inch baking pans that can go from oven to refrigerator to table. A large spatula will help lift and turn fillets without breaking them. Olive oil spray is a great convenience to keep fish from sticking. You can buy it ready to go or buy a refillable spray bottle, which you can fill with your favorite oil.

MARYLAND ROCKFISH CHOWDER

There are several species of fish called rockfish, but in Maryland, "rockfish" is another name for striped bass. The Maryland Watermen's Association holds a rockfishing tournament in Rock Hall, Maryland, each year. It seems that everyone in Rock Hall has a version of this dish.

YIELD | 12 SERVINGS

8	tablespoons (½ cup) unsalted butter	1	cup white wine (optional)
2	cups finely diced onion	1½	pounds new potatoes, peeled and cubed
2	ribs celery, finely diced	3	cups fresh or frozen corn kernels
2	pounds Maryland rockfish fillets or other firm whitefish, cut into cubes	2	cups finely diced carrots
		2	teaspoons Old Bay seasoning, or to taste
8	cups (two 1-quart containers) homemade vegetable stock or canned stock	1	teaspoon dried thyme
			Salt and pepper
1	can (28 ounces) diced tomatoes	⅓	cup minced fresh flat-leaf parsley, for garnish
2	bottles (8 ounces each) clam juice		

In a Dutch oven or heavy soup pot over medium heat, melt the butter and cook the onion, celery, and fish until browned, about 10 minutes.

One by one, add all the remaining ingredients except the parsley, stirring gently. Bring to a boil, lower the heat, and simmer, uncovered, for 30 minutes.

To serve the dish: Pour the soup into a warmed tureen and garnish with the parsley. Rockfish chowder is usually served with oyster crackers, but hot biscuits are also traditional.

CRAB CAKES WITH REMOULADE SAUCE

These are the real deal and a real treat. Unlike salmon cakes, which are better prepared with canned fish, crab cakes are best made with fresh crabmeat.

YIELD | 10 SERVINGS

1	large egg
1	tablespoon mayonnaise
½	teaspoon Dijon mustard
1	teaspoon Worcestershire sauce
1	pound backfin crabmeat
2–3	teaspoons Old Bay seasoning
	Pinch of baking powder
25	unsalted saltines, coarsely crumbled

	Juice of ½ lemon
	Salt and pepper
1	cup medium-grind cornmeal
4	tablespoons (¼ cup) unsalted butter
4	tablespoons olive oil
	Remoulade Sauce (recipe follows), for serving

In a large bowl, mix the egg, mayonnaise, mustard, and Worcestershire sauce. With a fork, toss the crabmeat lightly with the mayonnaise mixture. Stir in the Old Bay seasoning (to taste) and baking powder, then fold in the crackers and lemon juice. Lightly season with salt and pepper to taste.

Form the mixture into 10 (20 for a buffet) patties. Press just hard enough to hold each crab cake together. Pour the cornmeal into a shallow bowl and gently coat each cake.

At this point, if you are planning to cook the crab cakes in another kitchen, layer them with waxed paper in a flat plastic container, cover, and refrigerate for up to 24 hours.

In a large (preferably cast-iron) skillet, heat the butter and oil over medium heat until there is a slight sizzle. Cook the crab cakes until crisp and browned, 4 to 5 minutes per side. Drain on paper towels and serve immediately.

To serve the dish: These are best served within an hour of making. If you cannot do this, cool them on a wire rack for 15 minutes. Layer with parchment or waxed paper in a shallow pan, cover with foil, and refrigerate for up to 24 hours. Heat on one or two baking sheets in a 400°F oven for 10 minutes. Serve hot on a platter with cold Remoulade Sauce in a bowl alongside.

(continued)

Remoulade Sauce

YIELD | 2 CUPS

2	large egg yolks	½	cup minced celery
¾	cup olive oil	½	cup minced scallions
½	teaspoon Tabasco	¼	cup capers, minced
1	teaspoon Dijon mustard	¼	teaspoon sweet paprika
2	teaspoons fresh lemon juice		Salt and pepper

Whisk the egg yolks in a small deep bowl, using a balloon whisk. Continue whisking vigorously as you slowly and steadily dribble in the oil. In a few minutes, the mixture will achieve the consistency of mayonnaise. Incorporate the remaining ingredients, place in a covered container, and refrigerate immediately until ready to use.

When serving, do not leave at room temperature for more than 2 hours.

POTLUCK NOTE | *For recipes that call for eggs that are raw or undercooked when the dish is served, use either shell eggs that have been treated to destroy salmonella by pasteurization or another approved method, or pasteurized egg products. Treated shell eggs are available from a growing number of retailers and are clearly labeled.*

POACHED COD WITH LEMON-CAPER BUTTER SAUCE

This melt-in-your-mouth dish is only as good as the fish it is made with. It is very easy to make and to eat. It is especially good accompanied by White Beans with Gremolata (page 82).

YIELD | 10 SERVINGS

Fish

1½	quarts water	¼	teaspoon whole cloves
	Juice of 2 lemons	1	teaspoon coarse salt
1	medium to large onion, sliced	3	pounds cod fillets
¼	teaspoon black peppercorns		

Sauce

1	cup sweet unsalted butter		Finely grated zest of 1 lemon (see page 316)
⅓	cup small capers, rinsed and drained	⅓	cup minced fresh flat-leaf parsley, for garnish
	Juice of 2 medium lemons		

To make the fish: In a large Dutch oven or other pan with a large circumference, bring the water, lemon juice, onion, peppercorns, cloves, and salt to a boil over medium-high heat. Simmer for 10 minutes. Add the cod gently with a slotted spatula. Lower the heat to medium, and simmer until the fish flakes easily with a fork, 10 to 12 minutes.

To make the sauce: Melt the butter in a saucepan over medium-low heat. Stir in the capers. Reduce the heat to low and slowly stir in the lemon juice. Do not boil. Remove from the heat and stir in the lemon zest.

To serve the dish: Serve the poached cod on a warm platter, topped with the sauce, garnished with the parsley, and accompanied by White Beans with Gremolata served alongside in a warm bowl.

SPANISH-STYLE PAN-ROASTED RED SNAPPER WITH PAN-ROASTED POTATOES

Any green salad in the Salads chapter makes a good accompaniment to this dish.

YIELD | 10 SERVINGS

¼	cup olive oil		1	cup pimiento-stuffed Spanish olives + more for garnish
1½	cups diced sweet onion			
1	large bell pepper, diced		10	red snapper fillets (5 ounces each)
1	pound white mushrooms, sliced		1	teaspoon dried rosemary
1	cup whole blanched almonds (optional)		½	cup fresh orange juice
			½	cup fresh lemon juice
1	cup oil-soaked sun-dried tomatoes, drained and coarsely chopped, homemade or from a jar		½	cup chopped fresh flat-leaf parsley + sprigs for garnish
½	teaspoon coarse salt			Pan-Roasted Potatoes (recipe follows), for serving
¼	teaspoon ground white pepper			
½	teaspoon crushed red pepper flakes			

Preheat the oven to 400°F. Spray a 13-by-9-inch dish with olive oil. Heat the oil in a heavy skillet over medium heat. Add the onion and bell pepper and sauté until the onion is golden brown, about 7 minutes. Add the mushrooms and almonds and cook, stirring, until the almonds are golden brown, about 3 minutes. Lower the heat and stir in the tomatoes, salt, white pepper, red pepper flakes, and the 1 cup olives. Mix well and remove from the heat.

Spread half of the vegetable mixture on the bottom of the prepared baking dish. Set the fish fillets on top in a single layer, sprinkle with the rosemary, and pour over the orange and lemon juices, and sprinkle with chopped parsley. Cover with the remaining vegetable mixture. Roast until the fish flakes easily with a fork, 20 to 30 minutes.

To serve the dish: Serve in the baking dish or on a deep, warm serving platter, garnished with the parsley sprigs and additional olives. Serve the Pan-Roasted Potatoes alongside.

(continued)

| *To prepare the tomatoes yourself, place 1 cup sun-dried tomatoes in a small saucepan and cover with olive oil. Heat over medium-low heat just to a simmer. Remove from the heat and soak overnight. Drain the tomatoes and use. Refrigerate the oil in a covered container for another use, such as salad dressing. Use within a week.*

Pan-Roasted Potatoes

YIELD | 10 SIDE-DISH SERVINGS

2½	pounds new potatoes, scrubbed and cut in half	½–1	teaspoon Spanish paprika or other sweet paprika, or to taste
¾	teaspoon salt	1	teaspoon dried rosemary

Preheat the oven to 400°F. Spray a 13-by-9-inch baking dish with olive oil.

Place the potatoes in the prepared baking dish and spray them with additional oil. Season with the salt, paprika, and rosemary and roast until crisp and fork-tender, 40 to 45 minutes.

If you are serving this dish immediately, you can place the potatoes in the preheated oven while you are sautéing the ingredients for the snapper.

POTLUCK NOTE | *Although, like all fish dishes, this is best served immediately, it is sturdy enough to be cooled, covered, and refrigerated for 24 hours and reheated before serving. Heat in a 425°F oven for 10 minutes. The same is true of the potatoes.*

FILLET OF FISH EN PAPILLOTE

"En papillote" is the French term for food baked in parchment paper (more literally, "curled paper"). As the fish cooks, it steams in its own juices. This is a terrific potluck dish because you can make the fish packets, then refrigerate them for several hours before placing them on a baking sheet in a pre-heated oven. Everyone likes opening packages, so this dish is sure to please.

YIELD | 10 SERVINGS

10	circles (12 inches in diameter) of parchment paper	1	sweet onion, julienned
10	small new potatoes, peeled and sliced paper-thin	2	zucchini, julienned
		5	plum tomatoes, sliced lengthwise
10	sea trout (weakfish) or orange roughy fillets (4–6 ounces each)	2	teaspoons dried thyme
			Salt and pepper

Preheat the oven to 400°F.

Lay out the circles of parchment on a work surface. Fold each in half to make a crease, then open them up again. Spray with olive oil. As you proceed, keep all ingredients on one half of the circle and leave a 1-inch border around the edge.

Divide the potatoes evenly and fan them out on each half circle. Top with the fish, then add the onion and zucchini. Top with the tomatoes, thyme, and salt and pepper to taste. Fold each circle in half over the filling and, starting at one end, fold over the edges of the paper two or three times to seal the packets. Press tightly so juices don't leak out. You can place a few paper clips around the edges; just make sure to remove them before serving.

At this point you can refrigerate the fish packets for several hours.

Place the packets on two baking sheets and bake until the fish flakes easily with a fork, about 20 minutes.

To serve the dish: Serve immediately on individual plates or a large platter. If the packets are going to sit on a buffet table, cut a slit in each one to allow the steam to escape and stop the cooking.

SALMON BURGERS WITH ONION JAM

YIELD | 10 SALMON BURGERS

3½	pounds salmon fillet, skinned			Freshly ground black pepper
1½	cups finely diced red onion		3	egg whites, beaten until foamy but not stiff
1½	cups finely diced red bell pepper			Safflower oil, for sautéing
¼	cup minced fresh flat-leaf parsley			Onion Jam (recipe follows), for serving
2	cups fine fresh bread crumbs		10	hamburger rolls, toasted
	Juice of 1 lemon			
1	teaspoon dried thyme			
½	teaspoon dried rosemary			

Pick out all the bones from the salmon, cut it into 4-inch pieces, and mince with a sharp 8-inch chef's knife. Alternatively, pulse the fish a few pieces at a time in a food processor fitted with the metal blade. Do not turn the fish into mush.

In a large bowl, combine the salmon with the onion, bell pepper, parsley, and bread crumbs, then stir in the lemon juice, thyme, and rosemary. Season with black pepper to taste. Fold in the egg whites. Shape into 10 patties about ¾ inch thick. You can prepare burgers 12 hours in advance and keep them covered with plastic wrap in a single layer in the refrigerator.

On a griddle or in a large skillet brushed heavily with safflower oil, sauté the burgers in a single layer over medium-high heat until cooked through and golden brown on both sides, about 4 minutes per side. Repeat until all the burgers are cooked.

To serve the dish: Serve immediately, with the Onion Jam and toasted burger rolls. Or place the cooked burgers on a baking sheet and keep warm in a 200°F oven until ready to serve, up to 20 minutes.

Onion Jam

YIELD | 4 CUPS

3	tablespoons unsalted butter	¼	cup sugar
3	tablespoons extra-virgin olive oil	½	teaspoon ground allspice
10	medium to large onions, sliced and separated into rings	1½	cups red wine

Heat the butter and oil in a large sauté pan over medium heat. Add the onions and sauté for 4 minutes, or until transparent. Stir in the sugar and allspice, then lower the heat and stir in the wine. Cook, stirring frequently, until all the liquid has been absorbed, about 20 minutes. Onion Jam can be cooled, covered, and refrigerated for up to 3 days.

PAN-ROASTED SALMON WITH MINT PESTO

I am a salmon enthusiast because the fish is flavorful on its own, yet can stand up to strong season-ings and rich sauces. This dish is a springtime favorite—fresh mint is abundant then—but you can make it anytime. If you plan to serve it at a buffet or a light lunch, cut the salmon fillets in half.

YIELD | 10 SERVINGS

1	cup extra-virgin olive oil	¼	teaspoon coarse salt
4–5	cloves garlic, roughly chopped		Mint sprigs, for garnish
1	cup fresh mint leaves, large stems removed, and 1 tablespoon dried mint	12	salmon fillets (5 ounces each)
			Sea salt and freshly ground pepper
1½	cups toasted broken walnuts		

Preheat the oven to 360°F.

To make the pesto: Place ¾ cup of the oil, garlic, mint leaves, and dried mint in a small food processor and puree, but don't liquefy. Add the walnuts and salt and pulse until finely chopped. The pesto can be made 24 hours in advance, covered, and refrigerated. Bring to room temperature before spreading on the salmon.

To make the salmon: Pour the remaining ¼ cup oil in a 13-by-17-inch rimmed baking sheet, large enough to hold the salmon in one layer. Spread the pesto on the salmon fillets. Roast for 20 minutes. If possible, place the salmon under the broiler for the last 2 minutes of cooking time before serving.

To serve the dish: Serve from the baking sheet or, with the aid of a slotted spatula, place the pesto-topped fillets on a platter. Garnish with the mint sprigs, and offer sea salt and a pepper mill. Bow-tie pasta tossed with oil, garlic, and toasted walnuts makes a nice accompaniment.

POTLUCK NOTE | *To toast walnuts, spread them on a rimmed baking sheet and bake in a 400°F oven for 7 to 10 minutes, turning with a spatula after 4 minutes, until fragrant and lightly toasted.*

ROASTED SALMON FILLETS WITH MEDITERRANEAN SAUCE AND PANISSE FRIES

Though salmon isn't a Mediterranean fish, it takes well to the rich flavors of the region.

YIELD | 12 SERVINGS

3 tablespoons extra-virgin olive oil

12 salmon fillets (5 ounces each)

Juice of 1 lemon

Sea salt and freshly ground pepper

¼ cup minced fresh flat-leaf parsley + 2 tablespoons more, for serving

5 cloves garlic, sliced paper-thin

4 large tomatoes, seeded and cut into chunks, or 1 can (28 ounces) whole tomatoes, drained, seeded, and cut

5 zucchini, rinsed and sliced

1 cup black and green olives, pitted and sliced + 2 tablespoons more, for serving

1½ cups white wine

Panisse Fries (recipe follows), for serving

Grated zest of ½ lemon, for garnish

Preheat the oven to 375°F. Coat a 13-by-17-inch rimmed baking sheet with some of the oil.

Arrange the salmon in a single layer in the prepared baking dish, drizzle with the lemon juice, and season lightly with salt and pepper.

In a large bowl, mix the remaining oil with the ¼ cup parsley, garlic, tomatoes, zucchini, 1 cup olives, and wine. Spoon over the fish and bake until the fish is opaque all the way through, about 30 minutes.

This dish is best served immediately after cooking, so it's a good choice if you're hosting the potluck.

To serve the dish: Remove the fish and vegetables from the oven and transfer to a large warmed platter. Place the Panisse Fries around and garnish all with the lemon zest and the remaining 2 tablespoons each of parsley and olives.

Panisse Fries

On a recent trip to the Pacific Northwest, I had a terrific meal of fish served with Mediterranean vegetables and strips of panisse, a starch made from chickpea flour. You can think of it as a nice variation on polenta.

YIELD | 12 SIDE-DISH SERVINGS

3	tablespoons extra-virgin olive oil + more for greasing and frying	1	teaspoon herbes de Provence
3½	cups water	½	teaspoon salt
1	cup chickpea flour		Freshly ground pepper
¼	cup all-purpose flour + more for dusting		

Coat a 9-inch square baking pan with oil.

Pour the 3 tablespoons oil and water into a heavy-bottomed saucepan, bring to a low boil, and slowly whisk in the chickpea flour and the ¼ cup all-purpose flour, until well incorporated. Stir in the herbs, salt, and pepper to taste. Stir continuously over medium-low heat for 5 minutes, until the mixture thickens. Lower the heat and simmer for another 10 minutes, stirring often, until smooth, thick, and creamy. Pour into the prepared pan, evening it out with a rubber spatula. Brush with oil, cool, and cover and refrigerate for 3 hours or overnight, for up to 24 hours.

When ready to prepare for serving, cut across into thirds and then into 1-inch strips. Remove from the pan and place on a baking sheet. Dust with flour on both sides. Brush off any excess flour.

Heat oil ⅛ inch deep in a large, heavy sauté pan over medium-high heat. Sauté the strips for 2 to 3 minutes a side and drain on a baking sheet lined with paper towels. Place the fries on the serving dish with the salmon so that some of the sauce is absorbed.

POTLUCK NOTE | *Chickpea flour is readily available at most large supermarkets, as well as whole food and Indian specialty stores.*

FLOUNDER ROULADES FLORENTINE

"Roulade" is the French term for a thin slice of meat, fish, or poultry rolled around a filling and then cooked. "Florentine" usually means that the dish includes spinach. To stretch this dish to serve 12, simply purchase two more fillets and proceed with the rest of the recipe.

YIELD | 10 SERVINGS

Spinach

2	pounds rinsed spinach, with the water clinging to it		Salt and pepper
1	cup water	½	teaspoon nutmeg

Mushroom sauce

3	tablespoons unsalted butter	½	cup instant flour
1½	pounds button mushrooms, diced	1	cup cream
½	cup minced shallots		Dash of cayenne pepper, optional
	Salt and black pepper	½	cup Parmigiano-Reggiano cheese, grated
1	cup white wine		
2	cups milk		

Flounder

10	flounder fillets (5 ounces each, about 3½ pounds)	2	cups shredded Swiss cheese
	Salt and pepper		Ground nutmeg, for seasoning

Preheat the oven to 400°F. Spray a 13-by-9-inch baking dish with olive oil.

To make the spinach: Put the spinach and water in a large pot over medium heat. Stir in salt and pepper to taste. Cook, stirring constantly, until the spinach is cooked down, 5 to 7 minutes. Drain in a colander, pressing out as much liquid as you can. Transfer the spinach to a cutting board and mince, then transfer to a bowl and stir in the nutmeg. Set aside.

To make the mushroom sauce: Melt the butter in a sauté pan over medium heat and stir in the mushrooms and shallots. Sauté for 4 minutes, or until the shallots are golden brown. Lower the heat and stir in salt and black pepper to taste. Pour the wine over all and cook, stirring, until the wine is almost absorbed, about 5 minutes. Add the milk, flour, cream, and cayenne, if desired. Cook, stirring, until blended, then stir in the Parmigiano-Reggiano. Remove the sauce from the heat.

To assemble the roulades: Lay out the flounder fillets on a clean flat work surface and season lightly with salt and pepper. Place about 2 tablespoons of the reserved spinach at the broad base of each fillet and roll toward the point. Seal with a toothpick. Place in the prepared baking dish and cover with the mushroom sauce. Sprinkle the Swiss cheese over all and season with nutmeg to taste. At this point, the assembled dish can be covered and refrigerated for up to 24 hours. Bake until the fish is cooked through and flakes easily with a fork, 20 to 25 minutes, or transport cold and bake at your destination.

To serve the dish: Serve hot from the dish it was baked in—it is best to let each person remove the toothpick from his or her serving. A nice accompaniment to this dish is Wild Rice Casserole (page 76). Brown rice is good with this as well.

STIR-FRIED RICE WITH MUSHROOMS AND SHRIMP

This flexible dish incorporates a lot of precooked ingredients, and it is surprisingly delicious; each mouthful tastes a little different from the last. Cooked beef, pork, and/or chicken can be added or substituted for the shrimp, and it can be made with white or brown rice.

YIELD | 10 BUFFET SERVINGS

4	tablespoons peanut oil	¾	pound mushrooms, sliced
1	tablespoon grated fresh ginger	1	pound cooked large (24–30 per pound) shrimp
6	scallions, minced		
4	eggs, lightly whisked with 2 tablespoons water	2	cans (12 ounces) baby corn, drained and rinsed
3	cloves garlic, minced	⅓	cup light soy sauce or tamari
1	red bell pepper, seeded and cut in lengthwise strips	1	tablespoon sugar
		1	tablespoon sesame oil
7½	cups cooked white or brown rice		

Heat 2 tablespoons of the peanut oil in a wok or large sauté pan. Add half of the ginger, half of the scallions, and the eggs and stir until the eggs are just solid. Remove to a plate and set aside. Add the remaining 2 tablespoons peanut oil to the wok and stir in the garlic, the remaining ginger and scallions, and the bell pepper. Cook, stirring, until the scallions are slightly browned, about 3 minutes. Add the rice and cook until the grains are hot and free of clumps. Push the rice to the side of the wok, stir in the mushrooms and shrimp, stir in the corn, and cook until the shrimp are heated through, 3 to 4 minutes longer. Add the reserved cooked eggs and stir until broken up. Add the soy sauce or tamari, sugar, and sesame oil and mix well.

To serve the dish: Place in a warm serving bowl and serve with a deep serving spoon.

POTLUCK NOTE | *Cooked rice stays fresh refrigerated, tightly covered, for up to 1 week or frozen up to 6 months. To heat, add 2 tablespoons of liquid per cup of rice. Cover and heat about 5 minutes on top of the stove, or microwave on high about 1 minute per cup of rice.*

SHRIMP COCONUT CURRY WITH BASMATI RICE

A long time ago in a galaxy far, far away, I lived on the Spanish island of Ibiza for a year. Our neighbors, an Indian/French couple, cooked the most exotic dishes I had ever tasted from a home kitchen. This is only one of a variety of a seafood curries that we made and ate. You can personalize it after you have made it once or twice.

YIELD | 10 TO 12 SERVINGS

¼ cup clarified butter (see page 316) or canola oil

1 piece (2 inches) fresh ginger, minced

6 cloves garlic, minced

1–2 green, slightly hot chili peppers, such as Anaheim or poblano (ask your produce manager), seeded and thinly sliced, or to taste (optional)

2 tablespoons Madras curry powder

1 teaspoon ground cardamom

1 teaspoon ground cumin

1 teaspoon ground coriander

2 tablespoons packed dark brown sugar

4 medium to large onions, sliced

3 pounds ripe tomatoes, diced, or 2 cans (28 ounces each) diced tomatoes, drained

2 cups unsweetened coconut milk

3 pounds extra-large shrimp (25–30 per pound), peeled and deveined

1½ cups shredded coconut

½ cup minced fresh cilantro, for garnish

1 cup toasted coconut (see page 316), for garnish (optional)

Basmati Rice (recipe follows), for serving

Heat the ghee or oil in a large skillet over medium-low heat. With a wooden spoon, stir in the ginger, garlic, chili peppers, curry powder, cardamom, cumin, and coriander and cook until aromatic, 2 to 3 minutes. Stir in the sugar and onions and sauté until the onions are golden brown, about 7 minutes. Stir in the tomatoes and coconut milk and cook, stirring until the mixture comes to a low boil, 7 to 8 minutes. Stir in the shrimp and cook, stirring constantly, for 5 to 7 minutes. Do not overcook or the shrimp will be tough. Stir in the shredded coconut and remove from the heat.

To serve the dish: Transfer to a deep serving platter and top with the cilantro and, if you like, toasted coconut. Set a bowl of hot Basmati Rice alongside. Indian breads and Peach Chutney (page 98) are also good accompaniments.

Basmati Rice

YIELD | 8 CUPS

| 3 | tablespoons clarified butter (see page 316) or unsalted butter | 7 | cups water + 1 cup more, if needed |
| 4 | cups basmati rice, rinsed in several changes of water and drained | ¾ | teaspoon salt (optional) |

Heat the butter in a large heavy-bottomed pot with a tight-fitting lid over medium-high heat. Add the rice and stir for a few minutes, until it is shiny and almost translucent. Stir in the 7 cups water and bring to a boil. Stir in the salt. Cover, lower the heat, and simmer until the rice is tender, about 20 minutes. Check the rice after 15 minutes and add more water if the rice is cooking dry. Remove from the heat, transfer to a warm serving bowl, and fluff with a fork.

The rice can be made a day before serving. Line a large colander with cheesecloth, leaving enough overhang to cover the rice. Place the rice in the colander, cover with the cheesecloth, and cool. Refrigerate, covered with foil or plastic wrap. When ready to serve, remove the wrap and set the colander in a large covered pot with 2 inches of simmering water. Heat for 10 minutes, turn out in a warm serving bowl, and fluff with a fork.

TILAPIA FAJITAS WITH TOMATO SALSA, CHIPOTLE CREAM, AND GUACAMOLE

What delicious fun these are! They're even more fun with Perfect Margaritas (page 159).

YIELD | 12 SERVINGS (2 FAJITAS EACH)

3	pounds tilapia fillets, cut into strips		½	scant teaspoon garlic powder
¼	teaspoon freshly ground black pepper + more to taste			Juice of 1 orange
				Juice of 1 lime
½	teaspoon salt + more to taste		3	tablespoons extra-virgin olive oil
½	teaspoon ground cumin		1	large sweet onion, halved lengthwise and sliced
1	teaspoon ancho chili powder			
1	teaspoon dried oregano		2	green bell peppers, seeded and sliced
	Dash of cayenne pepper (optional)		1	red bell pepper, seeded and sliced

Accompaniments

24	soft flour tortillas (6 inches in diameter)		Tomato Salsa, Chipotle Cream, and Guacamole (recipes follow), for serving
2	cups shredded cheddar cheese		
3	cups shredded lettuce		
2	limes, cut in thin wedges		

Place the tilapia in an 8-by-8-inch baking dish. In a bowl, mix the ¼ teaspoon black pepper, the ½ teaspoon salt, cumin, chili powder, oregano, cayenne pepper (if using), garlic powder, and citrus juices and pour over the fish. Cover with plastic wrap and refrigerate for 30 to 45 minutes (no longer). Turn the fish once or twice.

Heat the oil in a large skillet over medium heat. Add the onion and bell peppers and sauté until the onions are golden brown, about 7 minutes. Season with salt and black pepper to taste. Remove the vegetables with a slotted spoon and reserve.

(continued)

Transfer the tilapia from the marinade to the skillet and sauté gently until the fish flakes easily with a fork, about 4 minutes per side. Return the onion and peppers to the skillet and stir.

Wrap the tortillas in foil (two stacks of 12 each) and heat in a 200°F oven or toaster oven for 5 minutes.

To serve the dish: Transfer the fish and vegetables to a deep serving platter and serve immediately with the tortillas, cheese, lettuce, and limes. Serve bowls of Tomato Salsa, Chipotle Cream, and Guacamole alongside so people can make their own fajitas.

Tomato Salsa

YIELD | ABOUT 2½ CUPS

1	large red onion, finely chopped		Juice of 1 orange
3	large ripe tomatoes, finely chopped		Juice of 1 lime
1	clove garlic, minced	⅓	cup chopped fresh cilantro
2	green chili peppers, seeded and finely chopped, or 1 can (4 ounces) chopped green chili peppers		Salt and freshly ground black pepper

In a large bowl, using a wooden spoon, mix all the ingredients by hand, crushing them together. It is better not to use a blender, as the salsa will get too mushy. Cover and refrigerate until ready to serve, up to 24 hours.

Chipotle Cream

YIELD | ABOUT 3½ CUPS

16   ounces (2 cups) regular or light sour cream

1   cup regular or light mayonnaise

⅓   cup sweet pickle relish, drained

⅓   cup minced shallots

¼   cup chopped fresh cilantro

1   tablespoon minced chipotle chili peppers, or to taste

In a large bowl, mix all the ingredients, cover, and refrigerate until ready to use, for up to 24 hours.

Guacamole

YIELD | ABOUT 3 CUPS

3   ripe avocados

     Juice of 2 limes

     Grated zest of ½ lime (see page 316)

3   cloves garlic, finely minced

½   cup finely minced sweet or red onion

3   tablespoons chopped fresh cilantro

1 or 2   serrano chili peppers, seeded and minced, or to taste

¼   teaspoon sea salt, or to taste

Peel, pit, and slice the avocados and place them in a medium mixing bowl. Mash with a fork and add the lime juice, lime zest, garlic, onion, cilantro, and chili peppers. Season with salt to taste.

POTLUCK NOTE | *Cooks in Mexico and other parts of the world mash avocados in a molcajete, a basalt mortar and pestle. If you make guacamole a lot, it's a good kitchen tool to have. It's also useful for making pesto, aioli, and other compound sauces. You can serve from it as well.*

PERFECT MARGARITAS

These are called perfect not because I say so but because no mixes or commercial mixes are used. As an accompaniment to fajitas (or any Mexican dish), they add a festive touch.

YIELD | 4 SERVINGS

	Ice cubes	½	cup fresh orange juice
6	ounces best-quality tequila		Juice of ½ lime
2	ounces Cointreau or triple sec		Lime slices, for garnish

Fill a shaker with the ice and add the tequila, Cointreau or triple sec, orange juice, and lime juice. Shake until chilled. Pour through a strainer into four margarita glasses. Serve straight up or over ice, garnished with lime slices. You can also salt the rim, as described below.

POTLUCK NOTE | *To rim the glass with salt, pour several inches of coarse salt in a shallow plastic container about 6 inches in diameter. Before pouring the margaritas, run a lime wedge over the rim of each glass and dip the rim in the salt. Wipe out any salt that falls into the glass. The salt can be covered and used repeatedly.*

VEGETABLES

POTLUCK EVENTS are the perfect occasions to fuss with vegetables, which are so often treated as an afterthought. Remember that you are making only one dish—so go for it. Julia Child once said that she thought the reason many people didn't like vegetables was because they were cooked like medicine. These recipes are anything but and will get as many oohs and aahs as anything on the table.

They are all from scratch because these days, almost every market has good-quality vegetables year-round. Generally speaking, if you do need (or want) to substitute, frozen products are better than canned. Fresh herbs have also become available in almost surprising abundance. If you need to buy more than a recipe calls for, freeze the remainder in a freezer bag, pushing out as much air as you can before sealing.

No special equipment is needed, but a good vegetable peeler and a mandoline with a metal blade are very useful. And, because many of the dishes are prepared in the oven, a 13-by-9-inch oven-to-table baking dish is essential. A comparably sized, covered plastic insulated container is also helpful for storing and transporting dishes. An 8-inch chef's knife, a small sharp paring knife, and a bird's beak knife will help you make almost anything here. Two colanders are useful for washing and draining.

There are other vegetable recipes scattered throughout the book as accompaniments and side dishes for other recipes, so check the index for additional choices.

STUFFED ZUCCHINI

10   small/medium zucchini (uniform in size, about 3 pounds total)

      Salt and pepper

3   eggs, lightly beaten

2   cups freshly grated Parmigiano-Reggiano cheese

½–1   cup dry bread crumbs

Preheat the oven to 425°F. Spray a baking sheet with oil.

In a large pot of boiling water, cook the zucchini until fork-tender, about 7 minutes. With a slotted spoon, transfer the zucchini to a bowl of ice water to stop the cooking. Leave in the water for 3 minutes. Remove and pat dry with paper towels.

Halve the zucchini lengthwise and scoop out the pulp, leaving a ⅓-inch-thick shell. Sprinkle the shells with salt and pepper and turn them upside down on paper towels to drain.

Squeeze the pulp dry and place in a food processor fitted with the metal blade. Add the eggs, cheese, and bread crumbs and pulse two or three times. Do not turn it to paste.

Wipe the zucchini shells dry, turn them cut side up, and fill with the zucchini mixture. For a decorative finish, use a pastry bag to fill the shells.

Place the stuffed zucchini on the prepared baking sheet and bake until golden brown and a bit puffed, about 17 minutes. At this point, if you are not serving them immediately, they can be cooled, covered, and refrigerated for up to 24 hours.

To serve the dish: Serve warm or at room temperature. If they've been made ahead and refrigerated, warm them in a 300°F oven for 15 minutes.

TOMATOES PROVENÇALE

This easy-to-make recipe is especially refreshing.

YIELD | 10 SIDE-DISH SERVINGS

10	tomatoes (uniform in size)	4	cloves garlic, minced
	Up to ½ cup extra-virgin olive oil	¾	cup fine dry bread crumbs
	Salt and pepper to taste		
½	cup chopped fresh flat-leaf parsley		

Preheat the oven to 400°F. Brush or spray one or two baking dishes or a larger roasting pan with olive oil.

Wash the tomatoes and cut off the top one-third of each tomato. Cut out the tough cores and discard.

Place the tomatoes cut side up in the prepared dish(es). Drizzle with ¼ cup of the oil and season lightly with salt and pepper. Roast for 10 minutes.

In a small bowl, mix the parsley, garlic, and bread crumbs.

Remove the tomatoes from the oven, brush with some or all of the remaining ¼ cup oil, and top each with the bread-crumb mixture. Return to the oven for 5 minutes, or until the topping is slightly browned. At this point, the tomatoes can be cooled, covered with plastic wrap, and refrigerated for up to 24 hours.

To serve the dish: If you've made the tomatoes and refrigerated them, heat them in a 250°F oven for 15 minutes and serve hot or at room temperature.

SAUTÉED BROCCOLI WITH GARLIC

YIELD | 10 SIDE-DISH SERVINGS

2½	pounds broccoli		½	teaspoon sea salt
¼	cup extra-virgin olive oil		¼	cup minced fresh flat-leaf parsley
6	cloves garlic, minced			

Trim the tough ends of the broccoli and pare the thick skin on the stalks. Cut each stalk into several stems and rinse.

Bring a large pot of water to a boil and blanch the broccoli for 5 minutes. Drain. The blanched broccoli can be cooled and refrigerated until you're ready to serve. It may take a little longer to sauté if it's cold.

Heat the oil in a large skillet over medium-high heat. Stir in the garlic and as soon as it sizzles, add the broccoli. Cook, stirring, until the broccoli is fork-tender, about 10 minutes. Stir in the salt and parsley.

To serve the dish: Transfer the broccoli to a serving bowl and serve hot.

GREEK-STYLE GREEN POLE BEANS

YIELD | 10 TO 12 SIDE-DISH SERVINGS

2½	pounds green pole beans, rinsed, strings and stem ends removed			Grated zest of ½ lemon
				Salt and pepper
4	plum tomatoes, diced		⅔	cup coarsely chopped toasted
3	tablespoons extra-virgin olive oil			hazelnuts (optional)
	Juice of ½ lemon			

Bring a large pot of water to a boil and boil the beans for 5 minutes, or until cooked but crunchy—taste one, as they vary. Drain. In a large serving bowl, toss the beans with the tomatoes, oil, and lemon juice. Stir in the lemon zest and salt and pepper to taste. Top with the hazelnuts, if desired.

To serve the dish: Serve hot or at room temperature.

CAULIFLOWER WITH OLIVE OIL AND LEMON

YIELD | 10 SIDE-DISH SERVINGS

1	large head cauliflower or 2 small	½	teaspoon freshly grated or ground nutmeg
⅓	cup extra-virgin olive oil + more for greasing	½	teaspoon sea salt
	Juice of 1½ lemons		Freshly ground pepper to taste

Preheat the oven to 400°F. Spray a large foil-lined baking dish with oil.

Rinse and drain the cauliflower. Cut off the thick stems and trim the leaves. Separate into 2-inch florets. Place in a single layer in the prepared baking dish and drizzle with the ⅓ cup oil and lemon juice. Sprinkle with the nutmeg and salt and season with pepper to taste. Roast, turning occasionally, until fork-tender, about 20 minutes.

To serve the dish: Transfer the cauliflower to a platter and serve hot or at room temperature.

POTLUCK NOTE | *Cauliflower is very pretty when steamed or simmered whole, but it's difficult to serve to a crowd. If you want to give it a try, bring two pots of water to a boil and simmer two 8-inch cauliflowers, trimmed of leaves and stems so they can stand upright on their own. Cook until fork-tender, about 30 minutes. Drain, stand on platters, and top with lemon juice, oil, and seasoning.*

STUFFED ONIONS

YIELD | 10 SIDE-DISH SERVINGS

10	sweet onions (uniform in size), unpeeled	⅓	cup chopped fresh flat-leaf parsley
2	tablespoons olive oil	½	teaspoon ground nutmeg
3	cloves garlic, minced	½	teaspoon ground cloves
⅔	cup white button mushrooms, diced		Salt and pepper
1½	cups coarse dry bread crumbs	4	tablespoons unsalted butter, melted

Bring a large pot of water to a boil and boil the onions in their skins for 20 to 25 minutes, or until fork-tender, then drain. Do not overcook.

Preheat the oven to 375°F. Spray a 13-by-9-inch baking dish with olive oil.

When the onions are cool enough to handle, cut about 1 inch off the top ends and carefully peel the outer skins, leaving the onions intact. With a teaspoon or small sharp knife, remove the centers of the onions, leaving about a ⅓-inch-thick shell. Be careful not to break the bottoms. Reserve both the centers and the scooped-out onions. Trim the root ends slightly so that the onions stand up on their own.

Heat the oil in a sauté pan over medium heat. Add the garlic and mushrooms and sauté for 5 minutes, until glistening. Chop the reserved onion centers and place them in a medium bowl. Stir in the mushrooms and garlic, then stir in 1 cup of the bread crumbs, parsley, nutmeg, and cloves. Season with salt and pepper to taste and stir until thoroughly blended.

Divide the mixture among the onions and fill gently. Sprinkle with the remaining ½ cup bread crumbs and drizzle with the butter. Place the onions in the prepared baking dish. At this point the dish can be cooled, covered, and refrigerated for up to 24 hours.

At your place or theirs, uncover, bring to room temperature, and pour 2 cups of water in the bottom of the pan. Bake until golden brown, about 20 minutes.

To serve the dish: Remove the onions from the baking dish and gently transfer to a serving platter. Serve warm or at room temperature.

GARLIC-ROASTED MASHED POTATOES

2½   pounds russet potatoes, peeled and held in a bowl of cold water

1   teaspoon coarse salt + more to taste

6   tablespoons unsalted butter, sliced, at room temperature

1   head roasted garlic, removed from skin and mashed (see page 316)

⅓   cup heavy cream

⅔   cup milk

Few turns of a pepper mill

½   teaspoon nutmeg (optional)

Cut the potatoes into 2-inch chunks and place in a large pot of cold water with the 1 teaspoon salt over medium-high heat. Boil uncovered for 20 minutes or until a piece is easily broken with a fork.

Drain the potatoes and place them in a bowl large enough to hold all the ingredients. Mash the potatoes with a fork, then, using an electric handheld mixer, mash with the butter, garlic, cream, and ⅓ cup milk. Add more of thre remaining ⅓ cup milk, if necessary, and season with salt, pepper, and nutmeg (if desired) to taste. Serve immediately or cool, cover, and refrigerate, for up to 24 hours.

POTLUCK NOTE | *The potatoes can be made a day in advance and heated in the top of a double boiler or in a shallow baking dish covered with foil in a 350°F oven for 15 minutes.*

SWEET POTATO CASSEROLE
WITH PECAN TOPPING

The sweet potato is indigenous to the Americas, as is the pecan. George Washington grew sweet potatoes at Mount Vernon, and variations of this dish have been made and eaten for hundreds of years.

YIELD | 10 SIDE-DISH SERVINGS

Potatoes

4	pounds sweet potatoes (4 or 5), scrubbed	1	teaspoon ground nutmeg
10	tablespoons unsalted butter, sliced, at room temperature	1	teaspoon ground cinnamon
½	cup packed brown sugar	½	teaspoon ground ginger
½	cup molasses	½	cup bourbon (optional)
			Salt and pepper to taste

Topping

½	cup packed light brown sugar	6	tablespoons unsalted butter, melted
½	cup packed dark brown sugar	2	cups broken pecans
½	cup cream		

To make the potatoes: Place the potatoes in a large pot of water, bring to a boil, and boil for 40 minutes, or until fork-tender. Drain and let cool.

Preheat the oven to 350°F. Spray a 13-by-9-inch baking dish with olive oil.

When they are cool enough to handle, peel the sweet potatoes and transfer to a large bowl. Mash, then stir in the butter, sugar, molasses, nutmeg, cinnamon, and ginger. Stir in the bourbon, if using, and season with salt and pepper to taste. Place in the prepared baking dish, and use a rubber spatula to spread it end to end and make some decorative swirls. At this point, the dish can be cooled, covered, and refrigerated for up to 2 days.

To make the topping: In a small bowl, mix the sugars together and sprinkle over the sweet potatoes. Drizzle the cream and butter over all and top with the pecans.

Bake until the sugar has caramelized, about 30 minutes.

To serve the dish: Serve hot, directly from the baking dish.

OVEN-ROASTED ROOT VEGETABLES

YIELD | 10 SIDE-DISH SERVINGS

6	tablespoons extra-virgin olive oil	1½	pounds small potatoes, peeled and cut into large dice
2	teaspoons coarse salt		
	Freshly ground pepper	10	small shallots, peeled and halved
1	celery root (about 1 pound), peeled and cut into large dice	2	tablespoons fresh thyme
			A few sprigs fresh thyme or ¼ cup chopped flat-leaf parsley, for garnish (optional)
3	carrots, scraped and cut into large dice		
4	parsnips, scraped and cut into large dice		

Preheat the oven to 425°F.

Place the oil, salt, and pepper to taste in a large bowl. Add all the vegetables and stir to coat with the seasoned oil.

If you are preparing this dish in another kitchen, you can transfer the oiled vegetables to a large plastic bag and carry the thyme in another small bag. Bring along two baking sheets and proceed at your destination.

Spread the vegetables on two baking sheets and roast, stirring occasionally, until well browned and fork-tender, about 45 minutes. Sprinkle with the thyme and mix. Roast for 2 to 3 minutes more.

These can be carried in a covered container and served warm at your destination. If you prefer them hot, heat in a single layer on a baking sheet in a 350°F oven for 6 to 8 minutes.

To serve the dish: Transfer the roasted vegetables to a serving platter and serve immediately. Garnish with the thyme sprigs or chopped parsley, if desired.

TWICE-BAKED POTATOES

Among the most welcome sides at a potluck are these very easy-to-make, satisfying potatoes.

YIELD | 10 SIDE-DISH SERVINGS

5	baking potatoes (uniform in size), scrubbed and dried	1	tablespoon + 1 teaspoon minced fresh chives
5	tablespoons unsalted butter, sliced, at room-temperature	2	cups grated cheddar cheese
16	ounces (2 cups) regular or light sour cream	6	strips crisp cooked bacon, crumbled, for serving
¼	cup heavy cream	6	scallions, thinly sliced, for serving
	Salt and pepper	16	ounces (2 cups) regular or light sour cream, for serving

Preheat the oven to 375°F.

Pierce the potatoes once or twice with a fork and spray with olive oil. Bake until fork-tender, 45 minutes to 1 hour. Remove from the oven and increase the oven temperature to 400°F.

Cut the potatoes in half lengthwise with a very sharp knife. Gently remove the potato flesh from the skins—leaving ¼ inch of potato attached to the skins to keep them firm—and transfer to a large bowl. Place the potato shells on a baking sheet. With a handheld electric mixer on medium speed, mash the potatoes and beat in the butter, sour cream, and heavy cream. Season with salt and pepper to taste and stir in 1 tablespoon of the chives and 1 cup of the cheese.

Carefully spoon the mixture into the potato shells, mounding the filling slightly in the middle. At this point, the potatoes can be refrigerated in a baking dish or plastic refrigerator container. Place them in a single layer and cover with plastic wrap.

To serve the dish: If serving the potatoes immediately after stuffing, top with the remaining 1 cup of the cheese and bake for 15 minutes, or until they are hot and the cheese is melted. If you've made them a day ahead, bring to room temperature before topping and baking. Serve in individual dessert bowls or from a large buffet platter with small bowls of the chives, bacon, scallions, and sour cream alongside.

POTATO-TURNIP GRATIN

This classic cooking style is suitable for many vegetables, but potatoes are most often used. In a slight twist, this recipe includes turnips as well as potatoes. (You can, of course, substitute additional potatoes for the turnips.) For the best flavor, choose turnips that are no larger than 2 inches across. The trick to this dish is cutting the vegetables uniformly thin. For the dish to bake properly, you want slices that are ¼ inch thick. This is a good time to use a mandoline.

YIELD | 12 SIDE-DISH SERVINGS

6	russet or white potatoes (about 2½ pounds total), scrubbed	¾	teaspoon freshly ground black pepper
6	turnips (about 1½ pounds total), scrubbed	½	teaspoon ground nutmeg
			Dash of cayenne pepper
½	pint (1 cup) cream	1	cup minced shallots
2	cups milk	1	teaspoon sea salt
1½	teaspoons fresh rosemary	1½	cups shredded Gruyère or Swiss cheese
1½	teaspoons fresh thyme		

Preheat the oven to 375°F. Spray a 13-by-9-inch baking dish or gratin baker with olive oil. Peel and cut the potatoes and turnips into ¼-inch-thick slices and place them in a large bowl of cold water.

In a heavy-bottomed saucepan, heat the cream and milk over medium-low heat until simmering. Remove from the heat and stir in the rosemary, thyme, black pepper, nutmeg, and cayenne.

Drain the potatoes and turnips and pat dry with paper towels. In a large bowl, mix the potato and turnip slices with the shallots and salt. Place half of the mixture in the prepared baking dish. Pour half of the cream mixture over the vegetables, then place the remaining vegetables on top of that. Pour the rest of the cream mixture over all and cover with the cheese. At this point, the dish can be covered with plastic wrap and refrigerated for up to 24 hours before baking and serving.

Bake until the vegetables are fork-tender, about 1 hour. If the top is not brown and bubbly, place under the broiler for 3 minutes. Let rest for 10 minutes before serving.

To serve the dish: If you've made the dish ahead, let it return to room temperature before baking. Serve hot, directly from the baking dish.

POTLUCK NOTE | *If you can't get fresh herbs, substitute 1 teaspoon of a dried blend such as herbes de Provence for 3 teaspoons of fresh.*

VEGETABLE FRITTATA

I don't know of a country or region that doesn't have a version of this dish.

YIELD | 10 SIDE-DISH SERVINGS

1	pound medium to thin asparagus, tough ends removed	6	extra-large eggs, lightly beaten
3	tablespoons olive oil + more for greasing	4	scallions, thinly sliced and separated into rings
2	russet potatoes, scrubbed and cut into ¼-inch slices		Salt and pepper to taste
6	extra-large egg whites, lightly beaten	½	cup shredded Fontina or Parmigiano-Reggiano cheese

Preheat the oven to 350°F. Spray a 13-by-9-inch oven-to-table baking dish with oil.

In a shallow skillet, bring some water to a boil, add the asparagus, and bring back to a boil. Lower the heat and simmer until the asparagus are tender, about 3 to 4 minutes. Remove from the water with tongs and drain on paper towels. Cut into 1-inch pieces.

Dry the skillet and heat the 3 tablespoons oil over medium heat. Add the potatoes and cook, turning once or twice, until crisp but not cooked through, about 8 minutes. With a slotted spatula, transfer to the prepared baking dish.

In a small bowl, whisk the egg whites until they are white and foamy but not stiff. In a large bowl, fold the egg whites into the beaten eggs. Stir in the asparagus and scallions. Season with salt and pepper to taste. Pour over the potatoes and top with the cheese.

Bake until the eggs are set and the top is golden brown in spots, about 20 minutes.

To serve the dish: Serve warm or at room temperature directly from the baking dish. This dish can be transported in a thermal container, but it is best not to reheat it because the eggs will get tough.

EGGPLANT PARMIGIANA

This dish has many steps, but don't let that scare you. In kitchens throughout southern Italy, Eggplant Parmigiana is made in many different ways. It is very forgiving and very delicious.

YIELD | 10 SERVINGS

3	pounds (2 or 3 large) eggplants
	Coarse salt
1	can (28 ounces) crushed tomatoes
4	ripe tomatoes, peeled, seeded, and diced, or 1 can (28 ounces) whole tomatoes, drained
4	cloves garlic, minced
⅓	cup olive oil + more for frying (or use canola oil for frying)
2	tablespoons sugar
2	tablespoons balsamic vinegar
1	teaspoon dried oregano
	Salt and freshly ground pepper

¾	cup all-purpose flour
1	cup fine dry bread crumbs or panko
6	extra-large eggs, beaten
¼	cup water
1½	pounds mozzarella cheese, cut into ¼-inch-thick slices
2	cups shredded Parmigiano-Reggiano cheese
1	cup shredded fresh basil
1½	cups freshly grated Parmigiano-Reggiano cheese, for serving

Cut the eggplants lengthwise into ¼-inch-thick slices and sprinkle both sides with coarse salt. Arrange the slices in layers in one large colander or two regular ones and cover with a heavy plate or pan. Let drain in the sink for 2 hours. This step will assure a good texture to the eggplant.

Place all the tomatoes, garlic, and the ⅓ cup oil in a medium saucepan over medium heat. Add the sugar, vinegar, and oregano, then season with salt and pepper to taste. Stir thoroughly, mashing the tomatoes against the side of the pan. Heat the sauce just to boiling, then stir, remove from the heat, and set aside.

On a baking sheet, combine the flour and bread crumbs or panko and stir with a fork. Lightly beat the eggs and water in an 8-by-8-inch baking dish.

When the eggplant has drained, rinse the slices and press them flat a bit to squeeze out the excess water, then place the slices on paper towels. Dredge the eggplant slices first in the flour mixture and then in the beaten eggs and set on a platter.

Heat 1 inch of oil in a cast-iron or other heavy skillet over medium-high heat until a drop of water sizzles. When the oil is sizzling, fry the eggplant two or three slices at a time until both sides are golden brown, about 3 minutes per side. Use a slotted spatula to turn the slices. Remove to paper towels and continue until all the eggplant is fried. Add more oil, as needed, after a few batches.

Preheat the oven to 350°F.

Oil an oven-to-table 15-by-12-inch baking dish. Spread 1 cup of the sauce over the bottom of the dish. Top with one-third of the eggplant. Cover the eggplant with one-third of the mozzarella and sprinkle with one-third of the shredded Parmigiano-Reggiano and one-third of the basil.

Make a second layer of eggplant, 1 cup sauce, and half of the remaining mozzarella, shredded Parmigiano-Reggiano, and basil. Repeat for the third layer.

Bake until the top is lightly browned, about 35 minutes. Allow to rest at room temperature for at least 10 minutes before serving, to cool and firm slightly.

If you are traveling with this dish, cover it with foil and heat it at your destination. You can also make it a day ahead, refrigerate, and heat.

To serve the dish: If you've made the dish just before going to your event, heat it covered with foil in a 350°F oven for 15 minutes. If you made it the day before, let it come to room temperature first. In either case, remove the foil for the last 5 minutes of heating. Cut into portions with a sharp knife, and serve directly from the baking dish. Serve with crusty Italian bread and the freshly grated Parmigiano-Reggiano.

CHINESE-STYLE VEGETABLE STIR-FRY

When I traveled in China, interviewing chefs and eating everywhere, I was amazed at how little oil was used in stir-fried dishes. The secret is to heat the wok with a little oil, coat all the ingredients, and finish cooking without adding more oil. The liquid in the vegetables and sauces will create enough steam, and if you use a cover, the vegetables will be more tender. If you have one, use a good heavy wok with a ring to sit over the hob of a gas stove. If you have an electric stove, a flat-bottomed wok will work almost as well. An electric wok can double as a serving dish.

YIELD | 10 TO 12 SERVINGS

¼	cup peanut or canola oil		12	dried whole Chinese mushrooms, soaked in hot water for 1 hour, drained, and halved (optional)
1	tablespoon minced garlic			
1	tablespoon minced fresh ginger		12	lotus root slices, soaked and drained (optional)
½	teaspoon crushed red pepper flakes		1	pound snow peas, stripped of strings
1	pound Chinese yard-long beans, cut into 4-inch pieces, or green pole beans		6	scallions, thinly sliced
3	carrots, julienned		1	tablespoon cornstarch
2	pounds baby or regular bok choy, rinsed and thinly sliced		2	tablespoons warm water
2	pounds Chinese broccoli or broccoli rabe, rinsed and dried, stems separated		1	cup vegetable broth
			¼	cup Shaoxing wine or dry sherry
1	pound white button mushrooms, sliced		¼	cup light soy sauce

Heat the oil in a wok over medium-high heat. Add the garlic and ginger and cook, tossing, until fragrant, about 3 minutes. Remove from the wok, stir in the red pepper flakes, and set aside. Add the beans to the wok and stir-fry until crisp, about 4 minutes. Lower the heat to medium and add the carrots, bok choy, and broccoli or broccoli rabe. Stir to coat the vegetables with oil. Stir in the mushrooms, lotus root, and snow peas and cook, stirring constantly, for 5 minutes, then stir in the scallions. Add the reserved garlic mixture. In a separate bowl, dissolve the cornstarch in the water and stir into the vegetable broth, then pour onto the vegetables. Cook for another 5 minutes.

Although this dish is best served immediately, it can be cooled and covered before adding the wine and soy sauce. It can be transported cold with the wine and soy sauce in a separate container.

To serve the dish: If serving immediately, stir in the wine and soy sauce, and serve from the wok or a deep serving dish. If you've made the dish ahead, heat in a covered wok or pot over medium heat for 5 minutes, stir in the wine and soy sauce, and stir until hot.

POTLUCK NOTE | *Yard-long beans resemble green beans but can grow to 3 feet in length. They are available at many Asian specialty stores, as are dried Chinese mushrooms, Shaoxing wine, and lotus root.*

CARROT-GINGER SOUP

This brightly colored soup perfumes the buffet table. The ingredients are available year-round, so it can be made whenever you like. It also freezes well and, more important, defrosts well.

YIELD | 3 QUARTS (12 ONE-CUP SERVINGS)

4	tablespoons olive oil		Grated zest of 1 orange
2	cups finely chopped sweet onions	1	tablespoon turbinado or brown sugar
2	cloves garlic, minced		
2	pounds carrots, finely diced		Salt and freshly ground pepper
12	cups vegetable stock	16	ounces (2 cups) crème fraîche or sour cream, for topping
2	tablespoons minced fresh ginger		
½	teaspoon salt	¼	cup minced crystallized ginger, for garnish (optional)
½	teaspoon ground ginger		
	Juice of 2 sweet oranges		

Heat the oil over medium heat in a Dutch oven or wide heavy-bottomed pot large enough to hold all the ingredients. Add the onions and garlic and sauté until the onions are transparent, about 3 minutes. Add the carrots and cook uncovered, stirring, until slightly softened, about 5 minutes. Add the stock, fresh ginger, salt, and ground ginger. Bring to a boil, lower the heat, stir, and simmer until the carrots are fork-tender, about 45 minutes.

In a covered blender, puree the soup in batches until very smooth. You may want to let the soup cool a bit before putting it in the blender in case it splashes.

Return the soup to the pot. Add the orange juice, zest, and sugar, and season with salt and pepper to taste. Stir and bring to a high simmer over medium heat. Lower the heat, stir, and simmer gently until the soup is hot throughout, about 3 minutes. Do not let the bottom scorch.

The soup can be cooled, covered, and refrigerated for up to 2 days.

To serve the dish: Serve very hot and offer crème fraîche or sour cream as a topping. Garnish with slivers of crystallized ginger, if desired.

SOUTHWEST VEGETABLE CHILI

This chili is one of the best potluck dishes I know. I have served it at many events with great success. The portobello mushrooms and hominy give it a very satisfying mouthfeel. You can, of course, adjust the heat and serve additional hot sauce on the side. This can be served as is or with rice.

YIELD | 12 TO 16 SERVINGS

3	tablespoons olive oil	½	teaspoon ground Aleppo chili pepper or ⅛ teaspoon cayenne pepper, or to taste
2	yellow onions, diced		
2	tablespoons minced garlic	1	package (12–14 ounces) frozen cut corn kernels
1½	pounds portobello mushroom caps (about 5 large), cut into 1½-inch cubes		
		2	cans (15.5 ounces each) black beans, rinsed and drained
1	large red bell pepper, scorched, skinned, and diced (see page 113)	1	can (20 ounces) hominy
2	zucchini, scraped, halved lengthwise, and sliced	2	cans (28 ounces each) diced tomatoes
3	tablespoons chili powder	¼	cup chopped fresh cilantro, for garnish
1	tablespoon ground cumin	24	ounces (3 cups) sour cream, for serving
2	teaspoons ground cinnamon		
2	teaspoons ground allspice	2	cups shredded cheddar or Jack cheese, for serving
3	tablespoons fresh oregano leaves or 1 tablespoon dried		
1	tablespoon salt	1	cup pickled jalapeño chili pepper slices, for serving

Heat the oil in a heavy saucepan or cast-iron skillet over medium-high heat. Add the onions and garlic and cook, stirring, until golden, about 5 minutes. Add the mushrooms and bell pepper, lower the heat, and cook, stirring, for 10 minutes. Remove the onions, garlic, and mushrooms from the pan and set aside. Add the zucchini to the pan, adding more oil if necessary, and cook, stirring, until lightly browned, about 5 minutes.

In a 6-quart Dutch oven or slow cooker, stir together the reserved onions, garlic, and mushrooms, and the bell pepper, zucchini, chili powder, cumin, cinnamon, allspice, oregano, salt, and Aleppo or cayenne pepper. Stir in the corn and beans. Rinse the hominy and use your hands to separate the kernels, then add to the pot along with the tomatoes. Stir well. Cover the Dutch oven and cook over medium-low heat for 3 hours, stirring occasionally. If using a slow cooker, set the heat to low and cook for 6 to 8 hours, or follow the manufacturer's directions.

If not serving immediately, let cool, cover, and refrigerate for up to 24 hours. Heat over medium-low heat for 15 to 20 minutes, or until hot, in your kitchen or at your destination. If transporting, carry in a thermal container.

To serve the dish: Serve directly from the cooking pot, garnished with the cilantro. Set out bowls of the sour cream, cheese, and chili peppers and squares of Jalapeño Corn Bread (page 269).

POTLUCK NOTE | *Ground aleppo chili is a mild, aromatic Middle Eastern spice.*

GAZPACHO WITH GARLIC CROUTONS

For hundreds of years, some form of this cold salad-and-bread soup has been eaten in southern Spain. The tomatoes are a New World addition. If you can get it, try using Spanish extra-virgin olive oil. In the Mediterranean, olives are as diverse as apples are in the United States; as a result, the oils vary. Gazpacho is thought of as a summer food, but it makes a great potluck luncheon dish instead of the usual salad.

YIELD | 3 QUARTS (10 ONE-CUP SERVINGS)

1	tablespoon sugar	1	green bell pepper, peeled, seeded, and diced (see page 113 for peeling instructions)
½	cup + 3 tablespoons Spanish (or other) extra-virgin olive oil	1	large Spanish onion, diced
4	slices French bread (crusts removed), torn into pieces	1	cup minced homemade or store-bought oil-packed sun-dried tomatoes
2	cloves garlic, peeled and sliced		
10	large ripe tomatoes, peeled, seeded, and chopped	6	cups tomato juice
2	jalapeño chili peppers, halved, seeded, and minced (optional or to taste)	3	tablespoons dry sherry or wine vinegar
		½	cup chopped fresh flat-leaf parsley, for garnish
3	cucumbers, peeled, seeded, and diced	½	cup chopped fresh cilantro, for garnish
1	red bell pepper, peeled, seeded, and diced (see page 113 for peeling instructions)		Garlic Croutons (recipe follows), for garnish

In a large bowl, stir together all the ingredients except the parsley, cilantro, and croutons. In batches, transfer to a covered blender or food processor and pulse for a few seconds until coarsely blended. Do not puree; this soup tastes best when bits of vegetables are still visible. Return to the bowl, cover, and refrigerate for at least 2 hours before serving or for 1 day.

To serve the dish: Remove from the refrigerator, stir, let rest for 15 minutes, and garnish with the parsley, cilantro, and Garlic Croutons. A nice accompaniment for this cold soup might be bowls of assorted olives and roasted almonds.

(continued)

Garlic Croutons

| 3 | slices whole wheat bread | 3 | cloves garlic, minced |
| ⅓ | cup Spanish or other extra-virgin olive oil | ½ | teaspoon garlic powder |

Preheat the oven to 400°F.

Remove the crust from the bread and cut into ½-inch cubes.

Mix the oil, garlic, and garlic powder in a bowl. Stir the bread in the oil mixture so that all sides are coated. Place on a baking sheet and bake until browned, about 10 minutes. Let cool on a rack and serve immediately, or store in an airtight container for up to 2 days.

DESSERTS

THESE VERSATILE DESSERTS, COOKIES, AND SWEETS are welcome at any meal as well as at teas, meetings, and open houses.

I've found that everyone likes great puddings of one kind or another. They are a very good dessert choice because portion control is self-determined. Most of these desserts can be made a day before they are to be eaten, removed from the refrigerator, and served with the chill off or at room temperature. The desserts here are complete as they are, but they're traditionally served with a dollop of whipped cream or a small scoop of ice cream. Any variety of sweet or sour cream blends, plain or frozen yogurts, or fresh berries is always welcome.

The cookies I've included are all easy to transport and can be made in advance and stored in the freezer or at room temperature. They're best packed between layers of waxed or parchment paper and carried in flat containers with tight covers. Most cookies can be layered with parchment or waxed paper and stored in an air-tight container for several days or a week. I have eaten 10-day-old biscotti with pleasure, but all baked goods unless otherwise specified are best a day or two after baking.

If you are going to be making lots of cookies, the biggest luxury is to have four 18-by-12-inch baking sheets so that you can put a second batch in the oven without waiting. Also useful are Silpat nonstick silicone baking liners. At 17 by 11 inches, they fit most baking sheets and can be used at temperatures up to approximately 475°F. To make the sweets in this chapter, you should have an 8-by-8-inch baking pan, a 9-by-9-inch baking pan, and a 13-by-9-inch pan that you can use for baking and serving small sweets.

DOUBLE CHOCOLATE PUDDING

The romance of chocolate is heady stuff. From homey puddings to artful confections, rich cakes, and chocolate moles that bite back, few people seem indifferent to its lure. This recipe is as much fun to make as it is to eat because of the chocolatey aroma.

YIELD | 10 SERVINGS

4	large egg yolks, at room temperature	1	cup (8 ounces) heavy cream
¾	cup sugar	2	teaspoons pure vanilla extract
2	cups whole milk	½	cup unsweetened cocoa powder
3	tablespoons cornstarch	4	ounces dark chocolate, melted
⅛	teaspoon salt		

In a bowl, beat the egg yolks and sugar until light.

In a medium saucepan over medium heat, bring 1¾ cups of the milk to the boiling point. Remove from the heat and slowly add the milk to the egg-and-sugar mixture, whisking constantly. Pour the mixture back into the saucepan.

In a measuring cup, whisk the cornstarch with the remaining ¼ cup of milk to form a smooth mixture. Add the cornstarch mixture and salt to the saucepan. Heat, stirring constantly, until thick enough to coat the back of a wooden spoon, 5 to 7 minutes. Add the cream and vanilla, stir, and remove from the heat.

Whisk in the cocoa and chocolate. Stir and pour into a serving bowl. Let cool thoroughly, cover with plastic wrap, and refrigerate until thick and cold, at least 4 hours and up to 24 hours.

To serve the dish: Serve cold with whipped cream, crème fraîche (or 1 cup heavy cream mixed with ¼ cup sour cream), and/or fresh raspberries.

POTLUCK NOTE | *To test the thickness of the pudding on the back of a wooden spoon, run the tip of a teaspoon through the coating. If it leaves a clear strip, the pudding is thick enough. To chill the pudding quickly, pour it into a metal mixing bowl, place in a larger bowl of ice water, and stir the pudding for 10 minutes. This ice-water bath is useful in many applications.*

BANANA PUDDING WITH MERINGUE

I thought my taste was way too sophisticated to even try banana pudding. When I was in Savannah, Georgia, interviewing Paula Deen before she became a household name, she suggested that I try her banana pudding. What had I been thinking? This is my potluck version. Thanks, Paula!

YIELD | 10 TO 12 SERVINGS

1½	cups vanilla wafer crumbs	¼	teaspoon salt
4	tablespoons (¼ cup) unsalted butter, melted	3	very ripe bananas, mashed but not pureed
2	cups whole milk	2	teaspoons pure vanilla extract
4	eggs, separated	3	ripe, firm bananas, sliced
¾	cup sugar	4–5	dozen vanilla wafers
¼	cup instant flour		Meringue (recipe follows)

Preheat the oven to 350°F.

In a small bowl, mix the wafer crumbs and butter, spread and press on the bottom of an 18-by-9-inch baking pan.

In a medium bowl, whisk together the milk and egg yolks.

In the top of a double boiler over simmering water, stir together the sugar, flour, and salt. Whisk in the egg-yolk mixture. Continue whisking to blend well and cook until the mixture thickens, 10 to 15 minutes. Stir occasionally to incorporate the thicker portion on the bottom of the pan. Remove from the heat and stir in the mashed bananas and vanilla. In the baking pan, alternate layers of the custard mixture, banana slices, and wafers, repeating two or three times.

Spread the Meringue on the pudding, using a spatula to seal the edges.

Bake until golden brown, about 15 minutes.

To serve the dish: Serve warm or cold. If you want to skip the meringue, sprinkle the finished pudding with a cup of fine vanilla-wafer crumbs and serve with whipped cream or a mixture of heavy cream and sour cream sprinkled with brown sugar.

Meringue

4	egg whites	⅓	cup superfine sugar
½	teaspoon cream of tartar	1	teaspoon pure vanilla extract

Using an electric mixer on low speed, beat the egg whites until frothy. Add the cream of tartar and sugar and beat until stiff, glossy peaks form. Add the vanilla toward the end.

POTLUCK NOTE | *If you want to skip the Meringue, sprinkle the top of the pudding with a cup of vanilla wafer crumbs to finish it and serve with whipped cream or a mixture of heavy cream and sour cream, sprinkled with brown sugar.*

TIRAMISU

Tiramisu, which translates literally as "pick-me-up," is an Italian dessert that traditionally consists of ladyfingers, mascarpone cheese, cocoa, espresso, liquor, eggs, sugar, and cream. Some culinary detectives think that it developed in Tuscany after World War I and was based on the British trifle, while others believe it dates back to the Renaissance. Certainly by the end of the 18th century, sugar, coffee, and cocoa were treats in the Friuli-Venezia region, as was creamy mascarpone cheese. So luscious is this dish that some say it was prepared for Casanova to keep his energy and spirits up. In any event, this dessert, in all its variations, inspires romantic stories.

YIELD | 12 SERVINGS

6	egg yolks	2	cups brewed or instant espresso, cooled
1	cup sugar	40	large ladyfingers or Savoiardi biscuits
⅔	cup marsala, port, or Madeira		
1	pound mascarpone cheese	3	tablespoons unsweetened cocoa powder
2	cups (1 pint) heavy cream whipped with ½ cup sugar		Shaved chocolate for garnish

In the top of a double boiler over simmering water, whisk the egg yolks, sugar, and wine. Stir constantly until the mixture is thick and just before the boiling point, about 4 minutes. Remove from the heat at the sight of any bubbles.

In a large bowl, beat the custard into the cheese until well incorporated. When it is at room temperature, fold in the whipped cream.

Place the coffee in a shallow bowl. Dip the ladyfingers or biscuits briefly into the coffee, then arrange in a single layer in a 12-by-9-inch serving dish. Top with a layer of the mascarpone mixture, then a layer of espresso-soaked ladyfingers or biscuits, and repeat, ending with a mascarpone layer. Smooth with a spatula.

When the cake is assembled, sprinkle with the cocoa from a shaker and chill for several hours. It can also be frozen very successfully and brought to refrigerator or room temperature before serving. Garnish with shaved chocolate before serving the tiramisu.

POTLUCK NOTE | *If you can't find ladyfingers or Savoiardi biscuits, you can use pound cake. Cut it into ¾-inch slices, then cut each slice into three strips.*

DOUBLE-RICH BUTTERSCOTCH PUDDING

I like this pudding so much that I once took a sample of it to one of my favorite restaurants and begged them to put it on the menu.

YIELD | 12 SERVINGS

9	tablespoons unsalted butter, cut into slices	3	cups whole milk
2½	cups packed dark brown sugar	6	large egg yolks
2	cups (1 pint) heavy cream	6	tablespoons cornstarch
		½	teaspoon salt

Melt the butter in a heavy saucepan over medium heat. Gradually stir in the sugar until incorporated. Cook until the mixture is smooth and simmering, stirring occasionally, about 5 minutes.

Meanwhile, heat the cream over low heat until warm.

Lower the heat under the sugar and gradually add the cream. Cook, stirring, until blended, about 2 minutes. Remove the pan from the heat.

In the top of a large double boiler, whisk the milk, egg yolks, cornstarch, and salt. Place over simmering water over medium heat, and gradually stir in the sugar-and-cream mixture. Stir or gently whisk constantly until the pudding thickens, about 12 minutes. Reduce the heat to low, cover, and cook another 10 minutes, stirring occasionally.

Remove from the heat and let cool for 10 minutes, still stirring occasionally. Pour into twelve 1-cup serving dishes or a 3-quart serving bowl. Chill thoroughly before serving.

The pudding can be refrigerated covered for 2 days before serving. Do not cover the pudding until it is cold, or steam will form.

To serve the dish: Serve cold, as is, or with dollops of whipped cream and/or toasted, finely sliced almonds.

S'MORES BREAD PUDDING

This dish, based on a childhood favorite, is really a meal in itself. I recommend it when the main course is a salad or other fish dish. Any leftovers can be frozen, brought to room temperature, and warmed in a preheated oven. But it won't be the same.

YIELD | 15 SERVINGS

12	ounces dark chocolate, chopped	1	cup milk
8	tablespoons (½ cup) unsalted butter, sliced	1	jar (16 ounces) marshmallow cream
2	pounds challah or baguettes, cut into 2-inch cubes	40	individual graham crackers, coarsely broken, in two uses
2	cups half-and-half	20	large marshmallows, halved horizontally
8	large eggs		
⅔	cup sugar	⅔	cup chocolate chips

Preheat the oven to 350°F. Lightly butter a 13-by-9-inch oven-to-table baking dish.

Melt the dark chocolate and butter in the top of a double boiler so that the bottom doesn't touch the water simmering in the lower half, then let it come to room temperature. In a large bowl, soak the bread in the half-and-half for 20 minutes for challah, 30 minutes for baguettes. In a large bowl, whisk together the eggs, sugar, and milk. Whisk in the chocolate-and-butter mixture and blend well, then pour over the soaked bread and mix thoroughly.

In a medium bowl, lightly mix the marshmallow cream with half of the graham crackers. (This will be messy and a good time to assist the rubber spatula with a gloved hand.)

Place half of the bread mixture in the prepared baking dish, spreading it out from edge to edge. Layer the marshmallow-cream mixture on top. Cover first with the remaining bread mixture, then with the remaining graham crackers. Top with the marshmallow halves and sprinkle with the chocolate chips.

Bake until firm, about 35 minutes. Remove from the oven and allow to cool. This pudding is best made and served without holding in the refrigerator.

To serve the dish: Serve at room temperature as is, or accompanied by whipped cream or vanilla ice cream.

POACHED PEARS WITH WHITE WINE
AND SHAVED PARMESAN CHEESE

I have had varieties of this dish in Italy, where fruit and cheese are combined in endless ways for a very refreshing end to a meal. The saffron is optional, but it has a lovely flavor.

YIELD | 10 SERVINGS

10	firm, ripe pears	2	tablespoons fresh lemon juice
1	large bowl of water with the juice of 1 lemon	2	teaspoons ground cinnamon
2	cups water	1	wedge (12 ounces) Parmesan cheese
2	cups white wine		Fresh basil leaves, for garnish (optional)
	Large pinch of saffron (optional)		
½	cup honey, mild if you are using saffron, strong if not		

Peel the pears, leaving the stems intact if possible, and core them from the bottom with a melon baller. Place in the lemon water so they do not discolor.

In a large pot, combine the 2 cups water, wine, saffron (if using), honey, lemon juice, and cinnamon. Place over high heat, bring to a low boil, and reduce the heat to medium.

Using a slotted spoon, remove the pears from the lemon water and add them to the poaching liquid. Simmer until fork-tender, about 35 minutes. Remove the pears with a slotted spoon, let cool, then refrigerate until cold.

Cook the poaching liquid until reduced by half, 30 to 45 minutes. Remove from the heat, let cool, then refrigerate until cold.

To serve the dish: Set the pears upright in a deep platter, douse with the poaching syrup, and surround with shavings of the cheese. Garnish with the basil, if using.

POTLUCK NOTE | *If preparing whole pears is too fussy for you, simply peel them, cut in half from top to bottom, core, and poach for 20 minutes. You can also eliminate the cheese and serve with a thick chocolate-fudge sauce.*

SUMMER PUDDING

This pudding couldn't be easier to make. Use any combination of ripe berries and, if you can find them, fresh currants. I've made this with conventional store-bought white, oatmeal, wheat, and raisin bread with equal success. It's most attractive made in a charlotte mold, but a 3-quart pudding mold or mixing bowl will do just as well.

YIELD | 12 SERVINGS

3	tablespoons unsalted butter, softened		½	pound (1 pint) blackberries, rinsed and halved
1	pound (1½ pints) strawberries, rinsed, hulled, and quartered		1	cup sugar, or to taste
1	pound (1½ pints) raspberries, rinsed		1	loaf sliced white bread, crusts removed
½	pound cherries, rinsed, pitted, and halved			

Grease a charlotte mold or 3-quart mixing bowl with 1 tablespoon of the butter. Line the bowl with plastic wrap, leaving extra to cover the pudding. Use about 1½ tablespoons of the butter to grease the plastic wrap.

In a large bowl, mix the fruit and dredge with the sugar. Taste and add a bit more sugar if you like, but keep in mind that too much will overpower the fruit.

Line the charlotte mold with the bread, overlapping where necessary. Start at the bottom and work up to ½ inch from the top of the bowl. Using a cup, add a layer of fruit. Cover the fruit with another layer of bread, pressing gently. Repeat until all the fruit is used. Finish with a layer of bread. Spread the remaining ½ tablespoon butter over all and cover with plastic wrap. Place a plate directly on top of the plastic so that it rests on the pudding, and weigh the plate down with cans from the cupboard. If you don't have a plate that fits, cut a piece of cardboard. Refrigerate for 8 hours or overnight.

To serve the dish: To unmold the pudding, remove the top plate and weights, and unfold the plastic. Place a flat platter that is larger than the rim of the bowl over the top and turn it upside down. Holding one hand on the open plastic wrap, gently loosen it all around the bowl onto the plate. Gently lift the bowl and you will have a perfect dome. Peel away the plastic wrap. Serve with whipped cream or custard sauce.

ROASTED SUMMER STONE FRUIT
WITH RICOTTA

Roasting fruit brings out its essence and sugar. This dish is the perfect light ending to any meal. It is very satisfying served cold either on its own or with a dollop of yogurt mixed with honey. You'll find your own combinations and accompaniments.

YIELD | 10 SERVINGS

1	pound firm, ripe red plums, washed, pitted, and halved (2 cups)	½	cup granulated sugar
		3	cups whole-milk or low-fat ricotta cheese
1	pound firm, ripe peaches, washed, pitted, and quartered (2 cups)	½	cup superfine sugar
		2	tablespoons fresh Meyer lemon or mandarin orange juice
1	pound firm, ripe apricots, washed, pitted, and halved (2 cups)	2	teaspoons Meyer lemon or mandarin orange zest (see page 316)
1	pound firm, ripe nectarines, washed, pitted, and quartered (2 cups)		

Preheat the oven to 400°F. Spray or brush a jelly-roll pan with oil.

Lay the fruit skin side down on the prepared pan and sprinkle with the granulated sugar. Roast until the edges of the fruit look brown and caramelized, about 20 minutes. Don't overcook, or the fruit will lose its shape. Remove from the oven and let cool.

In a medium bowl, using a flat whisk or large fork, mix the ricotta cheese, superfine sugar, lemon or orange juice, and lemon or orange zest. This mixture can be covered and refrigerated until ready to serve or carry to your destination.

To serve the dish: Arrange the fruit on a platter and intersperse with dollops of the ricotta mixture. The fruit is best served the same day, warm or at room temperature.

BAKED APPLES WITH BALSAMIC REDUCTION

Baked apples do not seem as popular as they once were, but I think you'll find that most people like them—I know I do. The balsamic reduction is a modern touch.

YIELD | 10 SERVINGS

1½	cups balsamic vinegar	1	teaspoon ground cinnamon
5	tablespoons + ⅔ cup firmly packed brown sugar	½	teaspoon ground nutmeg
10	medium/large red cooking apples	2	cups apple juice or water
½	cup currants, raisins, or dried cherries		

Preheat the oven to 375°F.

Place the vinegar and 5 tablespoons brown sugar in a small heavy-bottomed saucepan over medium-low heat and bring to the boiling point. Lower the heat and simmer—do not let it boil—until the liquid is reduced by half, 20 to 30 minutes. Remove from the heat.

Wash and core the apples with a corer or melon baller, leaving at least ½ inch on the bottoms. Remove a 1-inch strip of peel around the top of each apple and stand the apples upright in one or two 13-by-10-inch baking dish(es).

In a small bowl, mix the dried fruit, cinnamon, nutmeg, and the remaining ⅔ cup brown sugar. Spoon equal amounts into the center of each apple.

Add the apple juice or water to the baking dish to cover the bottom. Drizzle the tops of the apples with the balsamic reduction and bake until the apples are fork-tender, 30 to 40 minutes.

To serve the dish: Some people like this dish warm; others, cold—your choice. Carefully place the apples upright on a large platter with the syrup from the baking pan. If you prefer, you can plate them individually in deep dessert dishes with a little of the pan syrup over each apple.

BLUEBERRY GRUNT

A grunt, which is basically a fruit stew with dumplings, is so named because of the sound the boiling fruit makes as it pops air bubbles in the dough. It is a Southern specialty, and in a Daufuskie Island, South Carolina, cookbook, the instructions are to boil the berries, drop in the "doe," and cook on the back of a wood stove until done. And then, "Eat 'em hot er cold."

YIELD | 10 SERVINGS

Filling

1	cup water		1	tablespoon fresh lemon juice
1	cup turbinado or packed light brown sugar		1	teaspoon finely grated lemon zest
½	teaspoon cinnamon		3	pints (5 cups) fresh blueberries, rinsed
½	teaspoon ground nutmeg			

Topping

2	cups all-purpose flour		5	tablespoons unsalted butter, sliced and softened
1	tablespoon baking powder		¾	cup milk
½	teaspoon salt			
1	tablespoon + 1 teaspoon granulated sugar			

To make the filling: In a 3-quart cast-iron Dutch oven or any wide, heavy 3-quart pot with a lid, bring the water, brown sugar, cinnamon, nutmeg, lemon juice, and lemon zest to the boiling point over medium heat. Stir in the blueberries and return to the boiling point. Lower the heat and simmer, uncovered, stirring frequently, until the berries are somewhat crushed but still hold their shape, about 15 minutes.

To make the topping: In a medium bowl, blend together the flour, baking powder, salt, and granulated sugar. With a pastry blender or two butter knives, cut in the butter until the mixture resembles coarse crumbs. Add the milk and stir slightly with a fork, leaving the batter lumpy. To avoid hot splashes, remove the pot of berries from the heat and drop dough by the spoonful over the berries. Place the lid on the pot and cook over medium heat for 15 minutes. Don't peek during cooking or the dough will deflate. Let cool for 20 minutes before serving.

To serve the dish: At a buffet, use a deep serving spoon to serve from the pot it was cooked in. You can also plate it into individual dessert bowls.

DRIED WINTER FRUIT COMPOTE
WITH RAISIN SAUCE

This is another one of those dishes that you can make your own by choosing whatever dried fruit, liquor, and/or spice you prefer. Star anise and sliced lemon can be added, and honey can stand in for the sugar.

YIELD | 10 SERVINGS

1	pound dried figs, preferably whole, not pressed	3	quarts boiling water
½	pound dried plums, pitted and picked over for broken pits	¾	cup bourbon or any golden brown liquor such as brandy or scotch, or an equal amount of water
½	pound dried pears	½	cup sugar
½	pound dried apple slices	2	teaspoons ground cinnamon
½	pound dried mango or papaya		Raisin Sauce (recipe follows)
¼	pound dried blueberries		
¼	pound dried cherries, pitted and picked over for broken pits		

Place all the fruit in a large heatproof bowl and mix together. Pour the boiling water over the fruit. Let rest for 45 minutes, stirring two or three times. Drain the fruit and set aside 1½ cups of liquid.

In a saucepan large enough to hold all the ingredients, heat the liquor, reserved liquid, sugar, and cinnamon to the boiling point over medium-low heat. Add the drained fruit, lower the heat, and simmer gently for 30 minutes.

Let cool, remove to a serving bowl, cover, and chill for up to 24 hours before serving. This can keep longer, but the fruit will get softer.

To serve the dish: Place the fruit in a deep serving dish with a ladle, and accompany with the Raisin Sauce in a smaller bowl with a small ladle.

(continued)

Raisin Sauce

1	cup raisins, soaked in 1½ cups water for 24 hours, then drained	1	cup (8 ounces) heavy cream
2	cups light sour cream	½	teaspoon pure vanilla extract
		⅓	cup pure maple syrup

In a large bowl, mix all the ingredients, cover, and refrigerate for up to 24 hours.

POTLUCK NOTE | *For a dramatic presentation, make sure the compote is in a heatproof dish. Place ¼ cup bourbon in a long-handled soup ladle. Hold it at arm's length and light it with a long match. Tilt the flaming liquor into the compote. Wait until the flame goes out before inserting the serving spoon.*

CRUNCHY APPLE CRISP

In the fall, when markets have an abundance of apples, this is the dish to make. Mixing a variety of apples enriches the flavor. Pears can be substituted or mixed half-and-half with the apples. If you have them on hand, toss in a cup of frozen or dried cranberries.

YIELD | 10 SERVINGS

Filling

6	cups sliced assorted apples, such as Rome, McIntosh, and Granny Smith		1	teaspoon ground cinnamon
			½	teaspoon ground cardamom
¼	cup granulated sugar		¼	teaspoon ground cloves
1	tablespoon fresh lemon juice			

Topping

1	cup all-purpose flour		1	teaspoon ground cinnamon
1	cup rolled oats		10	tablespoons unsalted butter, sliced
1	cup packed brown or granulated sugar		½	cup chopped walnuts

Preheat the oven to 375°F. Lightly butter a 10-by-13-inch baking dish.

To make the filling: In a large bowl, toss the apples with the sugar, lemon juice, cinnamon, cardamom, and cloves. Layer on the bottom of the prepared baking dish.

To make the topping: In a medium mixing bowl, stir together the flour, oats, sugar, and cinnamon. With a pastry blender or two butter knives, cut in the butter until it resembles coarse crumbs. Do not overmix. With your hands, sprinkle the topping over the apples, then sprinkle the walnuts on top of that.

Bake until the apples are fork-tender, about 30 minutes.

To serve the dish: Serve hot from the oven or at room temperature. Cinnamon ice cream or low-fat vanilla yogurt mixed with cinnamon are great accompaniments.

GINGER-PEACHY COBBLER

There are as many cobbler recipes as there are states in the Union. In summer you can make cobblers with almost any stone fruit, and in winter you can use apples and pears. It's best to sauté winter fruit in some butter and sugar or maple syrup before putting it in the baking pan.

YIELD | 10 SERVINGS

Filling

6	cups sliced ripe peaches (about 8)	½	teaspoon ground nutmeg
⅓	cup packed brown sugar	⅓	cup minced candied ginger
½	teaspoon ground ginger	1	tablespoon fresh lemon juice

Topping

10	tablespoons cold unsalted butter, sliced	1	cup granulated sugar
2¼	cups self-rising flour	1	cup buttermilk or whole milk
⅛	teaspoon salt		

Preheat the oven to 375°F. Lightly butter a 13-by-9-inch baking dish.

To make the filling: In a large bowl, toss together the peaches, sugar, ground ginger, nutmeg, and candied ginger. Spoon into the prepared baking dish and drizzle the lemon juice over all.

To make the topping: In a large bowl, using a pastry blender or two butter knives, incorporate the butter, flour, and salt until the mixture resembles coarse crumbs. Stir in the sugar and milk only until incorporated. Drop by spoonfuls on top of the peach mixture.

Bake until the fruit is bubbling and the topping is golden brown, about 35 minutes. Cool at least 30 minutes, up to 3 hours, at room temperature.

To serve the dish: Serve warm or cold. Accompany with a pitcher of cold heavy cream, yogurt mixed with honey, or vanilla ice cream.

CHERRY CLAFOUTI

This is a traditional French "made at home" dish that is best served within an hour or two after it is made. Chilling toughens it a bit, so it is recommended that you make it just before leaving the house if you are taking it to an event. Think of it as a terrific last-minute dessert. If the oven will be free at your destination, consider bringing a baking pan and the ingredients in three plastic containers: one with the pitted cherries, with or without kirsch; another with the flour and sugar; and the third with the remaining ingredients.

YIELD | 10 SERVINGS

3½	cups sweet cherries, pitted	1	large egg yolk
¼	cup kirsch (optional)	1	cup milk
¾	cup instant flour	1	cup heavy cream
½	cup granulated sugar	2	teaspoons pure vanilla extract
4	large eggs		Confectioners' sugar, for dusting

Preheat the oven to 375°F. Lightly butter a 13-by-9-inch baking dish.

If using kirsch, place the cherries in a bowl, pour on the liqueur, and let soak for 15 minutes. Drain the cherries, then spread them in the prepared baking dish.

In a small bowl, mix the flour and sugar. In a large bowl, whisk the eggs and egg yolk, then whisk in the milk and cream. Beat in the flour mixture. Add the vanilla, stir, and pour the topping evenly over the cherries.

Bake until slightly puffed and browned, about 35 minutes. Let cool for 10 to 15 minutes before serving.

To serve the dish: Serve warm or cool, dusted with confectioners' sugar.

TRIPLE-CHOCOLATE COOKIES

These need no introduction; they are a chocoholic's dream come true.

YIELD | 36 TO 42 COOKIES

1½	teaspoons baking soda	6	ounces milk chocolate, coarsely chopped
2¼	cups flour	6	ounces white chocolate, coarsely chopped
1	cup (½ pound) unsalted butter	6	ounces dark chocolate, coarsely chopped
½	cup granulated sugar		
½	cup brown sugar		
2	eggs, lightly beaten		
1	teaspoon pure vanilla extract		

Preheat the oven to 375°F. Set out two baking sheets, unbuttered or lined with Silpat liners.

In a medium bowl, stir the baking soda into the flour.

In a large bowl, using an electric mixer, cream the butter and the sugars. Beat in the eggs and vanilla. Stir in the flour mixture, then stir in all the chocolate.

Drop the batter by heaping tablespoons 2 inches apart on the baking sheets. Bake until the edges darken slightly, 10 to 12 minutes.

Remove the cookies with a spatula to cake racks to cool completely. Eat within 24 hours.

POTLUCK NOTE | *Unless you think you are going to need all of the cookies, reserve a few from each batch and wrap them in plastic, then in foil. Label them clearly, being sure to include the date, and freeze. (Encircle anything you are freezing with masking tape—labeled with a waterproof marker—so it doesn't fall off and leave you with mystery packages.) In time you will have a terrific assortment of cookies that can be thawed and served at a spontaneous event.*

VERY CHOCOLATE BROWNIES

YIELD | 16 BROWNIES

⅔	cup all-purpose flour + more for dusting	8	ounces semisweet chocolate, chopped, or chocolate chips
¼	cup instant flour	3	large eggs
½	teaspoon baking soda	¾	cup sugar
¼	teaspoon salt	1½	teaspoons pure vanilla extract
6	tablespoons unsalted butter, sliced + more for greasing	¾	cup chopped walnuts (optional)

Preheat the oven to 325°F. Lightly butter and dust with flour a 9-by-9-inch baking pan.

In a small bowl, sift or stir together the ⅔ cup all-purpose flour, instant flour, baking soda, and salt.

Melt the 6 tablespoons butter and chocolate in the top of a double boiler set over simmering water. Remove from the heat.

In a large bowl, using an electric mixer, beat the eggs, sugar, and vanilla at medium speed. Add the chocolate mixture and continue beating for 1 minute. Add the flour mixture and beat on low for no more than 30 seconds. If using walnuts, mix them in with a spatula. Pour the batter into the prepared pan and spread evenly with a spatula.

Bake until a cake tester comes out clean, about 40 minutes. Cool in the pan on a rack and cut into squares.

The brownies are best served within a few hours but can remain in the pan, covered with plastic wrap, for up to 24 hours. Don't let the plastic rest on top of the brownies.

Apricot Squares (opposite)
Lemon Squares (page 212)
Raspberry Bars (page 213)

APRICOT SQUARES

Dessert bars and squares are welcome at any gathering. If you want to turn them into bite-size pieces, cut them into squares about 1½ by 1½ inches. Use a very sharp knife so they don't crumble.

YIELD | 16 SQUARES

Crust

½	cup granulated sugar	1½	cups all-purpose flour + more for dusting
2	egg yolks	¼	teaspoon salt
8	tablespoons (½ cup) unsalted butter, cut into slices	1	teaspoon pure vanilla extract

Topping

2	eggs, lightly beaten	½	pound dried apricots, plumped in simmering water for 3 minutes, then drained and minced
⅔	cup turbinado or packed light brown sugar		
		1	cup apricot or apple jelly, melted

Preheat the oven to 350°F. Butter and lightly flour an 8-by-8-inch baking pan.

To make the crust: In a large bowl, combine the granulated sugar and egg yolks and whisk until light. Add the butter and beat with an electric mixer until smooth. Blend in the 1½ cups flour, salt, and vanilla just until combined. Spread the batter evenly in the prepared pan.

Bake until golden, about 15 minutes. Remove from the oven and let cool for 10 minutes. Maintain the oven temperature.

To make the topping: In a medium bowl, stir together the eggs, turbinado sugar, and apricots. Spread over the crust. Drizzle the jelly over all. Return to the oven and bake until lightly browned, about 20 minutes.

Let cool completely and cut into sixteen 2-inch squares.

These are best served within a few hours but can remain in the pan, covered with plastic wrap, for up to 24 hours. Don't let the plastic rest on top of the Apricot Squares.

LEMON SQUARES

YIELD | 16 SQUARES

Crust

8	tablespoons (½ cup) unsalted butter, chilled and cut into pieces + more for greasing	⅓	cup packed light brown sugar
		1¼	cups all-purpose flour
		¼	teaspoon salt

Topping

1	cup granulated sugar	2	tablespoons unsalted butter, melted
2	large eggs		
½	cup fresh lemon juice (from 2–3 lemons)	3	tablespoons instant flour
			Confectioners' sugar, for dusting
1	tablespoon lemon zest (see page 316)		

Preheat the oven to 350°F. Lightly butter an 8-by-8-inch baking pan.

To make the crust: In a large bowl, using an electric mixer, cream the 8 tablespoons butter and brown sugar until light and fluffy. Add the all-purpose flour and salt and beat until just blended. Do not overmix.

Press the dough into the bottom of the prepared pan and bake until browned, about 15 minutes. Remove from the oven and let cool on a cake rack. Maintain the oven temperature.

To make the topping: In a medium bowl, using an electric mixer, beat the granulated sugar and eggs until light. Add the lemon juice and lemon zest and stir to combine. Stir in the butter and incorporate the instant flour until it disappears. Pour over the crust and smooth it from edge to edge with a spatula.

Bake until set, 20 to 25 minutes.

Let cool on a cake rack. Cut into sixteen 2-inch squares and dust with confectioners' sugar when completely cool.

Lemon Squares are best served within a few hours but can remain in the pan, covered with plastic wrap, for up to 24 hours. Don't let the plastic rest on top of the squares.

RASPBERRY BARS

YIELD | 18 BARS

Filling

2½	cups (1½ pints) raspberries, rinsed	1	tablespoon fresh lemon juice
2	tablespoons granulated sugar	1	tablespoon instant tapioca
2	tablespoons water	½	teaspoon ground cinnamon

Crust

1	cup all-purpose flour	¾	cup packed brown sugar
1	teaspoon baking soda	½	teaspoon ground cinnamon
¼	teaspoon salt	8	tablespoons (½ cup) unsalted butter, melted
1	cup quick-cooking oats (not instant)		

Preheat the oven to 350°F.

To make the filling: In a medium saucepan, combine all the filling ingredients. Bring just to the boiling point over medium heat, then reduce the heat and simmer, stirring frequently, for 5 minutes, or until slightly thickened. Remove from the heat.

To make the crust: In a large mixing bowl, stir together the flour, baking soda, salt, oats, brown sugar, and cinnamon. Stir in the butter until incorporated. Set aside 1 cup for topping. With your fingertips, press the remaining flour mixture into an ungreased 9-by-9-inch baking pan.

Bake the crust until pale brown, about 20 minutes. Remove from the oven but maintain the oven temperature. Using a rubber spatula, gently spread the filling over the hot crust. Sprinkle the reserved flour mixture over the filling. Lightly press the topping with the back of a spoon.

Bake until the filling is set, another 20 to 25 minutes. Let cool in the pan on a cake rack, then cut into 3-by-1½-inch bars.

These are best served within a few hours but can remain in the pan, covered with plastic wrap, for up to 24 hours. Don't let the plastic rest on top of the bars.

NEW YORK BLACK-AND-WHITE COOKIES

These cookies are available at just about every New York deli and diner. They have started making inroads in the other 49 states as well, but nothing beats the fresh-baked taste of these.

YIELD | 24 LARGE COOKIES

2½	cups all-purpose flour	1¾	cups sugar
2½	cups cake flour	4	eggs, lightly beaten
1	teaspoon baking powder	1	cup milk
½	teaspoon salt	½	teaspoon pure vanilla extract
8	tablespoons (½ cup) unsalted butter, sliced and softened + more for greasing	¼	teaspoon pure lemon extract
			Black and White Icings (recipe follows)

Preheat the oven to 375°F. Butter two baking sheets for the first batch or use Silpat sheets. They will be cooled, rebuttered, and used again.

In a medium bowl, using a fork, mix together the flours, baking powder, and salt.

In a large bowl, using an electric mixer, cream the 8 tablespoons butter, then gradually cream in the sugar until the mixture is light and fluffy. Beat in the eggs, milk, and vanilla and lemon extracts. Add 2 cups of the flour mixture and beat. Remove the beaters and stir in the remaining flour mixture until thoroughly incorporated. Do not overmix. Using a 2-tablespoon measure, such as an ice cream scoop, drop the batter 2 inches apart on the prepared baking sheets, about six cookies per sheet.

Bake in the top and bottom thirds of the oven until the cookie edges start to brown, about 20 minutes. If you think that your oven is unevenly heated—and most are—halfway through baking, reverse the cookie sheets from the top and bottom shelves and turn them around front to back, then continue baking.

Remove the baking sheets but maintain the oven heat. Using a spatula, transfer the cookies to a cake rack and let cool completely.

(continued)

Let the baking sheets come to room temperature, then butter and repeat, measuring 2 tablespoons of batter to make another 12 cookies on two sheets. Bake as before.

Make the icings.

When the cookies are cool, set them flat side up on waxed paper. Using a small offset spatula, spread white icing on half of each cookie. Then use a clean spatula to coat the other half of the cookie with chocolate frosting. Let set.

These are best served within 24 hours but can be layered with waxed paper and refrigerate for 2 to 3 days.

Black and White Icings

3½	cups confectioners' sugar	⅓	cup unsweetened Dutch-process cocoa powder
3	tablespoons light corn syrup	1½	ounces semisweet chocolate, melted
2	teaspoons fresh lemon juice		
1	teaspoon pure vanilla extract		
4–6	tablespoons water		

In a medium bowl, stir together the sugar, corn syrup, lemon juice, vanilla, and 1 tablespoon of the water until smooth.

Place half of the icing in another bowl. Sir in the cocoa and chocolate. Add more water as needed for a glossy icing.

DUTCH ALMOND COOKIES

In Dutch, these are called amandel koekjes. The word "cookie" comes from the Dutch "koekje," meaning "small cake." Almond paste is available at most supermarkets.

YIELD | 24 COOKIES

1½	cups all-purpose flour	½	cup packed brown sugar
1	teaspoon baking soda	2	large eggs, lightly beaten
8	tablespoons (1 cup) room-temperature unsalted butter, sliced + more for greasing	1	cup almond paste, loosely crumbled
½	cup superfine sugar	½	cup sliced almonds

Preheat the oven to 325°F. Butter two baking sheets.

In a small bowl, using a fork, stir together the flour and baking soda.

In a bowl large enough to hold all the ingredients, cream the 1 cup butter with an electric mixer and gradually beat in the sugars. Beat in the eggs. Mix in the flour mixture and incorporate the almond paste. Mix until smooth, then fold in the almonds. Using about 2 teaspoonfuls for each cookie, drop the batter 2 inches apart on the prepared baking sheets.

Bake until lightly browned, about 15 minutes. Transfer to a cake rack and let cool completely. Store in an airtight container for up to 1 week.

MADELEINES

Once made in convents and sold to raise money, these buttery, cakelike little cookies are the original bake-sale cookie. Marcel Proust described them as an "exquisite pleasure." Now, of course, you can find madeleines at coffee-shop chains, but they are not as good as these.

YIELD | 36 TO 40 COOKIES

2	eggs	2	teaspoons grated lemon zest
1	cup granulated sugar		Confectioners' sugar, for dusting
1	cup all-purpose flour		
12	tablespoons (¾ cup) unsalted butter, melted and cooled		

Preheat the oven to 350°F. Butter and lightly flour a madeleine pan. Prepare a bowl of ice water.

In the top of a double boiler over barely simmering water, beat the eggs and sugar until warm and blended, about 2 minutes. Remove from the heat and immerse the top of the double boiler in the ice water to stop the cooking. While it is in the water bath, beat with an electric mixer on medium speed until the mixture has almost doubled in volume, about 5 minutes. Remove from the ice water and alternately stir in the flour, butter, and lemon zest. Stir only until blended.

Use 1 rounded tablespoon of batter for each madeleine, or follow the pan manufacturer's directions.

Bake until a cake tester or toothpick comes out clean, about 12 minutes. Let cool for 2 minutes in the pan, then remove to cool completely on wire racks. Sprinkle with confectioners' sugar. Store in an airtight container for up to 3 days.

COCONUT JUMBLES

A jumble is simply a ring-shaped cookie. These easy cookies have an elusive, old-time taste.

YIELD | 30 TO 36 COOKIES

2	cups all-purpose flour	1	cup granulated sugar
½	teaspoon baking soda	2	large eggs, slightly beaten
¼	teaspoon salt	¼	cup sour cream
8	tablespoons (½ cup) unsalted butter + more for greasing	1⅓	cups sweetened coconut
			Confectioners' sugar, for dusting

Preheat the oven to 375°F. Butter two baking sheets.

In a small bowl, mix together the flour, baking soda, and salt.

In a large bowl, using an electric mixer, cream the 8 tablespoons butter until light and fluffy. Gradually beat in the sugar, then the eggs. Add the sour cream and coconut. Incorporate the flour mixture. Chill the dough for 30 minutes.

Take the dough by heaping tablespoons and roll each into a 5-inch rope. Shape into a ring and pinch the ends together. Place the rings on the baking sheets so that they do not touch.

Bake until golden brown, about 12 minutes. Remove from the oven and let cool for 5 minutes. Remove the jumbles to a cake rack, cool completely, and dust with confectioners' sugar. Store in an airtight container for up to 3 days.

PECAN BALLS

These literally melt in your mouth and require very few ingredients.

YIELD | 30 COOKIES

8	tablespoons unsalted butter, sliced and softened	1	cup coarsely ground pecans
2	tablespoons superfine sugar	1	teaspoon pure vanilla extract
1	cup all-purpose flour	½	cup confectioner's sugar

Preheat the oven to 300°F.

In a large bowl, cream the butter and superfine sugar until light. Gradually add the flour, pecans, and vanilla. Mix well. Using your hands, shape the dough into round smooth balls, using about 1 tablespoon of dough for each, and place 2 inches apart on ungreased cookie sheets. Bake until edges turn slightly golden brown, about 25 minutes.

Gently remove the cookies from the baking sheets and cool on a cake rack for 1 hour. Roll several times in a small bowl of the confectioner's sugar. Layer with waxed paper and store in a cookie tin. A flat plastic container with a lid is a good substitute but it can tend to let moisture in.

POTLUCK NOTE | *Pecans can be ground in a mini-processor. Process only for a count of 5—they should not be turned to dust.*

RUGELACH

These little rolled cookies are a simple, easy-to-make version of a traditional Jewish holiday treat usually made with a flour-and-oil-based dough.

YIELD | 48 COOKIES

Dough

8	tablespoons (½ cup) unsalted butter, chilled and cut into ½-inch pieces	¼	cup granulated sugar
		¼	teaspoon sea salt
8	ounces cream cheese, chilled and cut into ½-inch pieces	2	cups all-purpose flour

Filling

¾	cup raspberry or apricot preserves	1	tablespoon ground cinnamon
1	teaspoon unsalted butter	1	cup chopped walnuts
⅓	cup granulated sugar	⅔	cup raisins
¼	cup packed brown sugar		

Preheat the oven to 375°F. Line two baking sheets with parchment paper.

To make the dough: In a large bowl, using an electric mixer, cream the butter and cream cheese until light. Add the sugar and salt and blend thoroughly by hand, then incorporate the flour until just held together.

Place the dough on a lightly floured work surface and gather into a ball. Cut the dough into quarters, flatten slightly into disks, and enclose each in plastic wrap.

Refrigerate the dough for 1 hour or up to 24 hours. Bring to room temperature before rolling each disk into a 9-inch circle.

To make the filling: Melt the preserves and butter in a small saucepan. Remove from the heat and let come to room temperature. In a small bowl, mix the sugars, cinnamon, walnuts, and raisins.

To roll the cookies: Spread each circle of dough with the preserves and sprinkle the nut-raisin mixture evenly over all, gently pressing it into the dough with your fingertips or the back of a spoon. Cut each circle into 12 wedges (cut in quarters, then each quarter into three slices). Roll each slice from the wide side to the point and place on the prepared baking sheets. Chill for 30 minutes.

Bake until the edges are browned, 15 to 20 minutes. Let cool on a cake rack. The traditional way to cool rugelach is on brown paper grocery bags. Store in airtight containers for up to 5 days.

PEANUT BUTTER COOKIES

If you like peanut butter, you'll like these cookies. In fact, even if you don't like peanut butter, you may like these.

YIELD | 30 TO 36 COOKIES

1⅓	cups all-purpose flour	½	cup packed brown sugar
1	teaspoon baking powder	1	cup chunky peanut butter
½	teaspoon salt	1	large egg, lightly beaten
8	tablespoons (½ cup) unsalted butter + more for greasing	1	teaspoon pure vanilla extract
½	cup granulated sugar + more for the tops		

Preheat the oven to 350°F. Generously butter two baking sheets.

In a small bowl, stir together the flour, baking powder, and salt.

In a large bowl, cream the 8 tablespoons butter, the ½ cup granulated sugar, and brown sugar. Beat in the peanut butter, egg, and vanilla, then incorporate the flour mixture. Chill the batter in the refrigerator for 30 minutes.

Using a level tablespoon, shape the batter into balls and arrange on the prepared baking sheets, allowing enough room to flatten them.

Dip the tines of a fork in a small bowl of granulated sugar and flatten the cookies with a crisscross pattern. They will be about 1½ inches across.

Bake until light brown, 10 to 12 minutes. Remove the cookies from the oven and let cool for 10 minutes, then transfer to a cake rack to cool completely. The cookies can be stored in an airtight container for up to a week.

POTLUCK NOTE | *When a food contains peanuts, it is a necessary courtesy to make their presence known, as some people have severe allergies. If you are bringing an assortment of cookies, carry the ones with peanuts in their own container and serve on a separate, clearly marked dish.*

PINE NUT COOKIES

I love these cookies—the pine nuts remind me of the "Indian" nuts in the shell that we ate as kids.

YIELD | 24 COOKIES

2	large egg whites	½	cup granulated sugar
	Pinch of salt	¾	cup pine nuts (pignoli)
½	cup confectioners' sugar		
8	ounces almond paste, broken up into bits		

Preheat the oven to 300°F. Butter and lightly flour two baking sheets or line with Silpat sheets.

In a large bowl, using an electric mixer, beat the egg whites with the salt until quite foamy but not dry. Whisk in the confectioners' sugar, then incorporate the almond paste and granulated sugar until smooth.

Place the pine nuts in a shallow bowl. Keeping hands moist, take a scant tablespoonful of batter at a time and press the top into the pine nuts, making sure the nuts adhere. Drop 2 inches apart on the prepared baking sheets.

Bake until golden brown, 15 to 20 minutes. Cool thoroughly on racks, store in an airtight container, and eat within 24 hours.

Hazelnut Biscotti with Chocolate Icing (opposite)
Spiced or Not Hot Chocolate (page 229)

After living in Italy for a year, I became addicted to unfrosted biscotti with my morning latte—not an Italian custom but a very satisfying one. They are so dense and have no fat, and I am pleased to say that I came back the same size 6. The name "biscotti" translates as "twice" ("bis") "cooked" ("cotti"), which they are. They're delicious and well worth your time because they have a very long shelf life. For a special treat, these do well with chocolate icing. But what doesn't?

YIELD | ABOUT 36 BISCOTTI

1	cup hazelnuts		Pinch of salt
2	cups all-purpose flour	3	large eggs
⅓	cup unsweetened good-quality cocoa powder	1½	cups sugar
1	teaspoon ground cinnamon	¼	pound bittersweet chocolate
1	teaspoon baking powder	2	tablespoons unsalted butter
½	teaspoon baking soda	2	tablespoon chocolate liqueur, such as Godiva or Van Gogh

Preheat the oven to 350°F. Line two 18-by-13-inch baking sheets with parchment paper.

To remove the bitter brown skins from the hazelnuts, spread the nuts in a single layer on a rimmed, unlined baking sheet and toast in the oven for 7 to 9 minutes. Slide onto a clean tea towel. Fold the towel over them and, using your hands, rub them vigorously between the folds. Don't worry if some small bits don't come off.

Coarsely crush or chop the nuts and set aside.

In a medium bowl, stir together the flour, cocoa, cinnamon, baking powder, baking soda, and salt.

In a bowl large enough to hold all the ingredients, whisk the eggs and sugar. Stir in the dry ingredients, then the reserved hazelnuts. The dough will be quite thick and sticky.

Using your hands, divide the dough into two flat logs, each about 3½ inches wide and 10 inches long. Place both on one prepared baking sheet and bake until they are

(continued)

slightly browned and a toothpick comes out clean, 20 to 25 minutes. Remove from the oven and reduce the oven temperature to 300°F. Transfer the logs to a cutting surface. While they are still warm, cut into ½-inch slices.

Reline the used baking sheet with fresh parchment. Place the biscotti cut side down on the prepared sheets and bake for 20 minutes. Turn the oven off and, with the oven door ajar, let the biscotti sit another 10 minutes. Place on a rack to cool before icing.

Meanwhile, make the icing. Melt the chocolate and butter in the top of a double boiler over simmering water or in the microwave. Add the liqueur and stir.

When the biscotti are cool, drip or drizzle a scant teaspoon of chocolate icing along the cut side of each biscotti. Refrigerate to set the icing, about 2 hours.

SPICED OR NOT HOT CHOCOLATE

This crowd-pleaser needn't wait for the holidays—it's a treat on any cold day. If you like, it can be cooled and served over ice as a warm-day dessert drink. For a more conventional hot chocolate, omit the chili powder, cinnamon, and ginger and increase the vanilla to 4 teaspoons.

YIELD | 10 TO 12 SERVINGS

1½	cups water
5	tablespoons unsweetened cocoa powder
	Pinch of salt
8	cups (2 quarts) milk
1	cup hot chocolate powder
3½	ounces (1 bar) dark chocolate, chopped
2	cups chocolate chips

1	teaspoon ancho chili powder (optional)
1	teaspoon ground cinnamon (optional)
1	teaspoon ground ginger (optional)
2	teaspoons (double if spices are omitted) pure vanilla extract
½	pint (1 cup) heavy cream, whipped

In a medium to large saucepan over medium heat, bring the water to a low boil and stir in the cocoa powder and salt. Stir constantly until the cocoa is dissolved. Stir in the milk until barely simmering, then stir in the chocolate powder, chopped chocolate, and chocolate chips. Stir and add the spices, if using, and vanilla. This is a good place to use a wooden or Teflon whisk. Whisk until all the chocolate is melted and well incorporated. If you want, you can carry this ready-made cold, then heat and whisk it at your destination. If you have a large thermos or two that will keep it hot, use that.

Serve immediately, topped with dollops of whipped cream.

GREEN TEA CHAI

Chai is traditionally made with black tea, which can be substituted for the green tea in this recipe if you prefer. For a frosted drink, let the mixture cool, then pour over ice in a blender.

YIELD | 4 SERVINGS

2	cups water	¼	cup packed light brown sugar, or to taste
6	whole cloves		
8	whole cardamom pods, crushed	2	tablespoons loose green tea
½	teaspoon ground ginger or 1 teaspoon grated fresh	3	cups low-fat milk
		4	cinnamon sticks
½	teaspoon ground cinnamon	½	cup cream (optional)

Heat the water in a saucepan over medium heat just to a low boil. Add the cloves, cardamom, ginger, and ground cinnamon; lower the heat a bit, stir, and simmer for 10 minutes. Add the sugar and tea and remove from the heat.

Steep for 5 minutes. Strain and discard the tea leaves and spices. Return the tea to the pan over low heat and add the milk and cinnamon sticks. Heat just until hot, but do not boil.

Remove from the heat, stir in the cream (if desired), and pour into four glass mugs.

STRAWBERRY-BANANA SMOOTHIES

This is a delicious refresher and a good accompaniment to a light meal. Blueberries, raspberries, and peaches are just as good alone or in combination.

YIELD | 4 TO 6 SERVINGS

2 cups (1 pint) rinsed and hulled fresh or frozen strawberries

2 fresh or frozen bananas, cut into chunks

½ cup honey, or to taste

4 cups whole-milk, low-fat, or nonfat yogurt

2 cups crushed ice

In a blender, combine all the ingredients and cover. Blend at medium speed, then high, until smooth.

POTLUCK NOTE | *Overripe bananas can be peeled, sliced, and frozen for just this kind of use.*

PIES AND CAKES

BUNDT CAKES AND POUND CAKES, sheet cakes, shortcakes, and roulades are all "a piece of cake" to make, and they travel well. Sweet loaves can be sliced and carried on a tray tightly covered with plastic wrap. For layer cakes, layers can be made in advance, frozen (up to 2 months), and filled, frosted, and decorated when you want. You can also carry frosting in a disposable container to decorate at your destination. Pie shells made from gingersnaps, graham crackers, or chocolate wafers can be filled with a variety of sweets at home or just before eating.

I have always preferred making fruit tarts to pies because, though they look fancier, they're easier to make. When I was in Seattle and cherries were in season, I knew it was time to learn to make a real pie in a double crust. I now substitute pitted cherries for strawberries in rhubarb recipes. That said, any fruit in season, cut and roasted till the natural sugars caramelize, or raw and lightly macerated to enhance the flavors, makes a great base for desserts.

Use fruit in season, or freeze your own in the easiest way possible. Berries, dusted with sugar and placed in a freezer bag in a thin layer, can be frozen for months. Please don't use "artificial" anything. Use pure vanilla extract or vanilla beans. The same is true for almond extract and maple syrup. The supplies you need for baking are basic. Two 9-inch round cake pans, two 9-inch pie pans, one 13-by-9-inch sheet cake pan, one 17-by-12-inch jelly-roll pan, 10-inch pie pan, and 9-inch and 12-inch tart pans with removable bottoms will get you through most recipes. If you think you'll be making angel food cake more than once, consider purchasing a 10-inch springform pan, a 9-inch tube pan, and an angel food cake pan with legs.

Any of these cakes and pies can be served on your own serving dish or your host's. Some people I know enjoy finding single plates and platters at flea markets and yard sales that they can pass along.

234

A IS FOR APPLE PIE

YIELD | 10 SERVINGS

1	unbaked double 10-inch piecrust (page 245)	¼	cup brown sugar
		1½	teaspoons ground cinnamon
8	medium–large crisp, slightly tart assorted apples, such as Macoun, McIntosh, and Granny Smith	¾	cup + 2 tablespoons granulated sugar, or to taste
1–2	tablespoons fresh lemon juice	3	tablespoons instant flour
4	tablespoons unsalted butter	2	tablespoons heavy cream

Preheat the oven to 425°F. Place a baking sheet or foil-topped baking stone in the oven. (This catches drips and also gives the pie a hot surface on which to bake, preventing a soggy bottom crust.) Place the bottom half of the piecrust in a 10-inch pie pan.

Wash and dry the apples, then core and peel them. Cut into ½-inch-thick slices. You don't want them to be too thin.

In a large bowl, mix the apples with the lemon juice. Heat the butter in a large heavy skillet over medium heat and sauté the apple slices until golden at the edges, about 5 minutes. Remove from the heat.

Stir the brown sugar, cinnamon, and the ¾ cup granulated sugar into the hot apples, sprinkle with the flour, and stir. Let cool to room temperature.

Transfer the apple mixture to the piecrust and carefully place the rolled-out top crust on top. Pinch the edges together, making a thick, fluted edge.

With a single-sided safety razor blade, slit several vents in the top crust. Brush with the cream and sprinkle with the remaining 2 tablespoons granulated sugar. Wrap the edge of the crust in foil to cover the seam. Bake for 10 minutes, then reduce the heat to 375°F and bake until the crust is golden brown and the juice is bubbling at the vents, about 40 minutes. Remove the foil during the last 15 minutes of baking. If you think your oven is very uneven, turn the pie from front to back halfway through the baking time.

Remove the pie to a cake rack and cool at least 1½ hours before serving. Serve warm or at room temperature, with extra-sharp cheddar cheese or vanilla or cinnamon ice cream.

LEMON MERINGUE PIE

Meyer lemons, slightly sweeter than regular lemons and with a hint of mandarin orange, give this classic a "new" taste.

YIELD | 10 SERVINGS

Pie

1	extra-large egg	3	tablespoons unsalted butter, sliced, at room temperature
4	extra-large egg yolks		
1	cup granulated sugar if using Meyer lemons, or 1¼ cups for regular lemons	1	tablespoon lemon zest (see page 316)
	Juice of 3 Meyer or regular lemons	1	baked and cooled double 10-inch piecrust (see page 245)*

*Remaining pie dough can be used for tartlets.

Meringue

4	extra-large egg whites, at room temperature	½	cup superfine sugar
¼	teaspoon + ⅛ teaspoon cream of tartar		

Preheat the oven to 375°F, or simply leave the oven on if you have just baked the piecrust.

To make the pie: In a heavy saucepan, beat together the egg, egg yolks, and granulated sugar. Place over low heat and stir in the lemon juice. Stir in the butter and gradually increase the heat to medium. Stir constantly until the mixture thickens. If it coats the back of a wooden spoon and leaves a clear line when you draw your finger through it, it is thick enough.

Remove from the heat, stir in the lemon zest, and let rest for 5 minutes, stirring once or twice. With a rubber spatula, spread the filling from edge to edge in the piecrust.

Bake until the filling is set, 15 minutes. Remove the pie from the oven. Increase the oven temperature to 425°F.

(continued)

To make the meringue: In a large clean bowl, beat the egg whites with an electric mixer until foamy. Gradually add the cream of tartar and superfine sugar and beat until stiff, shiny peaks form.

To assemble and bake the pie: With the aid of a rubber spatula, mound meringue over the pie and, leaving the highest portion in the middle, gently spread it from edge to edge, covering all of the filling. Bake until lightly browned, 4 to 6 minutes. Do not overbake, or the meringue will shrink and toughen.

Let cool completely, at least 2 to 3 hours. This pie is best not refrigerated, as the texture of the meringue will change. However, most people are used to these pies being chilled, so do so if it is more convenient.

SWEET AND TART CHERRY PIE

This recipe really is easy as pie. If you want to make it a little more aromatic, you might add a splash of orange flower water or culinary rose water.

YIELD | ONE 10-INCH PIE

1	unbaked double 10-inch piecrust (page 245)	¾	teaspoon ground cinnamon
3	cups (about 1½ pints) sweet cherries, pitted	½	teaspoon ground nutmeg
3	cups (about 1½ pints) tart cherries, pitted	1	teaspoon pure almond or vanilla extract
1	cup sugar, or to taste	5	tablespoons instant tapioca
		2	tablespoons unsalted butter

Preheat the oven to 375°F. Place the bottom half of the piecrust in a 10-inch pie pan.

Pick over the cherries to see if there are any pits or chips still attached.

In a large bowl, mix the cherries and sugar. Let stand for 15 minutes. Stir in the cinnamon, nutmeg, and almond or vanilla extract, then the tapioca. Pour into the piecrust and dot with the butter. Cover loosely with the top crust and crimp the edges sealed by pinching with your fingers. With a single-edged safety razor, cut a few decorative slits to allow steam to escape.

Bake for 45 minutes. Some juices will bubble through. If it looks like the rim is getting too brown, cover the edge with a ring of folded foil. Let cool completely before serving.

PUMPKIN PIE

"Hurrah for the fun! Is the pudding done? Hurrah for the pumpkin pie!" (from "Over the River")

YIELD | 10 SERVINGS

4 cups fresh pumpkin puree from two 8- to 10-inch pie pumpkins or canned pumpkin

1 cup (1½ cups, if using canned pumpkin) heavy cream

3 egg yolks, lightly beaten

¾ cup brown sugar

3 tablespoons unsalted butter, melted

1 teaspoon pure vanilla extract

1 teaspoon ground cinnamon

½ teaspoon ground ginger

½ teaspoon ground nutmeg

¼ teaspoon ground cloves

¼ teaspoon freshly ground pepper

1 unbaked 9-inch deep-dish piecrust (page 245)*

Remaining pie dough can be used for tartlets

Preheat the oven to 350°F.

If using fresh pumpkins, scrub them with water only, no soap. Halve them and remove the seeds and stringy insides. Bake for 1½ hours, until more than fork-tender. Alternatively, peel, cube, and boil on the stove top until fork-tender, about 20 minutes. Puree the cooked pumpkin with an immersion blender or food processor. Blend in the cream.

In a large bowl, whisk the egg yolks with the sugar and butter. Whisk in the vanilla and spices, then fold in the pumpkin-cream blend. Pour into the piecrust and spread from edge to edge with a rubber spatula.

Bake until the edges of the filling start to brown, about 1 hour 10 minutes. If the rim of the piecrust looks like it is getting too brown after 30 minutes, cover with foil.

Remove from the oven and let cool. The filling will set more as the pie cools.

SWEET POTATO PIE

When you are cooking for a crowd, you really want to make a crowd-pleaser. Sweet potatoes appeal to almost everyone. In fact, there was a time when street vendors sold coal-roasted sweet potatoes wrapped in newspaper, much the way roasted chestnuts are sold in some cities in the winter today.

YIELD | 10 SERVINGS

4	cups mashed cooked sweet potatoes or yams (about 4 medium, or 1½ pounds)		1	tablespoon finely grated orange zest (see page 316)
¾	cup granulated sugar		¼	cup orange juice
¾	cup brown sugar		3	large eggs, lightly beaten
1	teaspoon ground cinnamon		1	can (12 ounces) evaporated milk
1½	teaspoons ground nutmeg		1	can (5 ounces) evaporated milk
¼	teaspoon salt		1	unbaked 10-inch piecrust (page 245)*
1	teaspoon pure vanilla extract			

Remaining pie dough can be used for tartlets.

Wash and dry the sweet potatoes and pierce the skin in several places with a fork. Bake in a 450°F oven for 45 minutes. Remove the peels and mash the sweet potatoes. Alternatively, wash and dry the sweet potatoes and drop them in slightly salted boiling water. Return to a boil and cook until fork-tender, about 20 minutes. Remove the peels and mash the sweet potatoes.

Preheat the oven to 375°F (or reduce the heat from 450°F if you've baked the sweet potatoes).

In a large bowl, using an electric mixer on medium-high speed, beat the potatoes, sugars, cinnamon, nutmeg, salt, vanilla, orange zest, and orange juice. Gradually add the eggs. When smooth, stir in the milk and mix well. Pour into the unbaked piecrust.

Cover the edge of the crust with foil and bake for 25 minutes. Remove the foil and bake for another 25 minutes. Let cool to room temperature or chill, and serve with dollops of whipped cream mixed with maple syrup.

PECAN TART

More people over the years have asked me for this recipe than any other. Okay, folks, here it is. The secret is out: NO corn syrup. This tart develops a unique custardy texture all its own that contrasts with the crisp crust and pecans. No substitutions. I can't tell you why, but pecans are the nuts of choice for this one.

YIELD | 9-INCH TART, 6 TO 8 SERVINGS; 12-INCH TART, 10 TO 12 SERVINGS

9-inch tart

1	partially baked 9-inch tart shell (recipe follows)	⅓	cup water
1	large egg	2	tablespoons unsalted butter
1	large egg yolk	1	teaspoon pure vanilla extract
1½	cups light brown sugar	2	cups pecan halves

12-inch tart

1	partially baked 12-inch tart shell	1	cup water
2	large eggs	4	tablespoons unsalted butter
3	large egg yolks	1½	teaspoons pure vanilla extract
3	cups light brown sugar	3	cups pecan halves

Preheat the oven to 350°F. Place a foil-lined baking sheet on the lowest shelf of the oven in case the filling bubbles over. Set a rack in the middle of the oven for baking the pecan tart. Set out the partially baked tart shell.

In a large bowl, whisk the egg(s) and egg yolks together.

In a heavy saucepan over medium-high heat, combine the brown sugar and water. Heat until the sugar dissolves, stirring constantly. Lower the heat to medium and bring to a slow boil. Maintain for 2 to 3 minutes, then stir in the butter and vanilla. In a slow stream, pour the syrup into the eggs, whisking constantly. Add the pecans and mix until fully coated. Carefully pour into the tart shell to within ¼ inch of the top.

Bake for 35 minutes, or until a cake tester comes out clean. Remove to a cake rack and let cool completely before removing the tart pan ring. It may be sticky, so have patience. You may need to use a narrow paring knife if sugar has gotten between the shell and pan.

RELIABLE TART SHELLS

A tart is basically a shallow open-faced pie. It's made in a tart pan, which has straight (not sloped) fluted sides. Metal tart pans have removable bottoms. This recipe can be doubled to make two 9-inch tart shells or one 12-inch tart shell.

YIELD | ONE 9-INCH TART SHELL

1 cup all-purpose flour + more for dusting

6 tablespoons unsalted butter, diced and frozen + more for greasing

2 tablespoons sugar

1 egg yolk

1–2 tablespoons ice water

Pinch of salt

Preheat the oven to 375°F. Lightly butter a 9-inch tart pan with a removable bottom and dust with flour.

Place the 1 cup flour and the 6 tablespoons butter in a food processor fitted with a metal blade and pulse for 4 seconds. Add the sugar and egg yolk and pulse for 5 seconds. Add 1 tablespoon of the ice water and salt and pulse until the dough forms a solid ball. If a ball doesn't start forming after a few pulses, add the second tablespoon of water.

Remove the dough from the processor, flatten slightly, cover with plastic wrap, and let rest for 30 minutes before proceeding.

Using a rolling pin, shape the dough into a thick circle, transfer it to the prepared tart pan, and press it out with your fingers, pushing the dough into the side of the pan. Smooth the dough evenly and prick in several places with a sharp-tined fork.

Line the shell with parchment paper and fill with pie weights or beans. Bake for 15 minutes. Remove from the oven to a level cooling rack. Remove the weights and parchment paper and proceed with the recipe that calls for a partially baked shell.

If you are using a filling that will not be baked, return the tart to the oven until golden brown, an additional 10 minutes. Let cool completely on the rack and add the prepared cold filling. This shell will be completely baked.

The shells can be cooled, left on the removable metal bottom of the tart pan, covered well with plastic wrap, and refrigerated for 2 days or frozen for up to 1 month.

PIECRUSTS

Single 9-Inch Crust

1⅓ cups all-purpose flour + more for dusting

½ teaspoon salt

2 tablespoons Crisco Stick

2 tablespoons sweet unsalted butter

3 tablespoons ice water

In a bowl large enough to hold all the ingredients, mix the 1⅓ cups flour and salt with a fork.

Using a pastry blender or two knives, cut in the Crisco and butter until the mixture is the texture of coarse meal. Sprinkle with the water, 1 tablespoon at a time. Toss lightly with a fork until the dough will form a ball. Press into a 5-inch disk and flour lightly.

For a single crust, roll the dough between sheets of waxed paper (or a designated silicone surface) 1½ inches larger than an inverted 9-inch pie plate. Using a flour shaker, dust the dough as you roll it out. Peel off the top sheet and gently fold in half, then in quarters. Open onto a pie plate. Peel off the other sheet and press dough gently with your fingertips to fit. Fold the edge under. Pinch a fluted edge with your fingertips.

To make a recipe calling for a single unbaked crust: Follow as directed in the recipe you are making.

To make a recipe calling for a prebaked piecrust: Heat the oven to 425°F. Thoroughly prick the bottom and sides of the crust with a fork (being careful not to tear the dough) at least 25 times to prevent shrinking.

Line the pastry with parchment paper or aluminum foil and lay some pastry weights over all. Bake for 10 minutes. Remove the pastry from the oven, but do not turn off the oven. Remove the weights and liner and return to the oven until golden brown, 3 to 5 minutes. Follow the pie recipe you are making for further baking.

Double 9-Inch Crust, Double 9-Inch Deep Dish Crust, or Double 10-Inch Crust

Double 9-inch crust

2	cups all-purpose flour	5	tablespoons sweet unsalted butter
1	teaspoon salt	5	tablespoons ice water
5	tablespoons Crisco Stick		

Double 9-inch deep dish or Double 10-inch crust

2⅔	cups all-purpose flour	8	tablespoons sweet unsalted butter
1	teaspoon salt	7–8	tablespoons ice water
8	tablespoons Crisco Stick		

In a bowl large enough to hold all the ingredients, mix the flour and salt with a fork.

Using a pastry blender or two knives, cut in the Crisco and butter until the mixture is the texture of coarse meal. Sprinkle with the water, 1 tablespoon at a time. Toss lightly with a fork until the dough will form a ball. Divide in half, press into two 5- to 6-inch disks, and flour lightly.

Roll each disk between sheets of waxed paper (or a designated silicone surface) 1½ inches larger than inverted pie plate. For a 9-inch deep-dish pie, roll dough 2½ inches larger than pan. Using a flour shaker, dust the dough as you roll it out.

Peel off the top sheet of waxed paper from one of the discs and gently fold the dough in half, then quarters. Open onto a pie plate. Peel off the other sheet and press the dough gently with your fingertips to fit.

Add the desired filling to the unbaked piecrust.

Remove the top sheet of waxed paper from the top crust. Lift the crust loosely onto the filled pie, thev remove the other sheet of paper. Trim to ½ inch beyond the edge of the pie plate. Fold the top edge under the bottom crust. Pinch a fluted edge together with your fingertips, a pie crimper, or the tines of a fork. Cut slits in the top crust to allow steam to escape.

Bake according to recipe instructions.

SUMMER STRAWBERRY SHORTCAKE

This classic summer crowd-pleaser is also very tasty with Rhubarb-Cherry Topping (page 248).

YIELD | 12 SERVINGS

Cake

2	cups self-rising flour	⅔	cup whole milk
⅔	cup granulated sugar	1	teaspoon pure vanilla extract
⅔	cup unsalted butter, sliced + more for greasing	1	jumbo egg, lightly beaten

Topping

4	cups (about 2 pints) strawberries	1	teaspoon pure vanilla extract
½	cup granulated sugar	1	tablespoon superfine sugar
½	pint (1 cup) heavy cream		Mint leaves, for garnish

Preheat the oven to 375°F. Butter only the bottom of a 13-by-9½-by-1-inch sheet pan.

To make the cake: In a large bowl, mix the flour and sugar. Cut in the ⅔ cup butter with a pastry blender or two butter knives until the mixture resembles coarse flakes. Mix in the milk, vanilla, and egg just until the batter is evenly moistened. Don't over-mix. Spread in the prepared pan. Bake until the top is golden brown and a cake tester comes out clean, 20 to 25 minutes.

To make the topping: Rinse the strawberries in cold water and dry on paper towels. Hull and quarter into a bowl. Sprinkle with the granulated sugar, stir, and let macerate. Cover and refrigerate until ready to use.

In a cold medium bowl, using a balloon or electric mixer on medium-high speed, whip the cream with the vanilla and superfine sugar until quite thick. Cover and refrigerate until ready to use.

To assemble and serve the shortcake: Cut the cake into 12 squares. Top with strawberries, a dollop of the whipped cream, and mint leaves. These can be placed on a large platter or individual dessert plates.

(continued)

RHUBARB-CHERRY TOPPING

This also makes a great topping for sorbet or vanilla ice cream.

¾	cup water		2	cups (about ¾ pounds, or 1 pint) cherries, pitted
1¼	cups sugar, or to taste		3–4	tablespoons instant tapioca
2	pounds rhubarb, leaves removed but not the strings, sliced into 1½-inch pieces			

In a medium-heavy saucepan combine the water, sugar, and rhubarb. Bring to the boiling point over medium heat, reduce the heat, and simmer for 10 minutes. Add the cherries, stir, and simmer for another 5 minutes. Sprinkle in the tapioca and stir until dissolved.

Remove from the heat and let cool. Place in a covered refrigerator dish until ready to serve, up to 3 days.

VANILLA—POPPY SEED POUND CAKE

YIELD | 20 SERVINGS

Cake

2	cups cake flour	¼	cup light brown sugar
1	teaspoon baking powder	1	tablespoon pure vanilla extract
½	teaspoon salt	4	large eggs, lightly beaten
1	cup (8 ounces) unsalted butter + more for greasing	3	tablespoons poppy seeds
1	cup granulated sugar		

Glaze

½	cup granulated sugar	1	teaspoon pure vanilla extract
⅓	cup water	1	tablespoon poppy seeds (optional)

Preheat the oven to 350°F. Lightly butter the bottom and sides of a 10-inch tube pan, preferably springform.

To make the cake: In a medium bowl, stir together the flour, baking powder, and salt.

In a large bowl, using an electric mixer, cream the 1 cup butter, then add the sugars and vanilla. Alternate beating in the eggs and the flour mixture. Stir in the poppy seeds, if using, in a stream. Pour the batter into the prepared pan and smooth lightly with a rubber spatula.

Bake in the bottom third of the oven for 1 hour 10 minutes, or until the top is lightly browned and a cake tester comes out clean. Let cool in the pan for 15 minutes, then turn the cake out on a cake rack over waxed paper. With a cake tester or toothpick, pierce the cake on the top and sides.

To make the glaze: In a small saucepan, heat the sugar and water over medium-low heat just to the boiling point, stirring, until the sugar is dissolved. Remove from the heat and stir in the vanilla and poppy seeds, if using.

To assemble the cake: Drip the glaze over the top and sides of the cake, spreading with a brush as you do. Gently tilt the cake as you cover the sides. Let the cake cool completely before serving.

PEANUT BUTTER LAYER CAKE

I know people who don't like to use the freezer. I was one of them. However, in a busy life, if you enjoy baking from scratch, the freezer is a terrific time-saving tool. This cake can be made from start to finish and served the same day or the next—or the layers can be baked, cooled thoroughly, wrapped in plastic wrap, and frozen for several weeks before thawing and assembling.

YIELD | ONE 9-INCH CAKE (12 SLICES)

Cake Layers

2½	cups all-purpose flour + more for dusting		1	cup peanut butter, at room temperature
1	tablespoon baking powder		6	eggs
½	teaspoon sea salt		2	teaspoons pure vanilla extract
8	tablespoons (½ cup) unsalted butter, sliced, at room temperature + more for greasing		1	cup sour cream
			1	cup hot water
2½	cups light brown sugar			

Frosting

3	egg whites		6	ounces milk chocolate, melted
¾	cup superfine sugar		1½	cups roasted peanuts, coarsely chopped
1	cup (8 ounces) unsalted butter, sliced, at room temperature			

To make the cake: Preheat the oven to 350°F. Lightly butter and dust with flour two 9-inch cake pans, preferably 2 inches deep.

In a small bowl, using a fork, stir together the 2½ cups flour, baking powder, and salt.

In a stand mixer with a paddle attachment or a large bowl and electric mixer, on medium to medium-high speed, cream together the ½ cup butter, brown sugar, and peanut butter. Add the eggs and vanilla and keep beating until well mixed. Incorporate the flour mixture, beat in the sour cream and water. Divide the batter among the prepared pans and bake until a cake tester comes out clean, about 35 minutes. Cool the cake in the pans on a cake rack for 10 minutes. Remove the cake from the pans and continue cooling. If the layers are domed, trim them horizontally so they're level for stacking.

To make the frosting: Simmer 2 inches of water in the bottom of a double boiler.

In a mixing bowl or the top of double boiler, whisk the egg whites and sugar until blended. Place over simmering water and whisk until the mixture is hot and the sugar dissolved. Turn off the heat and remove the mixing bowl from the pan of water.

Using an electric mixer, beat the mixture on high speed until thick and cool, about 5 minutes. Gradually beat in the butter and chocolate at medium speed until well incorporated.

To assemble the cake: Spread the frosting over each cake layer, stack them, then coat the top and sides generously. Sprinkle the peanuts over all. Refrigerate for at least 1 hour to set the buttercream. Serve at room temperature.

ICED DARK CHOCOLATE CAKE

YIELD | 10 SERVINGS

Cake

8	ounces dark chocolate, chopped	1	cup granulated sugar
1	cup (8 ounces) unsalted butter, sliced + more for greasing	1	cup all-purpose flour + more for dusting
6	large eggs, separated		Pinch of salt

Icing

¾	cup (6 ounces) unsalted butter, sliced, at room temperature	3	cups confectioners' sugar
⅔	cup unsweetened cocoa powder	1	teaspoon pure vanilla extract
	Pinch of salt	⅓	cup heavy cream

To make the cake: Preheat the oven to 400°F. Butter and lightly flour a 9-inch spring-form pan.

Melt the chocolate and 1 cup butter in the top of a double boiler. Stir until smooth and blended. In a large bowl, stir together the egg yolks and granulated sugar, then, with an electric mixer, beat in the 1 cup flour. Gradually stir in the chocolate mixture.

In a bowl, using an electric mixer, whisk the egg whites and salt at medium-high speed until stiff but not dry. Gently fold the beaten whites into the chocolate mixture until incorporated. Using a rubber spatula, pour the cake batter into the prepared pan.

Bake for 25 minutes, or until a cake tester comes out clean. Remove the cake from the oven and cool. Cover entirely with plastic wrap and store in the refrigerator. The cake can be made a day before it is needed.

To make the icing: With an electric mixer at low speed, cream the butter, cocoa, and salt. Gradually add the confectioners' sugar. Add the vanilla and cream, increasing the mixer speed to high. Beat until the icing is light and spreadable, about 4 minutes. Spread the icing over the top and sides of the cake. Refrigerate until 2 hours before serving.

BLUEBERRY CAKE

YIELD | 10 SERVINGS

1	cup sugar	2	teaspoons baking powder
¼	cup water	½	teaspoon salt
1	tablespoon fresh lemon juice	½	teaspoon ground cinnamon
1	teaspoon instant tapioca or cornstarch	1	egg
		½	cup milk
2½	cups (about 1½ pints) blueberries, rinsed and dried	6	tablespoons unsalted butter, sliced, at room temperature + more for greasing
	Grated zest of ½ lemon (see page 316)	1	teaspoon pure vanilla extract
1¼	cups all-purpose flour		

Preheat the oven to 375°F. Lightly butter a 9-inch baking pan.

In a medium saucepan over medium-low heat, stir together ½ cup of the sugar, water, lemon juice, and tapioca. Bring to a low boil and stir in the blueberries. Bring to a low boil again, stir, remove from the heat, and stir in the lemon zest.

In a small bowl, mix together the flour, baking powder, salt, and cinnamon.

In a mixing bowl, using an electric mixer at medium speed, beat the egg, milk, 6 tablespoons butter, vanilla, and the remaining ½ cup sugar. Gradually mix in the flour mixture.

Pour the batter into the prepared baking pan and lightly spread from edge to edge with a rubber spatula. Pour the blueberry mixture in an even layer over the batter.

Bake until a cake tester comes out clean, about 30 minutes.

Let cool for 1 hour before serving, or cool completely, cover with plastic wrap, and refrigerate for up to 24 hours. Bring to room temperature before serving.

CHOCOLATE-BUTTERMILK AMERICAN FLAG CAKE

Every summer, versions of this cake are presented at Fourth of July celebrations. This one uses a cake recipe that is tasty with any topping. Clearly, the white frosting can be a blank canvas for your imagination. Toasted coconut mixed with chopped toasted walnuts makes a delicious replacement for the berries when they are out of season.

YIELD | 12 TO 16 SERVINGS

Cake

½	cup buttermilk	½	cup canola or safflower oil
1	teaspoon baking soda	1	teaspoon pure vanilla extract
¼	cup unsweetened cocoa powder	2	large eggs
1	teaspoon ground cinnamon	2	cups all-purpose flour + more for dusting
1	cup water		
8	tablespoons (½ cup) unsalted butter, sliced and softened + more for greasing	2	cups granulated sugar

Frosting

2	packages (8 ounces each) cream cheese, softened	1	cup (about ½ pint) blueberries, rinsed and dried
3	tablespoons heavy cream	3	cups (about 1½ pints) raspberries or strawberry halves, rinsed and dried
2	tablespoons superfine sugar		
8	ounces marshmallow cream		

To make the cake: Preheat the oven to 350°F. Lightly butter and flour a 13-by-9-inch oven-to-table baking pan.

In a small bowl, mix together the buttermilk and baking soda.

In a medium saucepan over medium heat, stir together the cocoa, cinnamon, water, the 8 tablespoons butter, and oil. Bring to the boiling point, stirring constantly. Remove from the heat and stir in the vanilla and the buttermilk mixture. Beat in the eggs, then beat in the 2 cups flour and sugar until smooth. Pour into the prepared pan.

Bake until a cake tester comes out clean, 15 to 20 minutes. Let cool in the pan.

When the cake is completely cool, it can be covered and refrigerated for up to 2 days before frosting and decorating.

To make the frosting: In a medium bowl, combine the cream cheese, heavy cream, and sugar, then mix in the marshmallow cream by hand or with an electric mixer, beating until smooth and fluffy. Spread over the cooled cake. Refrigerate for 1½ hours before decorating.

To decorate the cake: Arrange the blueberries in a 5-inch square in the upper left corner of the cake to make the blue field of the flag. Starting and ending at the edges of the cake, arrange seven horizontal rows of raspberries, leaving white stripes in between.

CAROL'S OLD-FASHIONED GINGERBREAD

Carol is one of the best bakers I know. The first time I tasted this cake, she had carried all the ingredients in plastic storage bags in a canvas tote bag. The flour was in one plastic bag; the baking soda, spices, and salt in another; and the sugar in a third. She transported the butter and cream in a thermal container and also brought along her own 8-by-8-inch baking dish and a bowl. The results were perfect.

YIELD | 16 TWO-INCH SQUARES

2	cups all-purpose flour		⅓	cup sugar
2	teaspoons baking soda		1	large egg
2¼	teaspoons ground ginger		¾	cup molasses
½	teaspoon ground cinnamon		¾	cup cold water
¼	teaspoon ground cloves		¼	cup pure maple syrup
	Pinch of salt		½	pint (1 cup) heavy cream, whipped
5	tablespoons unsalted butter, sliced, at room temperature + more for greasing			

Preheat the oven to 350°F. Lightly butter an 8-by-8-inch cake pan.

In a small bowl, using a fork, blend the flour, baking soda, spices, and salt.

In a large mixing bowl, using an electric mixer, cream the 5 tablespoons butter and sugar until light and fluffy. Add the egg and beat until well incorporated. Scrape down the sides of the bowl and drizzle in the molasses, beating constantly. Add half of the flour mixture and mix until combined, then mix in the rest. Slowly pour in the cold water and stir until well incorporated. Pour the batter into the prepared cake pan.

Bake until a cake tester comes out clean, about 35 minutes. Place the pan on a cooling rack for at least 1 hour.

Mix the maple syrup into the whipped cream and serve with cake squares.

POTLUCK NOTE | *In the fall, stewed apples and pears are a welcome accompaniment to squares of gingerbread and maple cream.*

BREADS, ROLLS, AND MUFFINS

MEALS FOR WHICH different people make different courses are the ideal occasions to try baking bread. Baking is such a luxury in a busy life that attention should be paid to the quality of the ingredients. The first time may be the hardest but it also might be the most fun.

As far as equipment goes, "less is more" and "know thyself" are both good axioms. If you are going to be baking for a crowd, two of everything, including measuring spoons and measuring cup sets, is a good idea. Stock your kitchen with two 9-by-5-inch loaf pans; two baking sheets; two cake racks; one muffin tin for 12 regular-size muffins and one for mini-size muffins. Various bowls for mixing, proofing, and rising are handy. Pyrex or other transparent heatproof measuring pitchers are very useful in small, medium, and large sizes. Two wooden spoons, balloon whisks, rubber spatulas, a pastry blender and a package of one-side "safety" razor blades or a lame for slashing the crust of some yeast breads are practical. Thin wooden skewers to use as cake testers, a small spray bottle to moisten loaves and a good-sized trivet are helpful.

I recommend oven mitts that go halfway up your arm. More burns are caused by contact with the oven than with a pan.

If I had to recommend one luxury, it would be a stand mixer with a paddle and dough hook attachment. I know many people who bake a lot without one, using only a sturdy electric handheld mixer.

When you have seen as many professional kitchens as I have, you realize that terrific food is being made under the most diverse conditions all over the world.

Poppy Seed Rolls (opposite)
Parker House Rolls (page 260)

POPPY SEED ROLLS

These buns are quite good, they're easy to make, and they freeze well, so you can have them whenever you're in the mood.

YIELD | 16 ROLLS

2	packages active dry yeast (½ ounce)	1½	teaspoons sea salt
1	teaspoon sugar	5	cups bread flour
½	cup warm water	1	egg white, beaten
2	cups low-fat milk	2	tablespoons poppy seeds
2	tablespoons unsalted butter + more for greasing		

Butter a large mixing bowl and lightly butter a baking sheet.

In a large bowl, dissolve the yeast and sugar in the warm water and let stand for 5 minutes, or until it foams.

In a small saucepan over medium heat, scald the milk and remove from the heat. Add the 2 tablespoons butter and bring to room temperature. Stir the milk mixture and salt into the yeast mixture. Beat in 2 cups of the flour, then gradually add the remaining 3 cups.

Turn the dough out onto a lightly floured work surface and knead until smooth and elastic, about 10 minutes. Place the dough in the prepared mixing bowl and turn it to coat with a film of butter. Cover with a damp tea towel and let rise for 2 hours. Push the dough down and turn out onto a lightly buttered surface. Divide into four parts, then into four again. Roll each section into a round ball with a flat bottom. Place on the prepared baking sheet, cover, and let rise for 1 hour.

Preheat the oven to 375°F. Brush the tops of the rolls with the egg white and sprinkle with the poppy seeds. Bake until golden brown, about 15 minutes. Remove the rolls to cake racks and let cool.

These can be served immediately or frozen for later use. Let them cool completely and seal in plastic wrap in a single layer, then place in the freezer. When you want to serve them, bring to room temperature and heat in a 350°F oven for 5 minutes.

PARKER HOUSE ROLLS

These puffy, pocketlike rolls originated in the 1870s at the Parker House Hotel in Boston, one of America's oldest continuously operating hotels. They were so popular that versions of the recipe started appearing in the 1880s.

YIELD | 24 ROLLS

2	packages active dry yeast (½ ounce)	8	tablespoons (½ cup) room-temperature unsalted butter, sliced + 3 tablespoons melted
⅓	cup sugar		
½	cup milk, warmed	1	cup hot water
5	cups all-purpose flour	2	eggs, lightly beaten
¼	teaspoon salt		

Lightly butter two 13-by-9-inch baking pans.

In a large mixing bowl, combine the yeast, sugar, and warm milk. Stir and let sit until bubbly. Add 2½ cups of the flour, salt, and room-temperature butter and beat with an electric mixer on low speed until incorporated. Gradually add the water, beat at medium speed, and add the eggs. Add another 1½ cups flour and beat until thick, about 5 minutes more. Scrape down the sides of the bowl with a rubber spatula and turn the dough out onto a clean, floured work surface. Knead in the remaining 1 cup flour for 5 minutes to make a soft, smooth dough.

Shape the dough into a ball and place in the prepared mixing bowl, turning the dough so that it is coated. Cover the bowl and let the dough rise in a warm (about 80°F) place until doubled in size, about 1½ hours. Your finger will leave a small dent when you press the dough. Push the dough down and roll out on a floured surface to a ½-inch thickness. Cover lightly with a towel and let rest for 15 minutes. Using a sharp, floured 3-inch biscuit cutter, cut the dough into 24 circles. Brush the rims with some of the melted butter and fold the circles almost in half so that the top of each looks like the flap of a pocket, and pinch the edges together. Place the rolls in the prepared pans so that they do not touch. Cover with towels and let the rolls rise for about 1 hour.

Preheat the oven to 375°F. Bake the rolls until golden brown, about 15 minutes. Remove immediately from the pan and glaze with melted butter.

CHEDDAR CHEESE BISCUITS

2¼	cups all-purpose flour	6	tablespoons unsalted butter, sliced and chilled + more for greasing
1	tablespoon sugar		
1	tablespoon baking powder	1¼	cups coarsely grated extra-sharp cheddar cheese
1	teaspoon baking soda		
½	teaspoon salt	1¼	cups buttermilk
½	teaspoon freshly ground pepper		

Preheat the oven to 400°F. Lightly butter a large baking sheet.

In a large bowl, mix together the flour, sugar, baking powder, baking soda, salt, and pepper. Using a pastry blender or two butter knives, cut in the 6 tablespoons butter until the mixture resembles coarse meal. Slowly mix in the cheese so it doesn't clump too much. Add the buttermilk just until incorporated. Do not overmix.

Use about ⅓ cup batter for each biscuit and arrange on the baking sheet so that the biscuits do not touch. If the sheet is too small, use two. Bake until golden brown and firm to the touch, about 15 minutes.

These are best served fresh from the oven, but they can be cooled completely, wrapped in foil, and stored at room temperature for up to 12 hours. Reheat the biscuits, still wrapped in foil, in a 350°F oven for 4 minutes. Open the foil and leave in the oven for 1 minute more.

BLUEBERRY-CORN MUFFINS

If it seems like there are a lot of muffin recipes here, it's because I really, really dislike commercially made muffins. Depending on the fruit available, these fill the bill. This recipe makes 12 regular muffins or 36 mini muffins.

YIELD | 12 MUFFINS

1	cup all-purpose flour + more for dusting
1	cup fine cornmeal
1	tablespoon baking powder
1	teaspoon salt
8	tablespoons (½ cup) unsalted butter + more for greasing

1	extra-large egg
¾	cup milk
⅓	cup honey
⅓	cup sugar
2½	cups (about 1 pint) blueberries, rinsed and drained

Preheat the oven to 425°F for standard muffins, 375°F for mini muffins. Lightly butter and flour a standard 12-muffin pan or a 36-mini-muffin pan.

In a small bowl, using a fork, stir together the flour, cornmeal, baking powder, and salt.

In a medium bowl, cream the 8 tablespoons butter, then beat in the egg, milk, honey, and sugar by hand or with an electric mixer. Fold in the flour mixture and the blueberries. Spoon the batter into the muffin cups.

Bake until a cake tester comes out clean, 15 to 20 minutes. Let cool in the pan for 10 minutes, then remove the muffins to a cake rack.

RHUBARB-PECAN MUFFINS

These muffins are a bit tart and moist. When completely cooled, they can be individually wrapped and frozen. Thaw them before reheating.

YIELD | 12 MUFFINS

2	scant cups sliced fresh rhubarb (⅓-inch slices)	½	teaspoon baking soda
2	teaspoons finely grated lemon zest (see page 316)	½	teaspoon sea salt
		⅔	cup granulated sugar
3	teaspoons brown or granulated sugar	1	large egg, lightly beaten
		¼	cup canola or safflower oil
2	cups all-purpose flour	¾	cup milk
2	teaspoons baking powder	¾	cup chopped pecans

Preheat the oven to 350°F. Butter the bottom of a 12-muffin tin.

In a medium bowl, combine the rhubarb, lemon zest, and 3 teaspoons brown or granulated sugar.

In a large bowl, mix together the flour, baking powder, baking soda, salt, and ⅔ cup granulated sugar.

In a medium bowl, whisk together the egg, oil, and milk. Stir into the flour mixture, alternating with the rhubarb mixture. Fold in the pecans. Spoon the batter into the muffin cups.

Bake in the center of the oven until a cake tester comes out clean, about 25 minutes. Remove the pan from the oven and place on a cake rack to cool for 10 minutes. Remove the muffins from the pan and let them cool thoroughly on the cake rack.

MALTED MILK BALL MUFFINS

What can I say? Everyone likes these—except, of course, people who don't like chocolate.

YIELD | 12 MUFFINS

1½	cups all-purpose flour + more for dusting	1	large egg, beaten
½	cup unsweetened cocoa powder	¾	cup sour cream
½	cup + 1 tablespoon sugar	2	teaspoons pure vanilla extract
1	tablespoon baking powder	6	tablespoons unsweetened butter, melted and cooled + more for greasing
¼	teaspoon salt		
1	cup coarsely crushed malted milk balls (best available)	¼	cup milk

Preheat the oven to 375°F. Butter and lightly flour the bottom and sides of a 12-muffin pan or use paper liners.

In a large bowl, using a fork, combine the 1½ cups flour and cocoa powder. Stir in the sugar, baking powder, and salt, then add the malted milk balls.

In a small bowl, combine the egg, sour cream, vanilla, the 6 tablespoons butter, and milk. Add to the flour mixture and incorporate with a rubber spatula until just moistened. Do not overmix. Fill the prepared muffin tins two-thirds full.

Bake until a cake tester comes out clean, 16 to 18 minutes. Let cool in the pan on a wire rack for 5 minutes. Remove the muffins from the pan and let cool thoroughly on a cake rack.

FRANANA BANANA BREAD

This is one terrific banana bread. I have been making it for so long that people started calling it franana bread. The only variation I ever make is adding 1¼ cups of white chocolate chunks or chips or substituting them for the walnuts.

YIELD | 10 SERVINGS

1	cup whole wheat flour		1	cup honey
1	cup all-purpose flour + more for dusting		½	cup whole-milk plain yogurt
1	teaspoon baking soda		2	large eggs, lightly beaten
½	teaspoon sea salt		3	very ripe bananas, mashed
8	tablespoons (½ cup) unsalted butter, softened + more for greasing		⅔	cup coarsely chopped walnuts

Preheat the oven to 350°F. Lightly butter and flour a 9-by-5-inch loaf pan.

In a medium bowl, using a fork, stir together the flours, baking soda, and salt.

In a large bowl, beating by hand or using an electric mixer on medium speed, mix together the 8 tablespoons butter, honey, yogurt, and eggs until well incorporated. Mix in the bananas. Fold in the flour mixture and the walnuts.

Bake in the center of the oven until a cake tester comes out clean, about 1 hour. Let cool in the pan for 10 minutes, then on a cake rack until completely cool.

POTLUCK NOTE | *It is best to use unsalted butter in baking because you have better control of the flavor. If you use salted butter the recipes will be fine, however, and you don't really have to adjust the salt in the recipe. Please do not use margarine as a substitute because it is a mixture of solid and liquid fat and will affect the recipe.*

BOSTON BROWN BREAD

This bread is steamed on top of the stove in two 1-pound coffee cans. Why? No one seems certain, but my guess is that most home kitchens have had little use for cylindrical pudding molds and so made do with what was around the house.

YIELD | 12 SERVINGS

1	cup rye flour	2	cups buttermilk
1	cup whole wheat flour	1	cup molasses
1	cup medium cornmeal	1	cup currants or raisins
2	tablespoons baking soda	4	tablespoons unsalted butter, sliced, at room temperature
1	teaspoon salt		
¼	cup brown sugar		

Lightly grease two 1-pound coffee cans or cylindrical pudding molds. Start heating 2 to 3 quarts of water in a teakettle or pot.

In a medium bowl, using a fork, combine the flours, cornmeal, baking soda, salt, and sugar.

In a large bowl, beat together the buttermilk and molasses using a hand mixer or an electric mixer at medium speed. Mix in the currants or raisins, then beat in the flour mixture, followed by the butter. Pour the batter into the prepared cans, each no more than about two-thirds full. Cover each can loosely with a piece of buttered parchment or waxed paper, then top with a double fold of heavy-duty foil. Tie tightly with kitchen string or a rubber band. Trim the foil to 1½ inches from the top of each can so that the water doesn't seep underneath.

Place the cans side by side (without touching) on a rack in a Dutch oven or other heavy pan on the stove top. Pour hot water into the Dutch oven halfway up the sides of the cans. Steam over medium to medium-low heat, adding more hot water to maintain the water level, until a cake tester comes out clean, about 2 hours. Remove the cans from the water and let cool for 15 minutes before sliding the breads out of the cans.

The breads can be cooled completely, wrapped in foil, and refrigerated until needed. Heat, still wrapped in foil, in a 300°F oven, or in a colander over simmering water.

OATMEAL BREAD

This is a tasty, not overly sweet loaf. The cashews are a surprising and tasty addition to the batter.

YIELD | 10 SERVINGS

1	cup all-purpose flour + more for dusting	½	cup milk
⅔	cup oat flakes	½	cup honey
1	tablespoon baking powder	⅓	cup safflower or canola oil
2	large eggs, lightly beaten	½	cup raisins
½	cup whole-milk plain yogurt	½	cup chopped unsalted cashews

Preheat the oven to 350°F. Lightly butter and flour a 9-by-5-inch loaf pan.

In a medium bowl, using a fork, stir together the 1 cup flour, oat flakes, and baking powder.

In a large bowl, beat together the eggs, yogurt, milk, honey, and oil. Stir in the flour mixture, raisins, and cashews. Pour the batter into the prepared pan and level with a rubber spatula.

Bake in the center of the oven until a cake tester comes out clean, 50 to 60 minutes. Let cool in the pan for 10 minutes and then on a cake rack until completely cool.

JALAPEÑO CORN BREAD

The taste for "hot" food is rapidly advancing. This corn bread will be welcome as an accompaniment for soup and salads.

YIELD | 12 SERVINGS

1	can (16 ounces) creamed corn	¾	cup all-purpose flour
4	eggs, lightly beaten	1½	cups shredded Monterey Jack cheese, regular or hot
1	teaspoon sea salt		
1	tablespoon baking soda	¼	cup pickled jalapeño chili peppers, drained and chopped
2	cups buttermilk		
⅔	cup corn oil	2	tablespoons unsalted butter
2	cups stone-ground yellow cornmeal		

Preheat the oven to 375°F.

In a bowl large enough to hold all the ingredients, combine the corn, eggs, salt, and baking soda. Stir in the buttermilk, oil, cornmeal, and flour, then fold in the cheese and chili peppers. Mix well.

Put the butter in a 10-by-15-inch baking pan and place it in the oven until it melts, about 5 minutes, then brush up the sides of the pan.

Pour the batter into the pan and level with a rubber spatula. Bake until the corn bread begins to pull away from sides of the pan and a cake tester comes out clean, about 40 minutes. Cool in the pan on a cake rack.

To serve the dish: Serve right from the baking pan, or cut into squares and place on a serving platter.

EASY OLIVE BREAD

This bread is delicious on its own, or you can serve it sliced, toasted, and spread with a little garlic butter.

YIELD | 10 SERVINGS

1	cup all-purpose flour + more for dusting
1	cup whole wheat flour
1	tablespoon baking powder
1	teaspoon sea salt
2	tablespoons unsalted butter, melted
1	tablespoon olive oil + more for greasing

1	extra-large egg, lightly beaten
½	teaspoon dried rosemary
2	teaspoons grated lemon zest
½	teaspoon Aleppo pepper or crushed red pepper flakes
1	cup milk
1¼	cups black oil-cured or kalamata olives, pitted and coarsely chopped

Preheat the oven to 350°F. Lightly oil and flour a 9-by-5-inch loaf pan.

In a medium bowl, stir together the 1 cup all-purpose flour, whole wheat flour, baking powder, and salt.

In a large bowl, beat together the butter, the 1 tablespoon oil, egg, rosemary, lemon zest, and pepper or red pepper flakes. Stir in the flour mixture, alternating with the milk and beating after each addition. Fold in the olives. Pour into the prepared pan.

Bake until a cake tester comes out clean, about 1 hour. Let cool in the pan for 10 minutes, then remove the bread from the pan and let cool completely on a cake rack.

EASY WHOLE WHEAT BREAD

YIELD | 10 SERVINGS

1	large potato, peeled and diced	2	packages (½ ounce) active dry yeast
2	tablespoons unsalted butter + more for greasing	3	cups whole wheat flour or a multigrain mixture
¼	cup honey	¼	teaspoon salt
¼	cup warm water		

Generously butter a 9-by-5-inch loaf pan.

Bring 1½ cups water to a low boil and simmer the potato for 20 minutes, or until it falls apart at the touch of a fork. Strain the water through a fine-mesh strainer into a heatproof measuring cup and add the 2 tablespoons butter. Set the potato water aside.

Meanwhile, in a small bowl, stir the honey into the water until dissolved. Add the yeast, stir once or twice, and let stand until bubbly, about 5 minutes.

Place the flour in a large bowl and make a well in the center. Pour the yeast mixture into the center, cover with a towel, and allow to foam for 10 minutes. Add the potato water to the center of the flour and sprinkle the salt over all. Allow to foam for 20 minutes.

With a rubber spatula, work the flour from the center and thoroughly incorporate all the ingredients. Cover the bowl with a clean, damp kitchen towel and let rise until doubled, about 2 hours.

Turn the dough out onto a lightly floured surface and knead until smooth and elastic, about 10 minutes. Shape into a loaf and place in the prepared pan. Cover with a damp kitchen towel and let rise until doubled in the pan.

Preheat the oven to 400°F.

Bake in the center of the oven for 45 minutes. Let cool in the pan for 15 minutes, then turn out onto a cake rack to cool thoroughly.

ROSEMARY FOCACCIA

A distant cousin of pizza, this satisfying bread will soon be added to your can-do baking skills. Feel free to make it your own by changing the topping and adding or substituting pitted sliced olives, basil, minced oil-cured sun-dried tomatoes, or peppers. You can sprinkle it with finely grated cheese just when it comes out of the oven. You can even make it with no topping at all; just brush with a little olive oil and sprinkle on a little salt before baking. But don't call it "focach"—three syllables, please.

YIELD | 12 SERVINGS

Bread

1	packet (¼ ounce) active dry yeast		1	cup room-temperature milk
1	teaspoon sugar		1	cup room-temperature water
½	cup warm water		3	tablespoons extra-virgin olive oil + more for greasing
5–6	cups bread flour			
1	teaspoon sea salt			
1	tablespoon chopped fresh rosemary			

Topping

3	tablespoons extra-virgin olive oil		2	tablespoons chopped fresh rosemary
1	medium–large red onion, sliced			
6	cloves garlic, sliced		1–2	teaspoons coarse salt

Lightly coat a 17-by-14-inch baking sheet with olive oil. Coat a ceramic bowl with olive oil.

To make the bread: In a large bowl, dissolve the yeast and sugar in the warm water. Stir and let stand until bubbly, about 5 minutes. Stir in 1 cup of the flour, salt, and rosemary. Let rest for 5 minutes.

In a medium pouring bowl, mix the milk, room-temperature water, and the oil.

With a wooden spoon or the paddle attachment of a stand mixer set on low, alternately beat the milk mixture and the remaining 4 to 5 cups flour by the cup into the yeast mixture. When the dough starts to hold together, place on a lightly floured surface and knead until smooth and elastic, about 5 minutes.

(continued)

Place the dough in the prepared ceramic bowl. Rotate the dough so that it is coated in oil and cover the bowl with a clean, damp kitchen towel. Let stand for 2 hours, or until more or less doubled in volume. Gently deflate the dough in the bowl, turn it over, and let rise for another 45 minutes.

To make the topping: Heat the oil in a heavy skillet over medium-low heat. Add the onion and cook for 10 minutes, then add the garlic and cook until the onions are caramelized, another 2 minutes. Remove from the heat and let come to room temperature. With a slotted spoon, remove the onion and garlic to a small bowl. Reserve the oil in the skillet.

Preheat the oven to 400°F.

To assemble the focaccia: Stretch the dough into a 16-by-13-inch rectangle on a lightly floured surface. Cover and let rest for 30 minutes. Place on the prepared baking sheet and stretch gently to fit. With your fingertips, dimple the top of the dough, making indentations about 1½ inches apart and ¼ inch deep. Brush with the reserved olive oil and spread the onion and garlic over all. Sprinkle with the rosemary and coarse salt.

Bake until the edges are golden brown, about 30 minutes. Let cool on a rack for 15 to 20 minutes before serving.

If you must prepare ahead of time, let the cooked bread cool thoroughly, cover with plastic wrap and foil, and refrigerate for up to 24 hours. Remove all the wrapping and heat in a 350°F oven for 5 to 7 minutes.

HOLIDAY DISHES

ALL HOLIDAYS, FEASTS, and festivals are enriched when we feel we have participated in making them happen. There are few dining experiences more satisfying than the right food at the right time. I'd like to think that all the recipes in this book are suitable for special occasions. There are, however, in all traditions, foods we identify with certain celebrations.

All of these classic dishes will work at a potluck if you communicate with the other participants. Even the five-step Bûche de Noël is easy if it is the only dish you are making for a memorable gathering. Also, please keep in mind that you don't have to be celebrating a particular holiday to enjoy any of these recipes. I make the Mexican Chocolate Cake and Banana Rum Tart on many occasions because each is a very easy-to-make twist on an old favorite. Glazed ham or a leg of lamb can be enjoyed at any event, and sides such as Green Lentils with Pancetta (page 285) or Potato Pancakes (Latkes) with Chunky Applesauce (page 290) will accessorize any menu.

In a holiday spirit, it is good to remember that all events are about people. In any group, there are a few welcome guests who really just want to stay out of the kitchen; they can bring treats such as chocolate, olives, mustards, holly for the Christmas table, autumn leaves for Thanksgiving, beverages—or simply their enthusiasm and conversation.

ROAST TURKEY WITH EVERYTHING STUFFING AND OLD-FASHIONED GIBLET GRAVY

In the New World, turkeys were domesticated by the indigenous people of the Americas for centuries and continue to be an abundant food source here. When turkeys were imported by Europe, chefs as famous as Jean Anthelme Brillat-Savarin found many ways to cook them, and Impressionist painter Claude Monet was intrigued enough to create a wonderful painting of them.

YIELD | 10 SERVINGS

2	cups water
1	fresh (16–18 pounds) turkey; if using a frozen turkey, thaw according to package directions
	Salt and pepper
	Everything Stuffing (recipe follows)

	Up to 2 cups (1 pound) unsalted butter, melted
½	cup Dijon mustard
¼	cup all-purpose flour
	Old-Fashioned Giblet Gravy (recipe follows), for serving

Preheat the oven to 325°F and place an oven rack in the lowest position. Remove the other rack(s). Pour the water in a roasting pan and place in the oven.

Remove the turkey's giblets and reserve for the gravy. Rinse the turkey, pat dry with paper towels, and season lightly with salt and pepper. Stuff the large cavity of the turkey with Everything Stuffing. Place some in the smaller front cavity, fold the neck skin under, and fasten with a skewer. Don't pack with too much stuffing—any leftovers can be placed in an ovenproof casserole and baked separately.

Place the turkey on a Y-shaped rack and brush with ½ cup of the melted butter. In a small bowl, mix together the mustard, flour, and ½ cup of the butter and pat over the turkey. Place in the preheated roasting pan.

Roast, brushing occasionally with up to 1 cup of the remaining butter, until a meat thermometer inserted in the thickest part of the thigh (near the breast) registers 180°F and the drumstick moves easily up and down, 4½ to 5 hours. The temperature of the stuffing must be 165°F. Time the roasting so that the turkey is ready at least 20 to 30 minutes before serving; it needs to stand that long for proper finishing. Remove the turkey to a large platter. Stir the pan drippings and reserve 1 to 2 cups (amounts vary) for the gravy.

To serve the dish: There is no "right way"; it is up to you. Personally, I prefer to have someone carve the turkey as it is being served and spoon out the hot stuffing. Others like to slice the turkey onto a platter in the kitchen and place the stuffing in a bowl so that people can help themselves. Serve with Old-Fashioned Giblet Gravy in gravy boats or pitchers.

POTLUCK NOTE | *There will be leftovers. You may want to decide before the event who gets them. If you are hosting, they are certainly yours.*

Everything Stuffing

3	tablespoons unsalted butter	8–10	cups bread cubes (see Potluck Note on page 278)
3	tablespoons olive oil		
2	sweet Italian sausages, removed from casings	3	large eggs, lightly beaten
		¼	cup minced fresh flat-leaf parsley
2	hot Italian sausages (or 2 more sweet), removed from casings	¾	pound chestnuts, cooked, peeled, and coarsely chopped (see Potluck Note on page 287)
2	cups diced onion		
1	cup sliced white, cremini, or mixed mushrooms	1	teaspoon dried sage
			Salt and pepper

In a large heavy skillet, heat the butter and oil over medium heat. Add the sausage and move around with a spatula so that it breaks up into little pieces, but do not mince it. Sauté for 10 minutes, stirring occasionally, then stir in the onions and mushrooms. Sauté until the onions are golden brown, about 5 minutes. Turn off the heat and set aside.

(continued)

Place the bread cubes in a bowl large enough to hold all the ingredients, then stir in the eggs, parsley, chestnuts, and sage. Stir in the sausage mixture, along with any liquid in the pan, and mix thoroughly. If the mixture does not stick together, add up to 1 cup of water. Stir in salt and pepper to taste. The stuffing can be made a day ahead, cooled, covered, and refrigerated. Bring to room temperature before stuffing the turkey.

POTLUCK NOTE | *The only time I buy standard 1½-pound packaged white sandwich loaves is when I make stuffing. Preheat the oven to 250°F and place 25 bread slices on oven racks. Toast for about 15 minutes, until crisp but still pale. Tear into cubes.*

Old-Fashioned Giblet Gravy

3	cups water			Freshly ground pepper
4 or 5	whole cloves		1	cup diced white, cremini, or mixed mushrooms, sautéed
1	onion			Turkey liver, sautéed and diced
2	ribs celery, sliced (optional)		1–2	cups turkey pan drippings
	Turkey giblets (gizzard, heart, and neck)		½	cup wine or sherry
½	teaspoon dried thyme		⅓	cup instant flour
½	teaspoon salt + more to taste			

Place the water in a medium saucepan over medium heat. Insert the cloves into the onion and place in the water along with the celery (if using), giblets, thyme, ½ teaspoon salt, and a few grinds of pepper. Bring to a low boil and simmer for 45 minutes.

Remove from the heat and strain over a clean medium saucepan. Mince the giblets and add to the strained gravy along with the sautéed mushrooms and liver. At this point, the gravy can be covered and refrigerated until the turkey is done.

To continue, heat the gravy over medium-low heat and stir in the reserved pan drippings and wine. Stir in the flour and season with salt and pepper to taste. Serve hot.

CRANBERRY-KUMQUAT CONSERVE

YIELD | 8 CUPS

2	cups water
2	cups sugar
2	packages (12 ounces each) cranberries, rinsed
2	cups (about 1 pint) kumquats, rinsed and halved vertically

1 cup ginger packed in syrup, drained and sliced; reserve ⅓ cup of the drained syrup*

Store any remaining ginger and syrup in the refrigerator for future use. Jars of ginger in syrup are available in the Asian food sections of most large supermarkets Asian food shops or online. If it is not available, mince 1 cup candied dried ginger and add with the kumquats.

Bring the water to a boil in a heavy saucepan over medium-high heat. Stir in the sugar until dissolved. Stir in the cranberries and bring to a low boil, stirring constantly. Lower the heat to medium, stirring constantly, and boil until the berries start to pop, about 5 minutes. Add the kumquats, sliced ginger, and syrup. Stir, lower the heat to medium-low, and simmer for 5 minutes longer, stirring occasionally.

Transfer to a serving dish or refrigerator bowl and cool, cover, and refrigerate until ready to serve, up 24 hours.

POTLUCK NOTE | *Any leftover conserve is delicious spooned over vanilla ice cream.*

PUMPKIN CHEESECAKE
WITH GINGER-PECAN CRUST

This variation on a traditional pumpkin pie is a welcome treat.

YIELD | 12 SERVINGS

Crust

1½	cups crumbled gingersnaps (about 30 cookies)	7	tablespoons unsalted butter, melted + more for greasing
½	cup finely chopped pecans	¼	cup superfine sugar

Filling

3	packages (8 ounces each) cream cheese, at room temperature	½	teaspoon ground nutmeg
1	can (15 ounces) pumpkin puree	3	tablespoons crystallized ginger, minced
4	large egg yolks, lightly beaten	⅓	cup heavy cream
1½	cups superfine sugar	2	tablespoons cornstarch
1	teaspoon ground cinnamon	2	teaspoons pure vanilla extract

Preheat the oven to 400°F. Generously butter a 10-inch springform pan. Wrap foil around the outside bottom of the pan and up the sides a bit to cover and waterproof the seams. Simmer 6 cups of water in a kettle over medium heat.

To make the crust: In a medium bowl, mix the gingersnaps, pecans, the 7 tablespoons butter, and sugar. Press on the bottom and 1½ inches up the inside of the prepared pan. Chill in the refrigerator for 30 minutes, then bake for 10 minutes. Remove to a cake rack to cool. Maintain the oven heat.

To make the filling: In a large bowl or the bowl of a stand mixer, beat the cream cheese, pumpkin, egg yolks, and sugar at medium speed. When smooth and creamy, add the cinnamon, nutmeg, and ginger. Beat in the cream and cornstarch and add the vanilla.

Pour the cheesecake mixture into the crust and place in a roasting pan. Carefully pour the hot water into the roasting pan so that it reaches no more than halfway up the sides of the springform pan.

Place the roasting pan on the center shelf of the oven. Reduce the heat to 350°F and bake for 1 hour 10 minutes. The center of the cheesecake should still look a bit custardlike.

Remove the cheesecake from the roasting pan, remove the foil, and place on a cake rack to cool for 2 hours. Chill in the refrigerator for at least 4 hours. If the cake is not being served immediately, cover the top of the springform pan with plastic wrap, being sure to keep the plastic from touching the top of the cake.

Glazed Ham with Maple Mustard (opposite)
Sweet-and-Sour Red Cabbage (page 284)
Green Lentils with Pancetta (page 285)

GLAZED HAM WITH MAPLE MUSTARD

Ham for the holidays may go back to early Roman festivals, when pigs and boars were often roasted for celebrations. In modern history, Scandinavia and much of Western Europe celebrate Christmas from the Nativity to Twelfth Night with varieties of ham and roast pork. At Mount Vernon, George Washington savored the holidays with ham and oyster sauce as well as sweet potatoes and peanut soup. It is the maple syrup that gives this dish its American flavor.

YIELD | 10 SERVINGS

1 fully cooked, smoked, bone-in ham (about 8 pounds)	1 cup brown sugar
1⅔ cups grainy mustard	1⅔ cups pure maple syrup
	Small jar whole cloves

Preheat the oven to 325°F.

Score the ham through the rind in a traditional diamond pattern. In a medium bowl, mix together ⅔ cup of the mustard, brown sugar, and 1 cup of the syrup and coat the ham. Insert a clove into the center of each diamond. Place the ham on a rack in a roasting pan with 2 cups of water in the bottom.

Bake, basting occasionally, until a meat thermometer registers 140°F in the thickest part of the ham away from the bone, about 2 hours.

Discard the glazing mixture and let the ham rest on a platter for 30 minutes before serving.

In a small serving bowl, mix together the remaining 1 cup mustard and ⅔ cup maple syrup.

To serve the dish: The choice is yours. You can slice the ham in the kitchen and place it on a platter, or present the whole ham and carve it at the table—in which case, slice most of it and let people help themselves to seconds if it is a buffet. Serve with the maple mustard and any of your favorite mustards. Sweet-and-Sour Red Cabbage and Apples (page 284) and Green Lentils with Pancetta (page 285), each in an attractive serving bowl, are good accompaniments.

SWEET-AND-SOUR RED CABBAGE AND APPLES

This tasty side dish makes a bright accompaniment to the ham. It can be made several days before it is needed.

YIELD | 10 SIDE-DISH SERVINGS

3	tablespoons unsalted butter	½	cup packed brown sugar
1	head red cabbage (2 pounds), cored and shredded	½	red wine vinegar
		⅔	cup red currant jelly
4	apples, such as McIntosh or Empire, cored and thinly sliced	½	cup sweet wine, such as port + more if needed
½	teaspoon salt		

In a Dutch oven or other large heavy-bottomed saucepan with a cover, melt the butter over medium heat and stir in the cabbage and apples. Stir in the salt, brown sugar, and vinegar. Add the jelly and wine. Bring to the boiling point, then cover, lower the heat, and simmer for 20 minutes. Stir occasionally and add more wine if the mixture seems too dry.

If not serving immediately, let cool, cover, and refrigerate for up to 2 days.

To serve the dish: If you've made the dish ahead of time, heat it over medium heat for 10 minutes, or until hot. Place in a deep serving bowl with a deep serving spoon.

GREEN LENTILS WITH PANCETTA

YIELD | 10 SIDE-DISH SERVINGS

1	pound dried green lentils (about 2¼ cups)	2	cloves garlic, minced
2	tablespoons extra-virgin olive oil	6	cups chicken broth or water
5	slices pancetta or 4 slices smoked bacon, diced	½	teaspoon salt
1	medium/large onion, diced	2 or 3	sprigs fresh thyme or ½ teaspoon dried

Rinse the lentils and drain.

In a heavy-bottomed sauté pan or saucepan with a lid, heat the oil over medium heat. Sauté the pancetta or bacon until brown and beginning to crisp, 3 to 5 minutes. Remove to a paper towel with a slotted spoon.

Reduce the heat to medium-low and sauté the onion and garlic until the onion is translucent, about 5 minutes. Stir in the lentils. Add the broth, salt, and thyme and stir well. Cover, bring to a low boil, and simmer, stirring occasionally, until the lentils are tender, about 30 minutes.

Remove the cover, drain the lentils if necessary, and return them to the pan, along with the pancetta. The lentils can be cooled, covered, and refrigerated for 24 hours before serving.

To serve the dish: If you've made the lentils ahead, heat over medium-low heat, stirring frequently, until hot, about 10 minutes. Place in a serving bowl.

BÛCHE DE NOËL

A traditional French Christmas cake, Bûche de Noël, or Yule Log, is made to resemble a log out in the woods. There are four basic components: the cake, or roulade, that's brushed with rum syrup; the cream filling; the frosting; and the meringue "mushrooms." This is one of the few times that you need to like playing with your food. The preparation is very hands-on.

YIELD | 12 SERVINGS

Roulade

2	extra-large eggs	½	cup flour
1	extra-large egg yolk	2	tablespoons unsalted butter, melted + more for greasing
½	cup granulated sugar		Confectioners' sugar, for dusting
½	teaspoon pure vanilla extract		

Preheat the oven to 350°F. Lightly butter or spray a 17-by-12-inch jelly-roll pan and line with a Silpat liner or greased and floured parchment paper.

In a large heatproof bowl or the top of a double boiler, mix together the eggs, egg yolk, and granulated sugar. Place the bowl over simmering water to warm for 20 seconds. Remove from the heat and beat with an electric mixer for 5 minutes. Beat in the vanilla, flour, and 2 tablespoons butter until thick and creamy, about another 3 minutes. Pour the batter into the prepared pan.

Bake until the edges are very lightly browned and a cake tester comes out clean, about 10 minutes.

If you are using a Silpat, leave the roulade on the liner and place on a clean dish towel. Roll the cake up lengthwise, using the towel to tighten it. Place the wrapped roll on a rack. If you are using parchment, turn the warm roulade out onto a clean dish towel that has been dusted with confectioners' sugar. Roll and let cool on a rack.

Rum Syrup

2	tablespoons rum		1	teaspoon sugar
2	tablespoons water			

Heat all the ingredients in a small saucepan over medium-low heat, stirring, until the sugar is dissolved. Set aside.

Chestnut Pastry Cream

1	cup milk		1	cup fresh or canned chestnut puree
⅓	cup sugar			
3	large egg yolks, lightly beaten		½	pint (1 cup) heavy cream, whipped to firm peaks
½	teaspoon pure vanilla extract			
¼	cup instant flour			

In a medium heavy-bottomed saucepan over medium-low heat, whisk the milk and sugar until the milk reaches the boiling point, about 5 minutes. Whisk about ¼ cup of the hot milk into the egg yolks, then slowly pour the egg mixture back into the hot milk. Whisk in the vanilla and flour. Bring back to the boiling point, whisking constantly, until it thickens, 7 to 8 minutes.

Remove the pastry cream from the heat, transfer to a large bowl, and let cool. To hasten cooling, place in the refrigerator.

When the pastry cream is cool and you are ready to assemble the cake, mix together the pastry cream, chestnut puree, and whipped cream in a large bowl and set aside.

POTLUCK NOTE | *To cook chestnuts, use the sharp tip of a paring knife to cut an X through the shell on the flat side of each chestnut. Boil for 15 to 20 minutes or roast in a 400°F oven for 20 to 25 minutes. Peel the outer shell and inner skin and puree the chestnuts in a blender or ricer.*

(continued)

Chocolate Buttercream

6	ounces dark chocolate, melted	1	tablespoon pure vanilla extract
8	tablespoons (½ cup) soft, unsalted butter, at room-temperature	6	cups confectioners' sugar
		¼	cup heavy cream

In a large bowl, using an electric mixer at medium speed, beat together the chocolate and butter until well combined and fluffy. Add the vanilla and gradually beat in 4 cups of the sugar. Beat in the cream and add up to 2 cups of the remaining sugar to make a spreadable frosting. Set aside.

Meringue Mushrooms

2	large egg whites	½	cup superfine sugar
	Pinch of fine salt		Cocoa powder, for decorating
¼	teaspoon cream of tartar		

Preheat the oven to 200°F. Line a 13-by-9-inch baking pan with a Silpat liner or lightly buttered and floured parchment paper.

In a large bowl, whisk the egg whites, salt, and cream of tartar. Beat with an electric mixer at medium-high speed until soft peaks form. Gradually beat in the sugar, increasing the beating speed until the peaks are stiff and glossy.

Lightly fill a pastry tube (or a well-sealed plastic bag with a small hole cut in one corner) with a medium-small plain tip. With a gentle touch, place small, round dollops of meringue about ¾ to 1 inch in diameter on the prepared pan to make the mushroom caps. They will be slightly irregular, and some will have pointy tops, some not. This adds to their charm. Make some stems by pulling up on the pastry tube as you make little tails of meringue. Reserve a little of the meringue to glue the stems to the caps. You will have more than you need.

Bake for 1 hour 20 minutes. Remove from the oven and let rest for 20 minutes. Reduce the oven temperature to 180°F.

With the tip of a sharp paring knife, gently cut a small opening in the flat side of each mushroom cap. With a small tip on the pastry tube, place some unbaked meringue mixture in the opening and stick the stem in it. Repeat until all the stems and caps are assembled. Gently place back on the baking sheet. They will rest on their sides at an angle.

Return to the oven and bake for another 45 minutes. Remove from the oven and let cool in the pan for 1 hour. Remove the meringue mushrooms to paper towel–lined cake racks and let cool for another 2 hours. Before placing on the cake, lightly dust with cocoa.

To assemble the cake: Set the roulade, with the long edge facing you, on a flat surface covered with waxed paper. Brush with the Rum Syrup. Using a rubber spatula, cover with the Chestnut Pastry Cream, bringing it to within 1 inch of the long edge. Using the waxed paper as a guide, roll the cake into a log. Cut a slice from each end and reserve for two or three decorative branch stumps.

Frost the cake, including the ends, with the Chocolate Buttercream. Using a fork, make a bark pattern in the frosting. Cut the reserved end slices into thumb-shaped pieces—the stumps—frost them, and place on the log, using the frosting as glue.

Place the Meringue Mushrooms on and around the cake. If you have extras, place them in a single layer in a plastic bag and freeze them for another time.

Channukah

POTATO PANCAKES (LATKES) WITH CHUNKY APPLESAUCE

Because it uses a lot of oil, this dish commemorates the Channukah story of the miracle of the oil. Latkes are best served immediately, although you can refrigerate and reheat them. I have even frozen them and served them 2 weeks later with great success.

YIELD | 20 PANCAKES

2	pounds russet potatoes, peeled and held in a bowl of cold water to cover	1	teaspoon coarse salt
1	medium–large onion	3–4	cups canola or safflower oil
2	large eggs, lightly beaten		Chunky Applesauce (recipe follows), for serving
1	large egg yolk, lightly beaten	16	ounces (2 cups) sour cream, for serving
⅓	cup instant flour + more if needed		

Preheat the oven to 250°F.

Grate the potatoes on the medium shredder of a hand grater or with a food processor fitted with the medium shredding disk. Drain the potatoes and squeeze out extra moisture with a clean kitchen towel.

Grate the onion on a fine shredder or mini processor.

In a large bowl, mix together the potatoes, onion, eggs, egg yolk, ⅓ cup flour, and salt.

In a large heavy skillet, preferably cast-iron, heat ½ inch of the oil until it sizzles. Use a ladle or serving spoon equal to 2 tablespoons to drop pancakes into the hot oil. The pancakes should not touch, or they will stick together. They must be done in batches. Flatten slightly with the back of a spoon, but don't attempt to completely flatten them. Fry for 5 minutes, turn with a slotted spatula, and fry until crisp on the outside and well cooked inside, another 4 to 5 minutes. Repeat with the remaining pancake mixture. Add more oil to the pan after a couple of batches, as needed. Get it hot before frying more latkes.

Drain on paper towels and place on one or two baking sheets in the oven until ready to serve. Latkes taste best when served immediately, but they can be cooled, layered with waxed paper, and refrigerated for up to 24 hours.

To serve the dish: If you've made the latkes ahead of time, warm them in a single layer on one or two baking sheets in a 350°F oven until hot, about 10 minutes. Serve on a platter and accompany with bowls of Chunky Applesauce and sour cream.

Chunky Applesauce

YIELD | 8 CUPS

1	cup water
	Juice of 1 small lemon
½	cup sugar + more to taste
2	cinnamon sticks
1	teaspoon ground cinnamon
5	large sweet apples, such as Golden Delicious or Jonagold (about 2½ pounds)
5	large slightly tart apples, such as Rome or Northern Spy (about 2½ pounds)
1	teaspoon pure vanilla extract

In a large heavy saucepan with a lid, simmer the water, lemon juice, ½ cup sugar, cinnamon sticks, and ground cinnamon over medium heat.

Wash and core the apples, cut into eighths, then halve each piece crosswise. Stir into the saucepan, cover, and cook, stirring occasionally, for about 15 minutes. Uncover and continue cooking for another 10 minutes, stirring frequently with a wooden spoon and mashing the apples into a chunky sauce. If there is too much liquid (depending on the type of apples you use), continue to cook over low heat until some of the liquid has evaporated and the sauce is the texture that you want. Remove from the heat and stir in the vanilla.

Serve at room temperature, or let cool, cover, and refrigerate for up to 24 hours. Serve cold or at room temperature.

PEANUT SOUP

This weeklong spiritual celebration of African American heritage often features ingredients from Africa and the Caribbean. Peanuts are indigenous to both. Food etymologists believe that the nickname "goober" comes from the Kikongo word "nguba." George Washington Carver, an African American pioneer in agricultural science, developed many strains and uses of the peanut. But the main reason peanuts are part of holiday food: They are delicious.

YIELD | 10 SERVINGS

3	tablespoons unsalted butter, sliced
1	large onion, chopped
2	quarts chicken stock or broth
2	large tomatoes, chopped, or 1 can (15 ounces) diced tomatoes
2	yams, boiled and mashed
2	cloves garlic, crushed
1	piece ginger (2 inches), minced
	Salt, black pepper, and cayenne pepper
2	cups unsweetened crunchy peanut butter
½	pint heavy cream, warm
1	cup roasted peanuts, chopped

Melt the butter in a large stockpot over medium heat and stir in the onion. Cook, stirring, until the onion is golden brown, about 4 minutes.

Stir in the stock or broth, tomatoes, yams, garlic, and ginger and season with salt, black pepper, and cayenne pepper to taste. Bring to a low boil, lower heat to medium-low, and simmer until everything is well incorporated and hot. Blend with a long hand whisk.

Add the peanut butter and simmer for a few minutes more. Stir often to prevent the nut mixture from sticking. Simmer until the soup is thick and smooth.

To serve the dish: Pour into a warm tureen or deep bowl, swirl the heavy cream on top with a wooden spoon, and top with chopped peanuts.

SHRIMP AND CATFISH JAMBALAYA

Traditional food lore has it that the word "jambalaya" comes from "jambon" (French for "ham"), "à la" ("in the style of"), and "ya" (in one African dialect, the word for "rice"). Maybe, maybe not. This is another one of those forgiving classics, defined by whoever cooks it. This recipe is meatless for the sake of versatility, but feel free to use chunks of smoked ham or turkey.

YIELD | 10 TO 12 SERVINGS

¼	cup safflower or canola oil (or use the more traditional lard)	1½	teaspoons dried thyme
3	medium–large onions, diced	2	bay leaves (remove before serving)
3	medium–large red and green bell peppers, seeded and diced	2	cups medium-grain rice
3	ribs celery, sliced	2	cups thin tomato sauce + 2 cups more, if needed
¼–½	teaspoon cayenne pepper, or to taste	2	cups water
1	teaspoon black pepper	2	pounds catfish, cut into 2-inch chunks
1	teaspoon salt	1½	pounds shrimp, shelled and deveined
1	can (28 ounces) diced tomatoes	½	cup parsley, minced
6	cloves garlic, thinly sliced		
1	teaspoon dried oregano		

Heat the oil in a large Dutch oven or other stove-top casserole with a lid over medium heat. Sauté the onions, bell peppers, and celery for 7 minutes. Stir in the cayenne pepper, black pepper, and salt. Stir in the tomatoes and their liquid. Add the garlic, oregano, thyme, and bay leaves. Stir, bring to a low boil, and simmer for 5 minutes.

Stir in the rice, separating the grains. Add the 2 cups tomato sauce and water. Bring to a very low boil. Stir and cover. Cook over medium-low heat for 15 minutes. Stir in the catfish. Cover and simmer for another 10 minutes. Stir in the shrimp and simmer 5 minutes more. Make sure the rice is tender and the catfish and shrimp are cooked through, and remove from the heat. This dish is best served immediately, but it can be cooled, covered, and refrigerated for up to 1 day. Bring to room temperature and heat on top of the stove along with up to 2 cups tomato sauce so it is not too dry.

To serve the dish: Top with the parsley and serve from the pot.

BANANA RUM TART

YIELD | ONE 12-INCH TART (10 TO 12 SERVINGS)

Pastry Cream

2	cups whole milk		6	egg yolks
⅓	cup instant flour		½	teaspoon vanilla
6	tablespoons superfine sugar		2	tablespoons unsalted butter

Tart

1	prebaked 12-inch tart shell (see page 243)		6	firm, ripe bananas, sliced thin
			⅓	cup dark rum
5	tablespoons unsalted butter		1¼	cups apple or guava jelly
⅓	cup sugar		2	tablespoons kirsch, or any clear liqueur
3	tablespoons fresh lime juice			

To make the pastry cream: In a saucepan over medium heat, bring the milk to just below boiling. Remove from heat. In another saucepan, mix the flour, sugar, and egg yolks together. Slowly whisk the hot milk into the flour mixture over medium-low heat. Whisk continuously until the cream is smooth and thick, about 5 minutes. Remove from the heat. With a rubber spatula, stir in the vanilla and butter until creamy. Cool. The pastry cream may be covered and refrigerated for 24 hours.

To make the tart: Spoon the cooled pastry cream in the tart shell and gently smooth with a rubber spatula.

Heat 3 tablespoons of the butter in a heavy skillet over medium-low heat. Stir in the sugar and lime juice, and cook until golden brown, about 4 minutes. Stir the bananas into the butter mixture for 2 minutes to coat evenly. Remove from the heat and stir in the rum. With the aid of a spoon and a rubber spatula, spread the bananas over the pastry cream. Let cool.

For the glaze, melt the jelly and remaining 2 tablespoons of the butter in a small heavy pan, stirring constantly. Add the kirsch. Drizzle the glaze over the tart.

CHICKEN WITH DATES AND APRICOTS

Harira is a one-dish stew traditionally served to break the fast of Ramadan. This is a variation done in two parts, so that one can please vegetarians. A good dessert might be fresh figs stuffed with goat cheese and drizzled with flavorful honey. A beverage of mint tea sweetened with honey complements these aromatic dishes.

YIELD | 10 SERVINGS

2	whole chickens (3–4 pounds each), cut into eighths	1	cup dried apricots
2	cloves garlic, minced	1	cup dried pitted dates, halved lengthwise
½	cup orange juice	1½	cups chicken broth
1	teaspoon ground cumin	1	tablespoon minced fresh cilantro
½	teaspoon ground cinnamon	1	tablespoon minced fresh mint
5	tablespoons extra-virgin olive oil		Salt and pepper
1	medium–large onion, diced		

Wash and dry the chickens, then place in a large, flat baking dish. In a medium bowl, mix the garlic, orange juice, cumin, cinnamon, and 2 tablespoons of the oil. Pour the marinade over the chicken, cover, and marinate in the refrigerator for 4 hours, stirring occasionally.

Heat the remaining 3 tablespoons oil in a large Dutch oven or other heavy pot with a lid over medium heat. Sauté the onion until golden brown, about 5 minutes. Remove with a slotted spoon and set aside.

Drain the chicken and set aside the marinade. Sauté the chicken in the Dutch oven, turning frequently, until browned, about 10 minutes. Add the apricots, dates, broth, cilantro, mint, reserved onion and marinade, and salt and pepper to taste. Bring to the boiling point, stir, cover, lower heat, and simmer gently for 30 minutes. Remove the lid and simmer until the chicken is fork-tender, about 30 minutes longer.

The dish can be cooled, covered, and refrigerated for up to 2 days.

To serve the dish: Serve hot, with Rice, Lentil, and Chickpea Casserole (page 297). If you've made the chicken ahead of time, heat over medium-low heat, stirring occasionally, until hot, about 15 minutes.

RICE, LENTIL, AND CHICKPEA CASSEROLE

YIELD | 10 SERVINGS

3	tablespoons extra-virgin olive oil	1	teaspoon ground cardamom
2	onions, sliced	1	teaspoon crushed red pepper flakes, or to taste (optional)
2	teaspoons grated fresh ginger		
2	cups cooked rice	1	can (28 ounces) diced tomatoes
1	cup cooked lentils	½	cup minced fresh cilantro, for garnish
1	can (15 ounces) chickpeas, rinsed and drained		
		½	cup minced fresh flat-leaf parsley, for garnish
1	teaspoon ground cinnamon		
½	teaspoon ground nutmeg		

Heat the oil in a large heavy-bottomed saucepan over medium heat. Add the onions and sauté until well browned, about 5 minutes. Remove with a slotted spoon and set aside. Stir in the ginger and rice, stirring to separate the grains, and cook until lightly browned, about 5 minutes. Stir in the lentils and chickpeas, add the spices and reserved onions, and stir. Mix in the tomatoes with their liquid and bring to a boil. Reduce the heat and simmer for 30 minutes, stirring occasionally.

The rice and beans can be cooled, covered, and refrigerated for up to 2 days.

To serve the dish: If you've made the dish ahead of time, heat over medium-low heat until hot, about 10 to 15 minutes. Garnish with the cilantro and parsley and serve hot.

Cinco de Mayo

MEXICAN CHOCOLATE CAKE

The 15th of September is Mexican's true Independence Day and celebrates its separation from Spain in 1810. On May 5, 1862, the region of Puebla in Mexico won a huge victory against the French. Traditionally a local holiday, it has grown into an annual celebration of Mexican popular culture, with food and drink and music. Cinco de Mayo has become an American tradition celebrated more north of the Mexican border than south.

YIELD | 12 SERVINGS

Cake

1½	cups cake flour
1¼	cups sugar
⅔	cup cocoa or dark chocolate powder
1	teaspoon baking powder
1	teaspoon baking soda
2	teaspoons ground cinnamon
½	teaspoon cayenne pepper
1	teaspoon ancho chili powder
3	large eggs, lightly beaten

2	teaspoons pure vanilla extract
5	tablespoons corn, canola, or safflower oil
½	cup milk
1	tablespoon white vinegar
½	cup red jalapeño pepper jelly, such as Goya
2	tablespoons unsalted butter + more for greasing

Frosting

4	ounces dark chocolate, chopped
1	teaspoon ground cinnamon
3	tablespoons heavy cream
2	tablespoons unsalted butter

½	teaspoon pure vanilla extract
12	beautiful whole small, long red and green chili peppers, such as Fresno, Colorado, or Anaheim, for decoration

Cinnamon Whipped Cream

1	cup (½ pint) heavy whipping cream
1	tablespoon superfine sugar

¼	teaspoon pure vanilla extract
½	teaspoon cinnamon

(continued)

Preheat the oven to 350°F. Butter the bottom and sides of a 9-inch cake pan. Line the bottom with buttered parchment paper.

To make the cake: In a medium bowl, lightly stir the flour, sugar, cocoa or chocolate powder, baking powder, baking soda, cinnamon, cayenne, and chili powder with a fork.

In a large bowl, beat the eggs with an electric mixer until light and creamy. Beat in the vanilla and oil then mix in the flour-cocoa mixture, milk, and vinegar.

Pour into the prepared pan and bake for 30 minutes. Lower the oven temperature to 300° and bake until a cake tester comes out clean, about 25 minutes more.

Cool in the pan on a cake rack for 15 to 20 minutes. The cake will still be warm. Remove from the pan, turn upside down on a wire rack, and remove the parchment paper. Leave flat side up on the wire rack.

In a small saucepan, melt the jelly and 2 tablespoons butter. Spread on the top and sides of the cake while warm. Let cool completely, then cover the cake with the chocolate frosting.

To make the frosting: Place the chocolate, cinnamon, cream, and butter in the top of a double boiler. Set over simmering water until well blended and shiny. Remove from the heat and stir in the vanilla. When room temperature, frost the cake. Refrigerate.

To make the cinnamon whipped cream: Whip the cream in a medium-large bowl with an electric mixer on medium-high or with a balloon whisk. As it thickens, add the sugar, vanilla, and cinnamon. When stiff peaks form, cover the bowl with plastic wrap and refrigerate. Transfer to a serving bowl when ready to serve.

To serve the dish: Serve at room temperature with the cinnamon whipped cream in a serving bowl alongside. Garnish with the brightly colored peppers. Make sure to tell people that they are not marzipan. Or, if you are especially ambitious, make them from marzipan.

POTLUCK NOTE | *This cake can be made and kept in the refrigerator for several days before serving. When it is fully iced, the icing seals it and it will stay moist.*

POT-ROASTED BEEF WITH FRUIT AND VEGETABLES (TZIMMES)

The Jewish New Year is celebrated with sweet food; bitter and sour foods are avoided. This tradition is said to express the hope of good things to come. The apples, sweet potatoes, carrots, prunes, and orange juice in this traditional dish represent wishes for sweetness and abundance in the year to come. It is usually accompanied by round challah loaves and little dipping bowls of honey.

YIELD | 10 SERVINGS

½	pound pitted prunes, picked over for pieces of pits	½	teaspoon ground cinnamon
1	cup orange juice	2	cinnamon sticks (optional)
3	tablespoons extra-virgin olive oil	⅛	teaspoon ground cloves
5	pounds brisket (not corned beef)		Grated zest of 1 orange
	Salt and pepper	6	large carrots (about 1½ pounds), scraped and cut into 1-inch slices
2	cups sliced onions	4	sweet potatoes (about 1½ pounds), peeled and cut into 2-inch pieces
3	cloves garlic, minced		
⅔	cup beef broth		
2	tablespoons tomato paste	2	cups dried apple rings, each halved
1	teaspoon dried thyme	⅓	cup brown sugar
1	tablespoon minced fresh ginger		

Preheat the oven to 350°F.

In a small bowl, soak the prunes in the orange juice. Set aside.

Heat the oil in a large ovenproof Dutch oven or heavy roasting pan with a lid over medium heat. Season the brisket with salt and pepper, add it to the Dutch oven, and brown on all sides for 10 minutes. Add the onions and garlic and cook, stirring, until wilted, about 5 minutes. Remove the Dutch oven from the heat.

In a medium bowl, stir together the broth, tomato paste, thyme, ginger, ground cinnamon, cinnamon sticks (if using), cloves, and orange zest. Pour over the brisket.

(continued)

Cover the pan, place it in the oven, and roast for 1 hour 45 minutes.

Add the carrots, sweet potatoes, apples, and brown sugar to the brisket. Roast for another 45 minutes. Drain the prunes, discard the juice, and stir the prunes into the tzimmes. Roast for another 30 minutes, then check to see if the pan is dry. If so, add a cup of water.

Roast the tzimmes until the meat is fork-tender, 3½ to 4 hours total. Check every 30 minutes and add water if needed.

To serve the dish: Place the beef on a large platter and slice. Top with the fruit and vegetables and any pan juices. Serve with a serving fork and spoon.

HONEY CAKE (LAKECH)

YIELD | TWO 9-INCH LOAVES

4	tablespoons pareve (containing no milk or meat products) margarine
3	cups all-purpose flour
½	teaspoon salt
1	teaspoon ground cinnamon
¼	teaspoon ground cloves
½	teaspoon ground nutmeg
1	teaspoon cream of tartar
2	cups dark honey
1	cup orange juice
½	cup brewed black coffee

¼	cup sugar
2	tablespoons canola oil
1	extra-large egg, lightly beaten
½	cup fig conserve (optional)
½	cup raisins
½	cup diced dried apricots
½	cup pistachios
½	cup coarsely chopped walnuts
½	cup slivered almonds

Preheat the oven to 375°F. Coat two 9-by-5-inch loaf pans with the margarine.

In a large bowl, using a fork, mix the flour, salt, spices, and cream of tartar.

In another large bowl, mix the honey, juice, and coffee, then whisk in the sugar, oil, and egg. If using, add the fig conserve, stirring well so it isn't too lumpy, then add the raisins and apricots.

Using a wooden spoon, stir the honey mixture, pistachios, and walnuts into the flour mixture until well blended. Pour the batter into the prepared pans and sprinkle the almonds on top.

Bake in the middle of the oven for 15 minutes. Reduce the temperature to 350°F and bake until a cake tester comes out clean, another 45 minutes.

Let cool completely in the pans on a cake rack before removing the honey cakes from the pans. If not serving immediately, cover in parchment paper, wrap in foil, and keep at room temperature for up to 2 days.

MATZOHLA, BREAKFAST OF GENIUSES

One of the seasonal best-sellers of my business enterprises, Studio Food, was this amazing granola-like mixture. It was described in New York *magazine and sold across the country, from the Hamptons to Beverly Hills.*

YIELD | 4 QUARTS

1	cup canola oil	1½	pounds matzoh farfel
½	cup (¼ pound) unsalted butter	1½	cups (8 ounces) chopped pecans
1	cup water	2	cups (5 ounces) coconut flakes
1	cup packed brown sugar	2	cups raisins, soaked in orange juice and drained
½	cup honey	½	pound chopped dates
1	tablespoon ground cinnamon		

Preheat the oven to 400°F. Line four baking sheets with foil.

In a heavy saucepan over low heat, stir the oil, butter, water, brownsugar, honey, and cinnamon until blended.

Spread the farfel on the prepared baking sheets, pour the honey mixture over each, and stir. Bake for 12 minutes.

In a bowl, mix together the pecans, coconut, raisins, and dates. Place one-quarter of the mixture on each baking sheet of farfel and stir in with a rubber spatula. Bake for up to another 30 minutes. Stir frequently.

Remove from the oven and set the sheets on wire racks. Make sure the mixture is cool and dry, with no large clumps, before placing in 1-quart airtight containers, preferably not plastic. Matzohla will keep, covered and refrigerated, for up to 4 weeks.

To serve the dish: Serve as is or with additional dried or fresh fruit and milk in a bowl, or eat it by the handful as a snack.

LEMON-WALNUT FLOURLESS CAKE

This cake is made in many variations with the same ingredients. It is usually very moist, almost like a pudding cake.

YIELD | 12 SERVINGS

Cake

8	large egg yolks	⅓	cup potato starch
2	cups sugar	1	cup ground walnuts
	Juice of 2½ large lemons	1	tablespoon grated lemon zest (see page 316)
⅓	cup canola oil + more for greasing	5	egg whites, beaten to soft peaks
⅓	cup water		
¾	cup matzoh flour + more for dusting		

Topping

3	egg whites	¼	cup sugar
½	cup ground walnuts		Juice of ½ large lemon

Preheat the oven to 350°F. Grease a 9-inch square cake pan with canola oil and dust with matzoh flour.

To make the cake: In a large bowl, beat the egg yolks and sugar by hand or with an electric mixer until pale and fluffy. Beat in the lemon juice, ⅓ cup oil, and water. Beat or mix in the ¾ cup flour, potato starch, walnuts, and lemon zest. Fold in the beaten egg whites, and pour into the prepared pan. Bake for 25 minutes. Meanwhile, make the topping.

To make the topping: Beat the egg whites in a bowl, by hand or with an electric mixer, until white and foamy—old recipes say "like fallen snow." Stir the walnuts into the egg whites, then mix in the sugar and lemon juice. Set aside.

When the cake has baked for 25 minutes, remove it from the oven but do not turn the oven off. Spread the cake with the topping, return it to the oven, and bake for 10 minutes longer. Let cool in the pan on a cake rack. Serve warm, or let cool completely, cover with plastic wrap, and keep for 24 hours, or until ready to serve. The cake will be very moist.

ROAST LEG OF LAMB WITH ROSEMARY AND JUNIPER BERRIES

Eating lamb at Easter is an ancient tradition; there was a time in early church history when it was taken to the altar and blessed before it was cooked.

YIELD | 10 SERVINGS

1	leg of lamb (8–9 pounds)	2	tablespoons chopped fresh rosemary
1	teaspoon sea salt + more to taste	2½	cups chicken or vegetable stock
	Freshly ground pepper	1	cup gin
2	tablespoons juniper berries, crushed with a mortar and pestle or placed in a towel and hit with a hammer	3	sprigs rosemary, for garnish
			Pan gravy
6	cloves garlic, sliced lengthwise	2½	cups prepared mint jelly, for serving
4	tablespoons olive oil		

Preheat the oven to 350°F. Have ready a roasting pan that can take the heat on the stove top.

Trim the lamb of some but not all fat and rub with the 1 teaspoon salt, pepper to taste, and 1 tablespoon of the berries. With the tip of a paring knife, make about eight tiny cuts into the lamb and insert some of the garlic slices.

Heat the oil in the roasting pan over medium-high heat, then add the lamb and sear on all sides until well browned, turning occasionally, for 10 minutes. Add the chopped rosemary, stock, gin, and the remaining garlic and 1 tablespoon berries and bring to a low boil. Remove from the heat and cover with a lid or two layers of heavy-duty foil.

Transfer to the oven and roast for 2 to 2½ hours, turning the lamb after 1 hour, or until a meat thermometer reads 160°F for medium, 170°F for well done. Remove the lamb to a serving platter, garnish with the rosemary sprigs, and let stand for 20 minutes before carving. Strain the pan juices, skim the fat, and heat for a small amount of pan gravy. Season with salt and pepper to taste.

To serve the dish: Most people like to see the whole roast on a platter, perhaps surrounded by pan-roasted or steamed new potatoes and accompanied by fresh cooked asparagus. If you prefer, the roast can be sliced and placed on a warm platter. Serve the hot gravy in a gravy boat or pitcher, accompanied by the mint jelly in a bowl.

HOT CROSS BUNS

"One a penny, two a penny, hot cross buns" is an old British street sellers' cry. Written records relate that the buns have been an Easter treat for several centuries.

YIELD | 24 BUNS

Buns

1½	cups milk	½	teaspoon ground nutmeg
1	package (¼ ounce) + ½ teaspoon active dry yeast	½	teaspoon grated lemon zest (see page 316)
1	teaspoon + ½ cup granulated sugar	2	large egg yolks, lightly beaten
5	tablespoons unsalted butter, melted + more for greasing	4½–5	cups all-purpose flour
		1	cup currants
1	teaspoon salt	1	egg white, beaten

Icing

1	cup confectioners' sugar	2	tablespoons cream
½	teaspoon pure vanilla extract		Up to 3 tablespoons milk, if needed
2	teaspoons fresh lemon juice		

To make the buns: Scald the milk in a small pot over medium heat. Do not let it boil. Pour into a large bowl and let cool until lukewarm.

In a small bowl, mix the yeast, 1 teaspoon of the granulated sugar, and ¼ cup of the scalded milk.

To the larger bowl of cooled milk, add the 5 tablespoons butter, salt, nutmeg, lemon zest, and the remaining ½ cup granulated sugar. Stir well and incorporate the yeast mixture and egg yolks, stirring constantly. Gradually add 4 cups of the flour. The mixture will be sticky.

Add the remaining ½ to 1 cup flour and knead for about 5 minutes, until the dough is smooth and elastic. Cover the bowl lightly with a damp non-terry cloth kitchen towel and let the dough rest for 20 minutes.

Add the currants to the dough, turn out onto a floured surface, and knead for another 5 minutes.

Coat a clean bowl with melted butter and place the dough in it, turning the dough to coat. Cover the bowl with a damp non-terry cloth kitchen towel until the dough doubles in bulk, about 1½ hours.

Preheat the oven to 375°F. Line two large baking sheets with parchment paper or Silpat liners.

Divide the dough in quarters. Make six rolls out of each quarter and place them 1 inch apart on the prepared baking sheets. Cover lightly with clean, damp kitchen towels (not terry cloth) and let rise for 1½ hours.

Brush the tops lightly with the beaten egg white. Mark a cross on the top of each bun with a single-edged safety razor blade or a lame.

Bake the buns for 20 minutes, until browned. Remove to cake racks.

To make the icing: Put the confectioners' sugar in a bowl and stir in the vanilla, lemon juice, and cream. The mixture should have the consistency of toothpaste. If it doesn't, add the milk 1 tablespoon at a time until you get the desired consistency. Place the icing in a tightly sealed plastic bag with a small hole cut in the corner. Squeeze out the icing slowly, following the cross marks, to ice the buns.

TIPS FOR POTLUCKING

These days, luck plays only a small part in most of our gatherings—and sometimes there is not a pot in sight. But any time people get together, and some or all of them bring food to eat together, it's a potluck. It would seem from my travels that is the way America is eating today, and we are enjoying every moment of it. My favorite quote from a host is: "We like to eat. We especially like to eat good food. But we really, *really* like to eat good food with each other."

Dinner parties and small buffets tend to be very organized but sometimes, large events take on a life of their own. For example, I remember attending a very Happy New Year's party where we had everything from sushi to potato pancakes.

Whether your potluck is large or small, the following tips can help make your event a success.

The first three tips are: Communicate. Communicate. Communicate.

HOSTING

It is important to understand that even though you are hosting, you won't have total control. However, hosting the event is your main task. Your hospitality and generosity in opening your home (or establishing a special location) is a huge contribution and very rewarding. Think of it as taking the pressure off your guests to make a lot of decisions. Usually 2 to 3 weeks is enough of a heads-up for something simple; for a special event, you might want to start planning 1 to 2 months ahead.

The secret to success is organizing. Start with phone calls or emails to the people you think that you can count on and tell them what you have in mind. If someone on your list says that they don't think they can prepare anything, for whatever reason, never, *never* uninvite them. Suggest that perhaps they can bring a loaf of really great bread or just the pleasure of their company.

Whether you're the host or the guest at the next potluck, look through this book and see what strikes your fancy. The recipes are, as promised, crowd-pleasers. You might want to buddy up with one or more people who are invited and collaborate so that each of you makes something from a different chapter.

BY THE NUMBERS

Menu planning works something like this. If you are having 10 to 12 people at a potluck, you will want two or three appetizers, one main dish, two sides, a salad, good bread and butter (or extra-virgin olive oil for dipping), condiments, two desserts, and beverages. If the number of guests is doubled, simply have three or four appetizers, double the volume of the main dish or have two or three different ones, three sides, a large salad, and three desserts, along with the other elements of the meal. Sometimes there will be a guest who always likes to make salad or dessert. That's fine. Work with it. If there are too many offers for the same dish just politely say, "We already have three pasta salads. Please bring that delicious soup you make." Don't be too rigid. You can ask for a specific course but then see what people want to make. It's supposed to be fun.

When you are hosting ask people to bring food as finished and ready-to-serve as possible. Double check what guests need in the way of stove-top or oven use, refrigerator or freezer space. Do they need electric outlets? Will a heavy-duty extension cord be necessary? Let people know what to expect. Ask them if they are bringing food in or with a serving dish and inquire about any special utensils and condiments that may be needed. And don't forget ice. Often a large Styrofoam cooler will hold enough ice for a single event.

SERVING STATIONS AND TABLE SET-UP

If it's possible, set up "stations" as the pros do. One table, credenza, or buffet top for appetizers; one surface for the main portion of the meal; and another for coffee and dessert will go a long way to present your potluck choices at their best. A teacart or a folding table makes a nice bar and will keep spills at a minimum. One friend in a small apartment uses a sturdy ironing board as a serving table and covers it with a tablecloth over plastic. I used to be averse to those little TV tables, but they can come in very handy when you want to eat and drink at the same time.

PLEASE BE SEATED

If you want everyone seated at the same table and you don't have one with many leaves, you can make a T out of two tables. You can also rent a 72-inch folding table if you have the room and the budget for it. This size seats 10 to 12 comfortably. Some places will even rent just a tabletop that you can set on your own table to enlarge it. A friend rents three 4-foot tables for her parties; the rental fee is $25 for all three tables. The upside of rental: You don't have to worry about storing unwieldy tables between events! In addition, that assortment of folding chairs most of us have acquired look great with washable slipcovers that give them a clean and comfortable look. Of course, your choice depends entirely on the size of your home and your inclination.

MAKING ROOM

If you are hosting an event where you expect guests to mingle, clear furniture surfaces in the room where guests will be eating and drinking. It may look sparse before your guests arrive, but everyone will appreciate having a place to set down a plate or glass. Whatever you decide, remember that most people are thrilled to be out and about sharing good food and good company, and they're not worried about how you set up your dining area.

POTLUCK SERVING SIZES

Each recipe in this book lists the serving portions and amounts, and most of these recipes were created to serve 8 to 12 people. Before scaling up or scaling down a recipe, it's best to first cook (or bake) it as written. If you need a greater quantity for your potluck, I'd suggest making the recipe in two batches, rather than doubling it. That way, you won't have to adjust pan sizes and oven temperatures. However, many of these recipes can be easily doubled or halved to suit your crowd. If you double the recipe but don't really need as many as 20 to 24 portions, check the recipe to see if the remainder can be frozen for a later meal.

Potlucks offer an opportunity to taste and enjoy a sampling of many flavors. The larger the group, the more forgiving the menu. Guests will appreciate the two lasagnas and the two apple pies (and they were probably made with very different recipes). Everyone understands that if one dish is already empty on this end of the table, there's another dish over there that looks just as delicious. If more than 10 to 20 people are expected at an event, the serving size of each dish does not have to equal the number of guests, unless of course you volunteered to provide that amount.

TRY YOUR LUCK

I suggest that you ignore the old saw about not cooking something new when you are presenting food to others. What better time to expand your repertoire or elaborate on an old favorite! Since you are usually making only one dish for a potluck, stretch your skills a bit and try Fillet of Fish en Papillotte or Tiramisu. That being said, if you have never made a pie before and are worried about rolling out piecrust, it might be better to give the recipe a whirl a week or two before the event. For most dishes, though, if you think you can do it—you probably can.

GATHER YOUR INGREDIENTS

Read the recipe thoroughly before you go shopping. Make a list of ingredients that you may need to buy and check that you have the pans and tools needed. You can often improvise, but you don't want the crust rolled and the oven hot only to find out that your pie pan is not 10 inches across.

TAKING YOUR DISH ALONG

If you're traveling to a potluck, be sure to decide ahead of time how you will transport the dish. To keep cold food cold and hot food hot, refrigerate food before putting it into a cooled insulated container or heat food before putting it into a warmed thermal carrier. Cold gel packs are an inexpensive and effective coolant. You can also buy hot packs that can be heated in a microwave or regular oven. If you have the room to store them, inexpensive Styrofoam chests are very handy for cold or hot food. There are also insulated, soft-sided thermal carriers that zip closed and are very effective in keeping foods cold or hot.

FRESH FROM SCRATCH

Virtually all the recipes in this book call for fresh ingredients. These days, with few exceptions, supermarkets and specialty stores have abundant choices. And many, with a week or so notice, will get you what you want. Amazing! You can, of course, successfully make some substitutions. At the end of the day, once you get used to a mainly 'from scratch' kitchen, you will find cooking actually much easier and more rewarding.

Meat, poultry, fish and shellfish are best used fresh, rather than frozen, especially if you are going to freeze the dish you are making. If you do use these ingredients frozen, thaw them completely before cooking.

- I would request that no substitutes be made for fresh lemon, lime, or orange juice or the zest of their fruits. Artificial or processed citrus flavors always seem to give a chemical taste to dishes prepared with them.
- Garlic has some of the same issues. There really is no substitute for fresh garlic. It should almost never be served raw; if it is, discard the central green stem in each clove and thoroughly smash the clove. Pure garlic powder will give you the closest taste. Other forms are less dependable.
- To put it bluntly, I never use margarine because I don't like it. If you want to substitute margarine for butter for dietary reasons, it will often work.
- If a vegetable or a berry is out of season, you can substitute frozen for fresh. Canned foods, with the exception of tomatoes and beans, aren't as good.
- As far as salads go, try to avoid packaged mixed greens. They simply don't have the flavorful crunch you get from 2 or 3 heads of lettuce. Single-item packages, such as baby spinach or arugula, seem more appetizing.
- Try to use fresh herbs and whole spices that you mince or crush as needed for a recipe. To substitute dried herbs for fresh, use about ⅓ the amount of the dried. When you buy spices, put the date on them so that you know when they are no longer at their peak. Ground spices are good for about a year and whole spices for two.
- It is better to fill your own spray bottle with the oil of your choice than to use commercially prepared bottles, which have chemical propellants that eventually ruin the surface of your cookware.

SPECIAL DIETARY NEEDS

There are endless opinions about individual allergies, distastes, and dietary preferences. My position is that it is the responsibility of any adult with food concerns to honor them by taking charge of what they need to eat and not expect to a group meal to comply with their special needs. For instance, though the host should indicate the presence of peanuts, the person with the allergy should inquire. The same is true of shellfish or wheat or dairy products. If you are hosting, never push anyone to eat anything they don't want to. On the other hand, if you are a guest, ask before eating a dish that may not be good for you and set aside for yourself a good portion of the dish that you prepared.

A WORD ABOUT KITCHEN CLEANLINESS

Once a month, clean out your refrigerator. Throw away everything that's past its prime, especially "mystery" containers. The adage is "When in doubt, throw it out." Don't taste or ask anyone else to taste food you think is *off.* This will free up space to store a stew overnight or to chill bowls of cookie dough.

Use hot, soapy water. Wash your hands, utensils, equipment, and work surfaces thoroughly in hot, soapy water for 30 seconds before and after you come into contact with any food. Rinse equipment well and dry with paper towels or kitchen towels.

Take care not to contaminate. Don't cross-contaminate by letting bacteria spread from one food product to another. Keep raw meat, poultry, and seafood away from ready-to-eat foods. If you have drained a marinade from raw food, do not use it as is. You may continue basting whatever you are cooking, or bring it to a boil if you want to use it as a base for sauce. Never place cooked food on the same plate that was used for raw food without washing the plate first.

Call if you have questions. The USDA has great toll-free resources for consumers with food safety questions. Call the USDA Meat and Poultry Hotline at (888) 674-6854 or email at mphotline.fsis@usda.gov. The hotline is available in English and Spanish and can be reached from 10:00 a.m. to 4:00 p.m. (Eastern Time) on weekdays.

USEFUL KITCHEN HINTS

These culinary tips will help you prepare some of the recipes in *Crowd-Pleasing Potluck*.

HEAT SETTINGS

- High heat is for boiling only.
- Medium to medium-high heat is for sautéing and frying.

- Medium-low heat is for heating and keeping food hot.
- Low heat is for simmering and preparing sauces.

If you're using an electric range and need to move a pot from high to medium or low, it is better to have a second burner ready to go at the lower temperature, rather than waiting for the electric burner to cool down.

ROASTING GARLIC

To roast garlic whole, remove the outermost papery skins. Cut about ½-inch from the top of the head, trimming just enough to expose the tips of the garlic cloves. Place the garlic, root end down, in a baking dish or on foil and generously drizzle olive oil over the head. Cover tightly with foil and bake at 325°F until tender, about 45 minutes to 1 hour.

TOASTING COCONUT

Preheat the oven to 325°F. Place the shredded coconut in a single layer on a baking sheet, breaking up any clumps. Bake for about 7 to 10 minutes until golden brown. Every 2 to 3 minutes turn the coconut with a spatula so that it browns evenly. The coconut will crisp a bit as it browns. Remove the baking sheet from the oven and transfer the coconut to a cool baking sheet to stop the cooking.

MAKING CITRUS ZEST

The zest of citrus fruit is the thin, brightly colored portion of the outer peel; it's rich in flavorful oils and is used to infuse sauces and garnishes. For slivers of zest, use a citrus zester, vegetable peeler, or a sharp paring knife to remove strips of zest, taking care not to peel into the bitter white pith. Go slowly when peeling to create continuous strips of zest.

To grate zest, use a multisided grater or Microplane grater and rub the fruit back and forth; work over a plate to catch the grated zest. Rotate the fruit as you work, making sure that you do not remove the bitter white pith (or membrane) just underneath the peel. Be careful not to cut your fingertips when zesting because graters can be very sharp.

CLARIFIED BUTTER

This traditional cooking ingredient predates refrigeration. These days, it is best to store it in the refrigerator for up to 3 to 4 weeks. Slice 1 pound (4 sticks) of unsalted butter and place it in a small, heavy saucepan over medium-low heat. When the butter melts and starts to foam, lower the heat. Do not stir. Remove from the heat after five minutes when the surface is covered with foam. Skim off the foam and discard. You will see clear butter separated from the milk solids. Strain the clear butter into a clean glass jar or container (plastic is not recommended) that has a tight cover. Cool, cover, and refrigerate. Use clarified butter in recipes when it's called for and for sautéing; it has a higher burning point and a more delicate taste than whole butter.

THE SCOVILLE SCALE

Developed by chemist Water Scoville in 1912, the Scoville Scale was developed to measure the "heat" in chili peppers. The higher the number of Scoville units, the hotter the pepper. Peppers contain capsaicin, and the Scoville Scale measures the amount of capsaicin in various peppers. Bell or sweet peppers do not contain measurable amounts of capsaicin so they score zero on the scale. Habenero peppers, on the other hand, have a rating of 300,000 or more.

THE SCOVILLE SCALE	
Pepper	**Scoville Rating**
Bell pepper	*0*
Pepperoncini	*100–500*
Anaheim pepper	*500–1000*
Poblano pepper	*1,000–1,500*
Jalapeño pepper	*2,500–8,000*
Chipotle pepper	*2,500–10,000*
Wax pepper	*5,000–10,000*
Serrano pepper	*10,000–23,000*
Cayenne pepper	*30,000–50,000*
Thai pepper	*50,000–100,000*
Habenero pepper	*100,000–350,000*

MENUS

IN MANY WAYS the recipes in this book offer an embarrassment of riches. For the most part, you will be able to mix and match dishes to your heart's content. The following menus are just suggestions and takeoff points.

You know what you enjoy cooking and who will be eating. Some people like large amounts of a single dish, others like to taste a bit of everything. Some of the following are traditional, some are traditional with a twist.

The simplest meal prepared and shared with the gracious give-and-take of comfortable hospitality can be savored and remembered with more pleasure than any preparation that strains your goodwill. These menus will give you a good idea of the possibilities. I encourage you to explore the recipes in this book and make notes for your own menus so you can prepare for many delicious get-togethers.

Continental Breakfast

Strawberry-Banana Smoothies 233

Franana Banana Bread 265

Oatmeal Bread 268

Assorted Flavored Butters and Jams*

Deviled Eggs 20

Blueberry Cake 253

Coffee and Tea

Wedding Brunch

Dilled Shrimp 21

Smoked Salmon–Potato Cups 23

Vegetable Frittata 175

Assorted Mini Muffins
  (Breads, Rolls, and Muffins chapter; all muffin recipes can be made in
  mini sizes)

Poached Pears with White Wine and
  Shaved Parmesan Cheese 197

Madeleines 218

Welcome Wagon Buffet

Homemade Hummus 7

Roasted Eggplant Dip (Baba Ghanoush) 10

Crispy Pita Chips 14

Crudités

Salade Niçoise 27

Coq au Vin (Chicken In Wine) 92

Potato-Turnip Gratin 172

Greek-Style Green Pole Beans 164

Lemon Meringue Pie 237

The Big Game Buffet

Crudités

Baked Buffalo Chicken Wings **13**

Coleslaw with Raisins and Caraway Seeds **40**

Chili Mole **111**

Cooked Rice

Chili Dogs (hot dogs on warm buns topped with Chili Mole, page 111)

Jalapeño Corn Bread **269**

Assorted Cookies (Desserts chapter)

Fresh Fruit

Awards Show Buffet

Spicy Black Olives with Garlic and Herbs **4**
   and Seville-Style Olives **3**

Ginger-Roasted Almonds **5**
   and Spicy Pecans **6**

Basic Mixed Salad **34**

Mediterranean Stuffed Peppers **81**

Flounder Roulades Florentine **148**

Cherry Clafouti **207**

Hazelnut Biscotti with Chocolate Icing **227**

Church Social

Carrot-Ginger Soup **181**

Chicken Curry with Peach Chutney **97**

Shrimp Coconut Curry with Basmati Rice **152**

S'mores Bread Pudding **195**

After-Church Get-Together

Spinach Strawberry Salad with Poppy-Seed Dressing 33

Minestrone with Pesto 61

Southern Ham Casserole with Stewed Peaches 125

Parker House Rolls 260

Crunchy Apple Crisp 205

Informal Get-Together

Basic Mixed Salad 34

Poppy Seed Rolls 259

Moussaka 122

Pastitsio: Greek Macaroni and Cheese 64

Ginger-Peachy Cobbler 206

Lunch Meeting

Cobb Salad 28

Filet of Fish en Papillote 141

Wild Rice Casserole 76

Summer Strawberry Shortcake 247

Book Club

Mixed Spring Salad 35

Bestilla (Moroccan Chicken Pie in Fillo) 100

Lemon Squares 212

Raspberry Bars 213

Planning Committee

Country Salad with Lardons 31

Southwest Vegetable Chili 182

Jalapeño Corn Bread 269

Baked Apples with Balsamic Reduction 200

New York Black-and-White Cookies 215

Guests of Honor

Crab Cakes with Remoulade Sauce 135

Artichoke-Spinach Dip 17

Pork Crown Roast with Apple Stuffing and
Mustard Sauce 129

Poached Pears with White Wine and
Shaved Parmesan Cheese 197

Pine Nut Cookies 225

Triple-Chocolate Cookies 208

Vegetarian Dinner

Mixed Bean Salad 45

Pasta Squares with Roasted Vegetables 63

Easy Olive Bread 270

Dried Winter Fruit Compote with Raisin Sauce 203

Carol's Old-Fashioned Gingerbread 256

Bon Voyage Party

Assorted Hors d'Oeuvres 1

Fennel-Arugula-Parmesan Salad 30

Rosemary Focaccia 273

Roasted Rosemary-Garlic Chicken 103

Oven-Roasted Root Vegetables 170

Tiramisu 193

Birthday Party

Tapenade 11

Tuscan-Style White Bean Dip 15

Hot Crab Dip 16

Crostini 11

Stir-Fried Rice with Mushrooms and Shrimp 151

Tomatoes Provençale 163

Iced Dark Chocolate Cake 252

Summer Luncheon

Gazpacho with Garlic Croutons 185

Mediterranean Pasta Salad 42

Poached Cod with Lemon-Caper Butter Sauce 137

White Beans with Gremolata 82

Summer Pudding 198

Summer Supper, Outdoors or Indoors

Basic Mixed Salad 34

Gazpacho with Garlic Croutons 185

Salmon Burgers with Onion Jam 142

Parker House Rolls 260

Roasted Summer Stone Fruit with Ricotta 199

Apricot Squares 211

Autumn Dinner

Basic Mixed Salad 34
   with Blue Cheese Dressing 36

Chicken Satay Skewers 9

French Baguettes*

Tenderloin Roast with Rosemary-Chocolate-Wine Sauce 120

Polenta–Four Cheese Casserole 73

Greek-Style Green Pole Beans 164

A Is for Apple Pie 235

Winter Warm-Up

Mixed Spring Salad 35
   with Basic Vinaigrette 35

The Best Spaghetti and Meatballs 58

Eggplant Parmigiana 176

French Baguettes (with extra-virgin olive oil and sea salt)*

Dried Winter Fruit Compote with Raisin Sauce 203

Vanilla–Poppy Seed Poundcake 249

Springtime Celebration

Mixed Spring Salad 35

Mushroom and Asparagus Risotto 83

Pan-Roasted Salmon with Mint Pesto 145

Stuffed Onions 166

Stuffed Zucchini 161

Double Chocolate Pudding 189

Dutch Almond Cookies 217

Bereavement Meal

Greek Salad **29**

Aromatic Lentil Soup **85**

Roasted Turkey Breast with Orange-Cranberry Stuffing **107**

Oven-Roasted Root Vegetables **170**

Baked Apples with Balsamic Reduction **200**

Rugelach **222**

Surprise Shower

Assorted Hors d'Oeuvres (Hors d'Oeuvres and Appetizers chapter)

Boston Brown Bread **267**

Chicken Salad with Grapes and Walnuts **99**

Red-Skinned-Potato Salad **39**

Coleslaw with Raisins and Caraway Seeds **40**

Summer Strawberry Shortcake **247**

Thanksgiving

Roast Turkey with Everything Stuffing and Old-Fashioned Giblet Gravy **276**

Cranberry-Kumquat Conserve **279**

Sweet Potato Casserole with Pecan Topping **169**

Sautéed Broccoli with Garlic **164**

Pumpkin Cheesecake with Ginger-Pecan Crust **280**

Rosh Hashanah

Chopped Liver Pâté*

Pot-Roasted Beef with Fruit and Vegetables (Tzimmes) **301**

Roasted Barley Casserole **77**

Honey Cake (Lakech) **303**

Christmas

Glazed Ham with Maple Mustard 283

Sweet-and-Sour Red Cabbage and Apples 284

Green Lentils with Pancetta 285

Bûche De Noël 286

Channukah

Barbecued Brisket 117

Potato Pancakes (Latkes) and Chunky Applesauce 290

Sorbet and Berries*

Kwanzaa

Peanut Soup 292

Basic Mixed Salad 34

Easy Whole Wheat Bread 271

Creole Shrimp and Catfish Jambalaya 293

Banana Rum Tart 294

New Year's Day Open House

Assorted Hors d'Oeuvres (Hors d'Oeuvres and Appetizers chapter)

Seville-Style Olives 3

Ginger-Roasted Almonds 5
   and Spicy Pecans 6

Maryland Rockfish Chowder 133

Cheddar Cheese Biscuits 261

Shells Stuffed with Broccoli, Ricotta, Pine Nuts,
   and Raisins 53

Pecan Tart 242

Very Chocolate Brownies 209

Easter

Roast Leg Of Lamb with Rosemary and Juniper Berries 306

Cauliflower with Olive Oil and Lemon 165

Asparagus*

Hot Cross Buns 308

Cinco de Mayo

Steak Fajitas with Tomato Lime Salsa 115

Tilapia Fajitas with Tomato Salsa, Chipotle Cream,
and Guacamole 155

Mexican Chocolate Cake 299

Recipes for these menu items are not included in this book. Use your own favorite recipe, or visit a good deli and pick up ready-made.

INDEX

Underscored page references indicate sidebar notes. **Boldfaced** page references indicate photographs.

Conversion Chart

These equivalents have been slightly rounded to make measuring easier.

Volume Measurements

U.S.	Imperial	Metric
¼ tsp	–	1 ml
½ tsp	–	2 ml
1 tsp	–	5 ml
1 Tbsp	–	15 ml
2 Tbsp (1 oz)	1 fl oz	30 ml
¼ cup (2 oz)	2 fl oz	60 ml
⅓ cup (3 oz)	3 fl oz	80 ml
½ cup (4 oz)	4 fl oz	120 ml
⅔ cup (5 oz)	5 fl oz	160 ml
¾ cup (6 oz)	6 fl oz	180 ml
1 cup (8 oz)	8 fl oz	240 ml

Weight Measurements

U.S.	Metric
1 oz	30 g
2 oz	60 g
4 oz (¼ lb)	115 g
5 oz (⅓ lb)	145 g
6 oz	170 g
7 oz	200 g
8 oz (½ lb)	230 g
10 oz	285 g
12 oz (¾ lb)	340 g
14 oz	400 g
16 oz (1 lb)	455 g
2.2 lb	1 kg

Length Measurements

U.S.	Metric
¼"	0.6 cm
½"	1.25 cm
1"	2.5 cm
2"	5 cm
4"	11 cm
6"	15 cm
8"	20 cm
10"	25 cm
12" (1')	30 cm

Pan Sizes

U.S.	Metric
8" cake pan	20 × 4 cm sandwich or cake tin
9" cake pan	23 × 3.5 cm sandwich or cake tin
11" × 7" baking pan	28 × 18 cm baking tin
13" × 9" baking pan	32.5 × 23 cm baking tin
15" × 10" baking pan	38 × 25.5 cm baking tin (Swiss roll tin)
1½ qt baking dish	1.5 liter baking dish
2 qt baking dish	2 liter baking dish
2 qt rectangular baking dish	30 × 19 cm baking dish
9" pie plate	22 × 4 or 23 × 4 cm pie plate
7" or 8" springform pan	18 or 20 cm springform or loose-bottom cake tin
9" × 5" loaf pan	23 × 13 cm or 2 lb narrow loaf tin or pâté tin

Temperatures

Fahrenheit	Centigrade	Gas
140°	60°	–
160°	70°	–
180°	80°	–
225°	105°	¼
250°	120°	½
275°	135°	1
300°	150°	2
325°	160°	3
350°	180°	4
375°	190°	5
400°	200°	6
425°	220°	7
450°	230°	8
475°	245°	9
500°	260°	–